DIVINE THUNDER

The Life and Death of the Kamikazes

DIVINE
THUNDER

*The Life and Death of
the Kamikazes*

BERNARD MILLOT

Translated by Lowell Bair

The McCall Publishing Company
New York

Contents

Foreword

This book is neither a plea in favor of the Japanese suicide pilots of World War II nor a condemnation of the principles that motivated them. Besides telling their story in the context of the war, it examines the sources of the Japanese concept of suicide as a military weapon. The brief historical survey in the first chapter is intended to show the continuity between kamikaze tactics and the ancient Japanese heritage. Without this backward look it would be difficult to recapture the psychological climate of wartime Japan because the country is no longer the same: it has been transformed by the postwar American occupation.

CHAPTER

I

Amazing Japan

From the beginning of the Pacific war until late in 1944, a rather large number of Japanese pilots deliberately crashed into American ships. During this period, such acts resulted from individual initiative and accidental circumstances. In many cases the pilot had been so seriously wounded that he had no reasonable hope of survival, or else his plane had been so badly damaged that he could not have returned to his base. Suicide attacks, however, were not an exclusive Japanese specialty. They were sometimes made by pilots of other nations. We can cite two American examples.

Lieutenant Powers, a pilot aboard the carrier *Lexington*, had repeatedly sworn to his shipmates that he would hit a Japanese carrier. During the Battle of the Coral Sea, on May 8, 1942, he dived at the *Shokaku*, but instead of releasing his bomb and immediately pulling up as he should have done, he continued diving to make sure he would not miss. He was only about 150 feet from his target when he finally dropped his bomb. It struck the forward end of the enemy carrier's flight deck. Powers must have been aware that at such a low altitude he would not escape the blast of his own bomb. The other pilots of his squadron saw his plane pitch violently, then fall in a great shower of sparks and flame. The *Shokaku* was not sunk by his courageous attack, but it was removed from the theater of operations for more than a month, undergoing repairs in Japan.

On June 5, 1942, Captain Richard E. Fleming of the Marine Corps crashed his plane into the Japanese heavy cruiser *Mikuma,* striking one of the after turrets and causing a great explosion followed by an intense fire when his fuel burst into flame. His plane had been damaged a few minutes earlier by Japanese antiaircraft fire, but did not appear to be out of control. There was no doubt that he had crashed voluntarily, because the other members of his squadron were unanimous in saying that he could have tried to come down in the water and wait for an American ship to rescue him, as many other pilots did in similar circumstances. Fleming's attack was not immediately successful, but the *Mikuma* sank a few hours later as the result of the damage it had suffered.

Up to this point there was no fundamental difference between the conduct of the self-sacrificing Japanese pilots and that of their Occidental counterparts. But while many Western fighting men were willing to take great risks and could even conceive of making the supreme sacrifice in the heat of combat, they rejected the idea of premeditated suicide.

When the first grouped and coordinated kamikaze attacks took place on October 25, 1944, a common reaction in Western countries was to regard the Japanese suicide pilots as inhuman robots moved by obscure, mysterious impulses that had no relation to the psychological processes of the rest of mankind. But it would be a serious mistake to believe that those men had been transformed into mindless human bombs, or that they were nothing but well-trained animals blindly obeying insane orders. Such an uncritical view fails to take into account the deep-seated moral values of the Japanese people.

A Traditional Nation

The kamikaze attacks of World War II took the Western world by surprise, but the principle of deliberate self-sacrifice in war was not new to the Japanese. Their history abounds in examples of it. Moreover, the ancient traditions from which it springs have, unlike those of most other countries, survived the advent of modernism and industrialization. The structure of Japanese society held up under the pressure of rapid change, and its classes were able to retain their identity. The all-powerful shoguns [1] were reduced to the status of administrators, the daimyos [2] became the aristocratic ruling class, the samurai [3] formed the cadres of the new modern army. As far as the plebeian classes—peasants, laborers, craftsmen—were concerned, there was no notable change.

The Japanese were led to perform acts that Westerners may regard as excessive or even monstrous, but they were simply recognizing and putting into practice laws that followed logically from their long spiritual conditioning.

The Religious Basis

The Japanese have a deeply mystical turn of mind that is both a source and a product of their ancient Shinto religion. According to Shintoism, the Japanese people had a divine origin going back to the sun goddess Amaterasu, mother of the first emperor, Jimmu Tenno, whose reign began in 660 B.C.[4] From then on, the link between the imperial dynasty and its divine founder was never broken. Emperor Hirohito, who reigned during World War II, was the 124th direct descendant of the goddess Amaterasu.

Shintoism had two basic precepts: veneration of the emperor and his authority because of his divine essence, and

---

[1] *The shoguns governed large regions as representatives of the imperial authority. They usually acted as absolute rulers and referred decisions to the emperor only for the sake of form.*

[2] *The daimyos were suzerains who ruled their lands as feudal despots.*

[3] *The samurai were a warrior caste with a strict code of honor. They were employed by the daimyos and shoguns but maintained deep respect for the emperor.*

[4] *The Japanese calendar begins with that year. Our year 1940, for example, was 2600 in Japan.*

cultivation of great moral values and lofty virtues through ancestor worship.

The Japanese were also strongly influenced by the Chinese doctrine of Confucianism, but they were perhaps even more receptive to Buddhism, in its Chinese interpretation. It gave their religious thought its final coloration and, above all, its depth. Buddhist teachings such as the liberation of man from all earthly ties, the attainment of truth through insensitivity to suffering, renunciation of attachment to physical things, and an impassive attitude toward death became important elements of Japanese spirituality.

The Bushido Code

Since their whole history had been marked by constant local wars, with shoguns and daimyos fighting among themselves, each with his samurai and personal troops, the Japanese had always lived in a martial atmosphere. They tended to identify civic virtues with the qualities required of a good warrior. Religion and militarism were inseparable notions.

The Japanese gradually developed a special reverence for the noblest of their warrior heroes and many strove to imitate them, knowing that by heroic actions they could win a respect that would follow them after death and place them among the venerated ancestors.

The collection of principles that governed a samurai's conduct was known as the Bushido code. It taught honor, courage, loyalty, the ability to endure pain in silence, self-sacrifice, reverence for the emperor, and contempt for death. For centuries it was a code followed only by the samurai, but when Japan was opened to Western influence it was natural to make the ancient code part of the regulations of the modern army. It was also adopted by other social classes. Many Japanese commoners took pride in living by the noble principles of the samurai, who had by now become legendary heroes.

This emulation elevated Japanese morality. It also strengthened obedience to authority and enabled the ruling classes to count on the total submission of a large part of the population. The principles of the Bushido code were given a more political interpretation and made an integral part of the national ideology.

The Great Divine Mission

Belief in the divine origin of the Japanese people inevitably led to the notion of a chosen people with a great spiritual mission. This was the basis of the "Hakko Ichiu principle," according to which the Japanese were divinely predestined to dominate the world.

For centuries these ideas remained abstract and mythological, but when Japan became a modern industrial power they took on a more concrete meaning. They were the inspiration of many ultranationalistic secret societies and extremist parties, groups, and committees—organizations advocating different means of action but all having the same goal. They fostered a psychosis of national superiority which, in practice, was focused not only on necessary and legitimate economic expansion, but also on the political and military domination of Asia, perhaps even of the world.

From Morality to Suicide

The Japanese moral code held that voluntary death was better than living in shame. Suicide was regarded as an honorable act, free of the opprobrium often attached to it in Western countries. Reasons for it could vary from the deepest personal tragedy to humiliations whose seriousness would strike most Occidentals as highly debatable.

Seppuku,[5] the traditional method of suicide, involved a ritual that was as important as the act itself. It began with a meal to liberate the body from its natural needs and prepare the soul for the concentration required. Then the man about to die knelt on a mat, often facing in the direction of the emperor's palace as a sign of respectful submission. After several minutes of meditation, he bared his abdomen and made a deep vertical cut in it with a dagger or a sword. An aide, servant or friend then cut off his head with a samurai sword. Being chosen to perform this function was considered a great honor.

A keen sense of loyalty could lead to suicide: when an important or respected man died, his followers sometimes killed themselves to share his fate. As an example, we can cite the famous and true story of the forty-seven ronins, which passed into legend in the form of a lyric drama of the kabuki theater.

Asano, a daimyo lord, had forty-seven valiant samurai in his service. Kira, another daimyo, was his sworn enemy. One day in 1701, when they were both in the palace of a powerful shogun, Tokugawa, Kira treacherously provoked Asano into drawing his sword and wounding him. Asano was condemned to death for this sacrilegious act in the shogun's palace, but because of his rank he was allowed to commit ritual suicide.

His forty-seven samurai, or, more accurately, the forty-seven ronins (a ronin was a samurai who no longer had a master), swore to punish Kira for his infamous ruse. For more than two years they concealed their feelings to avoid attracting attention, then on December 14, 1703, they attacked Kira's palace, killed him, took his severed head and placed it on their dead master's grave, after which they all committed ritual suicide. Their remains, buried in the Sengakuju shrine, were venerated up to the time of World War II.

---

[5] *Seppuku, or ritual suicide, is better known in the West as hara-kiri, literally "belly-cutting," a term which because of its coarseness is seldom used in Japan.*

Military Consequences

Now that we have described some of the ideological elements of Japanese society, it will be useful to examine their effect on military developments.

Soon after the beginning of her rapid industrialization, Japan set about developing an effective army and navy. But while the organization and equipment of her new armed forces were modern, their spirit and discipline continued to reflect ancient traditions. The result was a brutal, rigid, totalitarian system which demanded a degree of courage, devotion, and obedience that went far beyond what was generally expected of soldiers in other countries. Even the ruthless discipline of the Prussian army before 1870 was mild by comparison.

Savage corporal punishment, sometimes for trivial offenses, was inflicted on recruits to give them boundless respect for authority in general and the military hierarchy in particular. Another purpose of this brutality was to harden the young soldier and build up his endurance. When he was beaten with a stick, for example, he had to remain silent and outwardly indifferent to his pain, otherwise all the other members of his unit would be given the same punishment. This created a feeling of solidarity and comradeship that was valuable in combat.

Saburo Sakai, later a fighter pilot, has described his experience as a sixteen-year-old naval recruit:

> The petty officers would not for a moment hesitate to administer the severest beatings to recruits they felt deserving of punishment. Whenever I committed a breach of discipline or an error in training, I was dragged physically from my cot by a petty officer.
>
> "Stand to the wall! Bend down, Recruit Sakai!" he would roar. "I am doing this to you, not because I hate you, but because I like you and want to make you a good seaman. *Bend down!*"

And with that he would swing a large stick of wood and with every ounce of strength he possessed would slam it against my upturned 'bottom. The pain was terrible, the force of the blows unremitting. There was no choice but to grit my teeth and struggle desperately not to cry out. At times I counted up to forty crashing impacts into my buttocks. Often I fainted from the pain. A lapse into unconsciousness constituted no escape however. The petty officer simply hurled a bucket of cold water over my prostrate form and bellowed for me to resume position, whereupon he continued his "discipline" until satisfied I would mend the error of my ways.[6]

No recruits were spared this treatment, not even those from rich and aristocratic families. Having long been accustomed to the worst hardships, the Japanese soldier naturally showed exceptional endurance in combat.

Another manifestation of this same outlook was the fact that no living Japanese soldier was given any decoration or promotion for outstanding bravery in combat. Devotion and heroism were required by the military code as a matter of course; it would have been improper to reward a man for them while he was still alive. If a hero was given a decoration or promotion, it was always after his death.

A further manifestation, logical to a Japanese but hard for an Occidental to comprehend, was the extreme disgrace attached to becoming a prisoner of war. Japanese soldiers were expected to die rather than endure the humiliation of defeat. Thousands of them, along with many civilians, committed suicide at the end of the war for that reason. And during the war the same attitude was a cause of injustice against soldiers who had been in combat and were home on leave: as the result of some recent defeat, not necessarily one in which they had been involved, they were often treated with animosity and contempt, sometimes even by their own families.

[6] Samurai, by Saburo Sakai, with Martin Caidin and Fred Saito, Ballantine Books, 1958, p. 18.

The Allies took very few prisoners in the whole course of the Pacific war.

In view of all this, it is easy to imagine the ferocity and fanaticism with which the Japanese fought in all the wars of their history, and particularly during World War II, when for the first time their homeland was seriously threatened.

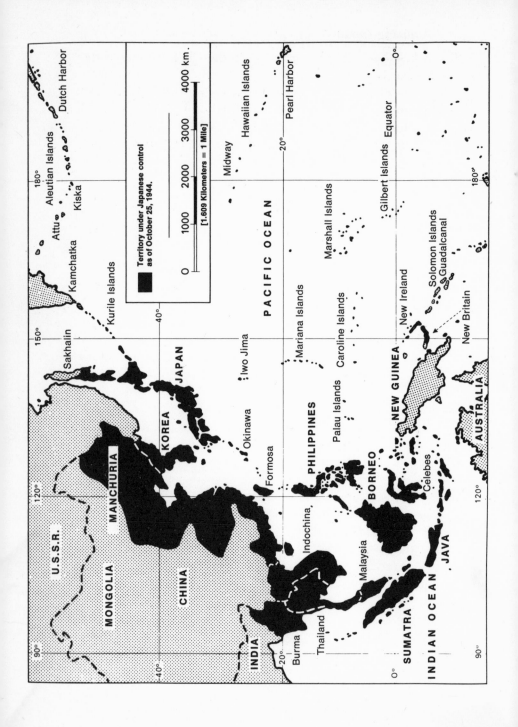

CHAPTER

II

The Path to Sacrifice

After the surprise attack at Pearl Harbor, the Japanese launched an assault against all of Southeast Asia, with spectacular success. For six months they won an uninterrupted series of resounding victories. During this period they had very few occasions to show their willingness for self-sacrifice, but in August, 1942, when the difficult Guadalcanal campaign began, the psychological aspect of the fighting changed.

The Japanese were forced to take the initiative for the first time. For months there were attacks and counterattacks with neither side able to gain the upper hand. Little by little, the Americans took the initiative, but the Japanese land, sea and air forces fought with an extraordinary bravery that foreshadowed the ferocity of battles to come.

Japanese infantrymen attacked with utter contempt for death. They charged directly into heavy American artillery and machine-gun fire with hysterical cries apparently intended to terrify the enemy as well as to raise their own fighting spirit. During these "banzai charges," [1] as soon as one assault wave was cut down it was replaced by another.

Some soldiers acted alone. They perched in palm trees, sometimes staying there for several days, and shot at any Americans who came within range, until they themselves were killed. Not one of them was ever captured alive. Some

---

[1] *The word* banzai, *literally "ten thousand years," was used as a war cry with the meaning, "May the emperor live ten thousand years!"*

shipwrecked sailors refused to be rescued by American ships. Those who were armed shot at their would-be rescuers while the others drowned themselves, preferring death to captivity.

In the numerous air-sea battles of the Guadalcanal campaign, several dozen Japanese pilots deliberately crashed into American ships, though none of these attacks resulted in a sinking. Judging from eye-witness accounts, in some cases the pilot had been wounded or his plane had been seriously damaged, but in others neither pilot nor plane showed any sign of having been hit. These men all acted on their own initiative, without orders from any higher authority.

A Typical Example

On October 26, 1942, the American carrier *Hornet* was attacked by a group of Aichi 99 dive bombers. One bomb struck the starboard side of the flight deck, two others exploded against the hull. When the bombers had pulled out of their dive, sailors aboard the *Hornet* saw the lead plane begin wobbling, then leave its formation. It came back toward the carrier and dived, showing obvious signs of damage.

The American sailors took shelter as best they could while all the ship's antiaircraft guns fired at the enemy plane. It was hit several times but kept coming. There was no doubt that it was going to crash into the *Hornet*. A few sailors, petrified by the inevitability of the outcome, stood watching the scene. It all happened very quickly. The plane struck the *Hornet*'s stack, tore off part of it, then plowed into the flight deck with a huge, blinding flash. Two of its bombs exploded, igniting its fuel.

A short time later, some Japanese Nakajima 97 torpedo planes appeared. They approached in small groups from both sides at once, flying at very low altitude. While their torpedoes were still moving through the water, one of the planes, whose pilot must have been wounded, headed straight for the *Hornet* without attempting any evasive movements. It was flying so low that American sailors lying on the deck were soon unable to see it. It first struck one of the forward antiaircraft mounts, then exploded near the forward elevator. The *Hornet* sank a few hours later, but according to survivors, it was not the two suicide attacks that had done the decisive damage.

Fury in the Aleutians

From that time on, the Americans witnessed an escalation of Japanese violence and fanaticism. They had a particularly bitter encounter with them in the Aleutian Islands, southwest of the Alaska Peninsula. On May 11, 1943, American amphibious forces landed on Attu, a rocky little island that was known to be weakly defended. Troops went ashore on both sides of Chichagof Harbor, in Holtz Bay to the north and Massacre Bay to the south. They made slow progress even though the Japanese put up only a token resistance while the bulk of their troops withdrew to the heights overlooking Chichagof Harbor. From those ideal positions, they harassed the two invading groups and prevented them from joining each other. The Americans had to bring all their reserves of about 11,000 men ashore.

Although American ships and planes pounded the Japanese positions without letup, the situation remained almost unchanged for more than two weeks. A tight blockade prevented any supplies or reinforcements from reaching the Japanese but they continued to hold out against repeated American assaults.

On May 28 the colonel in command of the Japanese garrison had to recognize that defeat was inevitable. There was no more food and very little ammunition. His original force of 2600 men had been reduced to about a thousand. By Occidental standards, he would have been perfectly justified in surrendering under those circumstances, since he no longer had the means to continue fighting. That was not his decision. Late in the afternoon he called his men together, described the situation to them and exhorted them to launch a suicide attack to kill as many enemy soldiers as possible. He spoke of the hand-to-hand combat that the ancient samurai warriors had cherished and the lofty traditional virtues that led to self-sacrifice for the sake of the emperor.

His men all declared that they were ready to die for eternal Japan. That evening the sick and wounded who were unable to take part in the last charge were all killed. They were either shot in the back of the head or given powerful injections of barbiturates.

During the night the Japanese silently came down from their defensive positions. Many of them were armed only with knives and bayonets. They infiltrated the American outposts and killed the sentries without making a sound.

They then reassembled, still in silence, and just before dawn, shrieking wildly, they charged the enemy encampments. Many Americans were taken by surprise and killed in their sleeping bags. The slaughter was horrible; the Japanese, in the grip of a murderous frenzy, struck from all sides at once. American tents collapsed, red with blood. Some Americans fled in panic and fell a short time later, caught by the Japanese. At the height of their rage, the Japanese burst into an American field hospital and massacred the patients.

At dawn, American soldiers succeeded in organizing an effective counterattack. When the surviving Japanese, numbering about 500, were cornered, they began committing suicide. Some cut open their bellies, others exploded grenades against their chests. Except for a handful of wounded men who were captured alive, the entire Japanese garrison on Attu perished. Their incredible attack cost the Americans about 600 dead and 1200 wounded.

The Murderous Stages of the Reconquest

There were many other combats all over the Pacific during which the Japanese had occasion to apply the same tactics. Whether in New Guinea or the central Solomon Islands, ruthless Japanese onslaughts led the Americans to dread the terrible and bewildering determination of their enemies.

On November 30, 1943, American amphibious forces opened a new front in the central Pacific by landing on Tarawa, one of the Gilbert Islands. The marines quickly ran into fierce resistance that stopped their advance for three days. It ended only when all the Japanese defenders had died, either in combat or by suicide and after inflicting very heavy losses on the invaders.

Hopping from island to island, the Americans were inexorably closing their gigantic pincers on the Japanese empire. With their growing material superiority, they steadily strengthened their control of the air and the sea and increased the disproportion between the opposing forces. In June, 1944, they landed in the Mariana Islands. After what they had already suffered from the incredible ferocity of Japanese resistance, it would have been hard for them to imagine that they might have to fight even more savage battles, yet that was what happened.

By July 6, 1944, American marines had occupied two-thirds of the island of Saipan, in the Marianas, and were preparing to clear its northern end of enemy forces. On July 7, at dawn, nearly 3000 Japanese hurled themselves at the American lines, shrieking and singing the warrior hymn *Umi Yakaba*. Most of them were armed only with bayonets or even clubs.

They charged the marines in successive waves, suffering enormous losses. In some places, bodies were piled so high that the Americans had to move their machine guns in order to have an open field of fire. The Japanese were determined to die; they continued running and shouting until they fell, either dead or wounded. The Americans fought for every inch of ground, sometimes driven back, sometimes slipping in pools of blood.

The first attack waves were followed by a horde of sick and wounded men, limping, covered with bandages, holding each other up. They had left the hospitals and infirmaries, determined to take part in the last banzai charge. (Three hundred other wounded men, unable to stand, had been killed in their beds; they were found later, lying in their own blood.) The Americans eventually reconquered the terrain, but they had lost 668 men.

The next day, July 8, the marines set out to take Marpi Point, the last part of the island still in enemy hands. Several hundred Japanese soldiers had gathered there, along with a large number of civilians who had fled before the American advance. The marines moved forward without encountering any serious resistance and soon reached a rocky area that ended with cliffs overhanging the northern coast. They were horrified by what they saw: hundreds of Japanese, both soldiers and civilians, were committing suicide.

Soldiers were shooting themselves in the mouth or letting themselves be killed by their noncommissioned officers before groups of haggard civilians. The latter, men, women and children, were begging the soldiers to kill them. Other civilians, holding each other by the hand, ran to the edges of cliffs, jumped off and were killed on the rocks below. Three young women, sitting on large stones, were combing their hair; when they had arranged it in accordance with a rite whose meaning was all too clear, they stood up, walked hand in hand to the edge of a cliff and disappeared. Fathers cut their small children's throats or strangled them before leaping from the top of a precipice. Many civilians who had taken refuge in cliffside caves committed suicide by walking into the ocean until they drowned.

When the Americans finally reached the edge of the cliffs, some of them were overwhelmed with nausea when they saw the hundreds of bloody corpses below. Despite all their efforts, they were unable to stop that collective suicidal madness. They took no prisoners, and only a few young children survived.

With each step in the American reconquest, and with the growth of the threat to Japan herself, Japanese resistance became increasingly tenacious and violent. An extraordinary climax became inevitable.

Tacit Sacrifice

As we have seen, from the beginning of the Pacific war a certain number of Japanese pilots had intentionally crashed into American ships. In the early part of the war these suicide attacks were relatively rare, but during the last months of 1943 and the first part of 1944 they became more frequent. At first, local Japanese commanders had little knowledge of them. But by the middle of 1944 they were one of the main subjects of conversation among Japanese fliers and no officer could be unaware of them.

Besides admiring the heroism of their self-sacrificing comrades, the pilots also reflected on the results it had achieved. They all realized that the inherent vulnerability and fragility of their planes [2] decreased their chances of survival when they had to confront the Americans' formidable antiaircraft fire and Grumman F6F Hellcats. Nor was it any secret that the Japanese were unable to produce enough planes to make up for the enormous losses they were suffering. And finally, because of the gasoline shortage, new pilots were being graduated from accelerated Japanese flying schools with inadequate training. The result of all this was that a large number of Japanese planes were unable to reach a given

[2] *In the design of Japanese military aircraft, protective armor had been sacrificed to increase speed and maneuverability by saving weight. This gave the Japanese an advantage at the beginning of the war, but from then on they made no appreciable improvement in the quality of their planes, which were soon outclassed by American fighters that combined superior strength and excellent performance in spite of their greater weight.*

target, and the general effectiveness of Japanese aviation declined.

Base commanders, squadron leaders and ordinary pilots thought about these agonizing problems and tried to find a solution. They did not need much imagination to make a comparison between conventional tactics and the suicide attacks that were already in their minds. Although some of them were repelled by the idea, many others considered it with enthusiasm. They all talked about it among themselves and commented on the depressing uncertainty of their usual procedures. Whole squadrons were often unable to carry out their missions because they were largely or totally wiped out by American defenses before they could even reach their objectives. If a few planes did manage to get through, their bombs and torpedoes were likely to be wasted because of the lack of experience and training of most Japanese pilots. Brave men and many aircraft were thus lost in vain.

Repeated failures of this kind led some pilots to consider *jibaku* [3] as the only way of inflicting great damage on the enemy. "Since I'm going to be killed anyway," their reasoning went, "I may as well make it count for something." Monstrous though a premeditated suicide attack may seem to us, we must recognize that it was extremely effective: one pilot could often do more damage than a whole squadron.

All this was a slow process, and the idea was not fervently accepted by all Japanese pilots. To some of them, the idea of deliberate suicide, decided in advance, was an insurmountable obstacle. But to the great majority, *jibaku* was a noble act that filled them with exalted enthusiasm. And on a practical level, it seemed to them the only way of countering the overwhelming superiority of the enemy's forces and reversing the dangerous situation into which Japan had been driven.

Some of them also thought that even if it should fail to inflict decisive destruction, it might at least intimidate the Americans and make them willing to negotiate an honorable end to the war. These men felt that their spiritual superiority and moral strength, demonstrated by their self-sacrifice,

[3] *A suicide attack; the word "kamikaze" was not used until later.*

would unnerve and discourage "those cowardly Yankees." [4]

For the moment, these drastic ideas had no influence beyond the theater of operations. A few unit commanders discreetly and unofficially transmitted them to the high command in Tokyo but their suggestions were rejected.

The pilots who accepted the principle of suicide tactics most wholeheartedly were, as a general rule, those whose religious or patriotic sentiments were most highly developed. *Jibaku* offered them a chance to attain two goals: first, to inflict losses on the enemy that might make him lose the advantage of his material superiority; and second, to die bravely in the purest style of ancient Japanese tradition. Those who succeeded in returning from conventional missions in which most of their comrades had been shot down were convinced that their survival was only temporary and that they should make the best possible use of it.

The Mysterious Mission

The first organized suicide operation apparently took place in the middle of 1944, but it remained unknown to both the Japanese and the American high commands.

In June of that year, the Japanese expected the Americans to follow up their conquest of the Marianas by attacking Iwo Jima, a small volcanic island about 700 miles north of Saipan. Iwo Jima was weakly defended and could have been invaded easily. (The American high command did not see fit to invade it at that time and thereby made a serious strategic mistake. Realizing the great importance of the island, the Japanese began fortifying it heavily and building up large stocks of munitions, so that when the Americans finally did take it they had to pay a very high price for their victory.)

On June 20 a squadron of 30 Zero [5] fighters was sent from

---

[4] *This was how Japanese propaganda had always depicted the Americans, soldiers and civilians alike.*

[5] *The nickname, used by both the Japanese and the Americans, of the most common Japanese naval fighter plane.*

Yokosuka, Japan, to reinforce the air units already based on Iwo Jima. When the pilots had landed on the dusty runways, they learned that an American naval force [6] had attacked the island on the two previous days.

During the approach, the American destroyers *Charrette* and *Boyd* sank a small 1900-ton Japanese freighter, the *Tatsutagawa Maru,* and in the first air raid ten Zeros were shot down in flight and seven bombers damaged on the ground. The airfield was attacked by 54 carrier-based planes the following day. The American pilots reported destroying 63 Japanese planes on the ground. This figure was exaggerated, but in any case Iwo Jima had now been plunged into the war.

To help the Japanese garrisons in the Marianas, the air commander of Iwo Jima sent groups of Betty [7] bombers to attack the American invasion forces every night. No more than one or two planes from each group succeeded in returning, riddled with bullet holes. Within a very short time the whole bomber force of the island had melted away like snow in sunlight. Jill [8] torpedo planes were then sent on the night missions, with no better results.

On the morning of June 24 there was another large-scale air raid against Iwo Jima. Alerted by radar, more than 80 Zeros flew off to intercept the attackers. A few minutes later, fierce air fighting broke out. The Americans did not escape without losses, but they downed nearly half of the Japanese planes.

On July 3 a new American air attack devastated Iwo Jima. While Avengers [9] were bombing the runways and planes on the ground, Hellcats [10] shot down 20 of the 40 Zeros that had gone up to fight them. The next day, July 4, American Inde-

[6] *Admiral Clark's Task Group 58-1 (carriers* Hornet, Yorktown, Belleau Wood, Bataan) *and Admiral Harrill's Task Group 58-4 (carriers* Essex, Langley, Cowpens).
[7] *The Mitsubishi G4M, a twin-engined navy medium bomber.*
[8] *The Nakajima B6N Tenzan, a single-engined torpedo-bomber.*
[9] *The Grumman TBF Avenger, a single-engined navy torpedo-bomber that carried a crew of three.*
[10] *The Grumman F6F Hellcat, a single-engined navy fighter, somewhat less maneuverable than the Zero, but faster and less fragile.*

pendence Day, the carrier planes returned to complete their work of destruction. The Zeros went up again, but within a few minutes 11 of them had been shot down. Installations on the island were severely damaged and many planes were destroyed on the ground.

When the American raiders had disappeared over the horizon and the dust and smoke cleared, the full extent of the disaster became apparent. There were now only eight Jills and nine Zeros left on Iwo Jima.

The staff officers of the base met to consider the problem of how they were to continue operations. They decided to send all their remaining planes to attack the American fleet that had been sighted about 500 miles south of Iwo Jima. The pilots assigned to the mission were told to assemble in front of the tent of the command post. Captain Kanzo Miura mounted an improvised platform and looked at each one of them before he began to speak:

> You will strike back at the enemy. From now on our defensive battles are over. You men are the fliers chosen from the Yokosuka Air Wing, the most famous in all Japan. I trust that your actions today will be worthy of the name and the glorious tradition of your wing.
>
> In order for you to perpetuate the honor which is ours, you must accept the task which your officers have put before you. You cannot, I repeat, you cannot hope for survival. Your minds must be on the word *attack!* You are but seventeen men, and today you will face a task force which is defended perhaps by hundreds of American fighter planes.
>
> Therefore, individual attacks must be forgotten. You cannot strike at your targets as one man alone. You must maintain a tight group of planes. You must fight your way through the interceptors, and . . . *you must dive against the enemy carriers together!* Dive—along with your torpedoes and your lives and your souls . . .
>
> A normal attack will be useless. Even if you succeed in penetrating the American fighters, you will only be

shot down on the way back to this island. Your death will be ineffective for our country. Your lives will be wasted. We cannot permit this to be.

Until you reach your targets, the fighter pilots will refuse to accept battle with the enemy planes. No bomber pilot will release his torpedo in an air drop. No matter what happens, you will keep your planes together. Wing to wing! No obstacle is to stop you from carrying out your mission. You must make your dives in a group in order to be effective. I know that what I tell you to do is difficult. It may even seem impossible. But I trust that you can do it, that you will do it. That every man among you will plunge directly into an enemy carrier and sink the vessel . . . You have your orders.[11]

According to custom, the pilots should have replied with enthusiastic "banzais," but this time there was only a heavy silence. It was obvious that they were all deeply absorbed in thought. For several months, Japanese pilots had been going on missions from which they often had very little chance of returning; everyone knew it, but there was always a slight glimmer of hope. Each man could cling to the idea that perhaps his turn had not yet come. Now it was different: death had been decided and ordered, it was present even before the mission began. Yet most of the assembled pilots reacted with a calm determination that underscored their exceptional courage. "A samurai," says the Bushido code, "lives in such a way that he is always ready to die." The code does not prescribe suicide, but in this case self-sacrifice had an undeniable military value and it was accepted on that basis.

The other pilots, those who had not been assigned to the mission because there were no longer any planes for them, brought gifts which, though necessarily modest, had the value of an offering, a token of affection and reverent respect for the men they already regarded as heroes.

When the time came, the 17 planes took off and headed south-southeast. When they were still more than 60 miles

[11] Samurai, by Sakai, Caidin and Saito, pp. 220-21.

from their objective, American fighters began pouring out of the clouds in a seemingly endless stream. The Japanese tightened their formation, remembering that they had been ordered not to fight back if attacked.

A few minutes later it became impossible to obey that order. The enemy fighters came in from all sides and immediately shot down two of the bombers. The Zeros and the remaining bombers fought fiercely, trying to escape at the same time, but one by one they began falling in flames.

Assailed by more than 60 Hellcats, the few surviving Japanese were finally able to take refuge in a storm cloud. They ran into violent turbulence and blinding rain, but they had escaped being methodically executed by the Hellcats. After flying through the storm for a long time, they emerged into calm air and a clear sky. No Hellcats in sight. But where was the American fleet?

They searched for it until twilight, without success. They all knew it would be senseless to exhaust their fuel and fall into the ocean. They had accepted a suicide mission, but with the understanding that they would end it by crashing into an enemy ship. Even so, they felt that they would be dishonored if they returned to Iwo Jima. After a painful inner debate, they headed back, intending to wait for a new opportunity to strike their blow at the enemy.

It was dark when the five surviving planes, four Zeros and a Jill, landed on Iwo Jima. Their pilots expected to be punished for having disobeyed orders. Instead, they were received with warm sympathy. Everyone at the base knew that their decision to return was not motivated by cowardice but only by a desire for a chance to make their deaths more meaningful.

That chance never came. The next day an American naval force hurled thousands of tons of shells at Iwo Jima, ravaging the whole island and destroying all four of the remaining Zeros.

The suicide raid was not reported as such to the Japanese high command because it was too revolutionary at the time and would have aroused disapproval. On the American side, no one was aware of the Japanese pilots' intentions, so American reports mentioned the air battle only as the interception of an ordinary enemy raid.

An Idea Takes Form

Although the nature of the raid just described was unknown to the Japanese high command, the idea behind it was already spreading. At first, individual suicide attacks had not been reported beyond the level of unit commanders, but increasingly large numbers of them were not being brought to the attention of the highest authorities. Squadron leaders had courageously [12] begun sending in reports praising the merits of suicide tactics and describing the willingness of most of their men to carry them out.

Many proposals were made, too many to mention specifically here. As an example, we can take that of Eiichiro Jyo, captain of the carrier *Chiyoda*. After the disaster of the Mariana Islands, he submitted his ideas to his superiors: "No longer can we hope to sink the numerically superior enemy aircraft carriers through ordinary attack methods. I urge the immediate organization of special attack units to carry out crash-dive tactics, and I ask to be placed in command of them." [13]

Captain Jyo's valor and outstanding record carried great weight and his viewpoint influenced a number of high army and navy commanders. From then on, official communiqués exalted the heroism of pilots who, acting individually, deliberately crashed into enemy ships.

Shortly afterward, unit commanders were urged to develop new and more effective methods of attack, but no specific

[12] *In the Japanese armed forces, such unrequested expressions of opinion bordered on insubordination.*
[13] The Divine Wind, *by Rikihei Inoguchi, Tadashi Nakajima and Roger Pineau. Ballantine Books, 1968, p. 25. Captain Jyo died in the Battle of Leyte Gulf on October 25, 1944, the day when the first organized suicide attacks began.*

recommendations were made. Did the high command want to avoid taking responsibility for suicide tactics, or did it simply want to encourage unit commanders to devise better procedures within a conventional framework? Its members were apparently divided on that delicate subject. As in all countries, there were officials caught up in the toils of bureaucracy who had only a hazy view of the military situation and the combatants' state of mind. Others, whose work brought them into closer contact with the men who were doing the fighting, had a more realistic outlook. Some of them realized the importance of the new methods that had been proposed but they were not yet numerous enough to bring about a decision. The situation would have to become still worse before the high command as a whole changed its mind. Meanwhile the idea of suicide tactics continued to spread and take more definite shape.

Certain high-ranking Japanese officers, convinced that launching a great air offensive based on suicide attacks was the only way to keep the American pincers from closing in on Japan, gathered often to discuss their ideas. One of them even ventured into a working session of the general staff to cite a passage in a book on the pioneers of aviation.

This passage quoted the answers given by a great French aviator, Jules Védrines, to questions from a delegation of civilian and military dignitaries concerning the future of the airplane in case of war. Védrines believed that military aviation could play an important role, and the usefulness he attributed to it was soon to be confirmed by World War I, even beyond what he had foreseen.

Trying to find a flaw in his reasoning, someone stated that airplanes would surely be powerless to break a naval blockade, which was one of the great obsessions of the time. Védrines replied without hesitation: "Let's say I'm attacking a naval squadron that's blockading a port. Nothing can stop me from diving full speed into a battleship, with 400 kilograms of explosives in my plane. I'll be killed, of course, but the battleship will be blown up, and that's what counts."

It was a surprising answer from an Occidental, but it put

an end to the discussion. Védrines' personality and the calm courage he had shown in his previous exploits made it impossible to think that what he had said was nothing but braggadocio.

The principle of the aerial suicide attack had thus been stated more than 30 years before that summer of 1944. Under certain conditions, it seemed to offer a chance of inflicting maximum destruction with a minimum loss of life and matériel. There were many debates on the subject in Tokyo but they led to no decision. A few weeks later, however, the long-rejected idea began to have practical effects.

Skip Bombing

In August, 1944, when the Americans gained control of all the Mariana Islands, the Japanese began sending reinforcements to the Philippines, convinced that they would be the next invasion target. It was then that unit commanders were instructed to seek more effective methods of attack. It was the first time the general staff had given such an important prerogative to subordinates.

This surprising change in the usually rigid attitude of the Japanese military hierarchy had been caused by uneasiness over the morale of bomber and torpedo plane pilots. It had been dropping so alarmingly that Tokyo had considered taking disciplinary action against them. They were discouraged by their bitter failures in the past few months. They had seen large numbers of men and planes sacrificed for insignificant results. Pilots often took off on missions without any hope of either success or survival. Bombing and torpedo raids had become almost useless. Enemy defenses were so powerful that many pilots simply turned back when they encountered them, without even trying to get through. When reports convinced the general staff that the disciplinary measures they had in mind could do nothing to correct this disastrous situation, they resigned themselves to letting unit commanders choose other tactics.

Japanese fighter pilots, however, had not lost their determination. When the instructions from Tokyo arrived and Admiral Kimpei Teraoka, commander of the First Air Fleet, based in the Philippines, decided to study the technique of skip bombing, he realized that he could no longer expect anything from his bomber and torpedo plane pilots. He knew that he would have to count on the higher morale of his fighter pilots and the greater speed of their planes.

Skip bombing involves a principle known to children all over the world: an object thrown almost horizontally a short distance above water will bounce off the surface several times, continuing in its original direction, before it finally sinks. Nearly everyone has at one time or another thrown pebbles in this way to watch them hop across the water.

With skip bombing, as Admiral Teraoka conceived it, the idea was to equip fighter planes with slightly modified 550-pound bombs and train the pilots to drop them at the lowest possible altitude as they approached their targets. The bombs would skip across the surface of the ocean and strike the enemy ships in their vulnerable sides. It was such a simple and promising idea that the high command approved it and the fighter pilots were eager to try it.

The chosen units began their training in the Bohol Strait, off the island of Cebu, Philippines. But when the first trial runs were made it became clear that the technique was not as simple as it had seemed in theory. It required a degree of self-confidence, judgment and skill that was often lacking in hastily trained young pilots. Experiments showed that the pilot had to drop his bomb from a dangerously low altitude when he was less than a thousand feet from his target. He then had only two seconds in which to avoid colliding with the target ship, while at the same time trying to escape from enemy antiaircraft fire and fighters.

Only an expert pilot could judge his altitude with precision while flying close to the surface of the water at high speed.

Furthermore, the technique could not be used when the sea was rough, because the bomb would then sink immediately instead of skipping. In training, it was not uncommon for a pilot to fly too close to the water and plunge into it, sending up a huge geyser of foam. Yet many pilots volunteered, knowing that even if they succeeded in surviving the hazardous training they would have little chance of escaping death in a real attack.

Early in September, 1944, American carrier planes began bombing Japanese airfields in the Philippines to prepare for the coming invasion. They destroyed more than half of the 500 Japanese planes there, either on the ground or in the air.

Because every available fighter plane was now needed for the defense of the Philippines, the training program for skip bombing was discontinued. The technique was thus abandoned before it was used in combat. Later events were to lead Japanese pilots, in the same state of mind, to use different tactics and carry them to their sublime conclusion.

CHAPTER

III

The Philippines:
Birthplace of the Kamikazes

In war, one adversary is sometimes able to deduce where the other will strike next. He can then take special defensive measures, although he will not shift all his forces from other sectors, because an error of judgment is always possible. This was the case with the Japanese in 1944: they had become convinced that the Philippines would be the target of the Americans' next leap forward.

In mid-August, Tokyo learned that the enemy forces were regrouping in the Marianas. The high command knew that the Americans planned to bring Japan to her knees by a series of amphibious operations leading to an invasion of the home islands. They had a choice of several routes, but the Japanese believed that General MacArthur's determination to reconquer the Philippines at any cost would weigh heavily in the balance. This proved to be correct. Furthermore, having learned the extent of American military power from bitter experience, they were inclined to believe that the enemy might create a diversion or direct his efforts against several different points at once. To cope with this possibility, they devised the Sho ("Victory") Plan, which would bring into action practically all of Japan's remaining air and sea forces.

In the first half of September, as related in the preceding chapter, there were highly effective American bombing raids against Japanese airfields in the southern Philippines. On September 15, American amphibious forces landed on Pele-liu, one of the Palau Islands, about halfway between the Marianas and the Philippines. Shortly afterward, the Americans extended their air strikes to the northern Philippines. These developments confirmed the assumptions of the Japanese. There could be little doubt that the Philippines were the Americans' next major objective.

The Philippines were not only the last important bastion on the way to Japan but also the last geographical protection of shipping from the Dutch East Indies, which was essential to Japan's war economy. If the Americans regained control of the Philippines, they would cut off that vital source of supplies and force Japanese defenses back to the home islands.

A Critical Situation

Japan's war effort depended on obtaining petroleum and raw materials from conquered territories. Early in 1942, a steady stream of tankers and freighters began bringing these products to the home islands and delivering fuel and manufactured articles on their return voyages.

The United States realized the importance of the sea lanes between Japan and the Dutch East Indies, and soon began a submarine war of extermination. As the number of ships plying these lanes diminished, Japan's economic situation became more and more precarious. By the summer of 1944, the systematic destruction of her merchant fleet by American submarines had reached such proportions that seaborne supplies were inadequate to meet the needs of the war effort. The drastic fuel rationing that had to be imposed even on the armed forces had many repercussions. It severely limited the number of sorties that could be made by ships and planes, for example, and dangerously reduced the amount of flight training given to pilots before they were sent into combat.

To keep even the thin trickle of supplies flowing, the Philippines had to be defended at all costs. That was why most of the air and sea forces still fit for combat were assigned to the Sho Plan. So far, however, there were only strong presumptions about the Americans' next move. It still seemed quite possible that they might strike at several points simultaneously, which would spread Japanese defenses and make them less effective.

On October 6, 1944, a diplomatic dispatch from Moscow informed the Japanese general staff that the Americans would attack the central Philippines during the last ten days of October. This Soviet indiscretion relieved the Japanese of their last doubts. Admiral Soemu Toyoda, Commander in Chief of the Combined Fleet, want to Manila soon afterward to confer with the local navy commanders, give them the precious information, and work out the special arrangements of the Sho Plan. Everything was now focused on defending the central Philippines.

Although Japan had just gained an important strategic advantage, the essential part of the plan still remained to be carried out: the available forces had to be grouped and located in such a way that they would be able to drive the Americans from Philippine waters. But heavy losses of ships and planes, the inadequacy of Japanese industry, shortages of reinforcements and supplies, and a certain deficiency in command all combined to weaken what was to have been an unshakable defense.

The Sho Plan specified that the navy was to concentrate its forces for a great surface and air engagement that would wipe out the bulk of the American fleet. Japanese navy pilots eagerly discussed the most effective ways of attacking the enemy. Some racked their brains to devise new methods; others had already begun to consider large-scale use of suicide attacks.

The Pilots' Attitude

The defense of the Philippines was to be a combined effort—
badly coordinated, as it turned out—of land, sea and air
forces, but for the moment we will consider only its aerial
aspect because the first volunteers for collective suicide missions were pilots.

Since mid-September 1944, Japanese pilots had been stiff-
ening their determination, as is shown by the many proposals
for attacks that they made to their superiors. In these proposals, the survival of the pilots involved was always prob-
lematical and was sometimes disregarded altogether. The
primary concern was to inflict maximum destruction on the
enemy; it mattered little whether the pilots had to be sacrificed or not. This new outlook was extremely widespread. It
was inspired, as previously noted, by the proud Japanese
heritage, and by the example of the increasingly numerous
pilots who crash-dived against enemy targets.

The American invasion of Peleliu, in the Palau Islands,
made the Japanese fliers still more impatient for action. The
few messages that came from Peleliu gave them an idea of
the intensity of the fighting there. It was obvious that if the
Americans took the Palau Islands there would be nothing to
stop them from attacking the Philippines within a short time.

To support the heroic defenders of Peleliu, many Japanese
officers proposed launching air strikes in the hope of breaking the American encirclement of the island. Rear Admiral
Masafumi Arima, commander of the 26th Air Flotilla, took
the initiative in ordering several raids, but the weather was
so bad at this time that the planes were often prevented even
from taking off. And the few missions that were carried out
did no serious harm to the enemy. Nevertheless, those few
raids showed the pilots' extraordinary will to fight, no matter
what their chances of survival. The progression from courage
to heroic suicide was well under way.

One detail is revealing: knowing that their days were numbered, many Japanese fliers reduced their personal belongings to a strict minimum and kept them in a small bag or box, so that sending those last keepsakes to their families would be a simple matter. In some cases the pilot even addressed the container to his parents in advance and wrote his own name with the next highest rank, anticipating the posthumous promotion given to officers killed in combat.

The Long Wait

Every day since the beginning of September, reconnaissance planes had been flying out from the Philippines to look for the expected American fleets. Japanese commanders were impatient to learn the enemy's intentions, but for long days nothing was sighted. Tension became so great that this was a disappointment rather than a relief.

The same tension was responsible for the unfortunate Davao incident. As the result of air raids against Davao on September 9 and 10, lookouts in the area were expecting an enemy landing at any moment. Deluded by either emotion or fatigue, some of them announced the arrival of an American invasion fleet. Defense plans were put into effect and the news was transmitted to all Japanese forces in the Philippines. There were movements of troops and airplanes while new messages reported that enemy tanks were moving inland.

There had actually been no landing at all. The incident was caused by a misinterpretation of a telegram urging vigilance, which the lookouts had mistaken for an alert. Order was quickly restored, but the dispersion of forces prompted by the false alarm had one serious result: many of the planes shifted to Luzon were later destroyed by bombing raids against airfields in the northern Philippines.

The atmosphere of uncertainty and strained expectancy continued for another month. Finally, early in the afternoon of October 12, a Japanese reconnaissance plane sighted the

American armada. After such a long wait, the news was received with a kind of satisfaction and relief. The enemy had showed himself at last and the Japanese were determined to deal him a staggering blow that would discourage him from attempting a landing.

Air strikes were immediately ordered. They were limited by bad weather and those planes that were able to take off soon ran into almost impenetrable enemy defenses. The Japanese suffered heavy losses without damaging a single American ship. Discouraging though they were, these raids continued to be launched.

Admiral Arima's Example

This was probably the period when the idea of suicide tactics made its most rapid progress in the minds of Japanese pilots. Facing death with almost no chance of inflicting it on the enemy in return, they were gnawed by helpless anger and frustration. Then something happened which, though not momentous in itself, had important later consequences.

On the morning of October 15 a reconnaissance plane spotted a large group of American ships off the island of Luzon. It included several aircraft carriers. Since the beginning of the Pacific war, carriers had been the key to naval battles and were therefore the prime targets to strike. As soon as the message was received, Japanese commanders decided to launch a massive raid. Squadrons from both the army and the navy air forces were assembled for the first time and ordered to attack in two waves.

The second wave, composed of 13 Suisei dive bombers and 16 Zeros from the navy, with 70 fighters of several different types from the army, was ready to take off when Rear Admiral Masafumi Arima, commander of the 26th Air Flotilla of the First Air Fleet, arrived at the airfield wearing flight gear, without any insignia of his rank. He had decided to lead the second attack in person.

His subordinates looked at him in consternation. It was against regulations: a flag officer was not supposed to take part in a combat mission. In reply to questions from the officers present, Admiral Arima said that he wanted to make a personal check on the conditions under which his men were fighting; to avoid violating regulations, he had removed the insignia of his rank and even scratched off the word "Admiral" from his binoculars. This answer deceived no one. The officers all tried to persuade him not to go on the mission.

Arima had been living with great austerity for several weeks, refusing to sleep in the comfortable house that had been provided for him in Manila, spending long periods of time in meditation and sharing the precarious life of his men. He was liked and respected by everyone for his kindness, understanding, tact and unshakable faith in victory. While the officers watched in dismay, he got into one of the Suisei dive bombers and was the first to take off.

His group sighted the American formation 280 miles east-northeast of Manila and prepared to attack it. It was Task Group 38-4, commanded by Rear Admiral Ralph E. Davison, cruising off Luzon.

Patrols of American fighters, alerted by radar, flew to intercept the Japanese. American superiority in both number and quality was again decisive, as it had consistently been for many months. The formidable Hellcats decimated the Suisei bombers and their fighter escorts.

But one Japanese plane was able to hide in a cloud layer and continue its approach. It was Admiral Arima's bomber. Witnesses saw it come out of the sheltering clouds and dive as though to make a conventional attack. It headed for an American carrier and prolonged its dive until a huge orangish-red flame suddenly rose from the enemy ship. Admiral Arima had crash-dived into the *Franklin* (CV-13), Admiral Davison's flagship. Fire raged through it and set off successive explosions of powder magazines that worsened the already serious damage. The crew struggled to save the ship. Only after long hours of sometimes superhuman effort could they be sure it was not going to sink. Listing and unable to resume aerial operations, it had to withdraw to a repair base.

Some of Admiral Arima's subordinates were not surprised when they learned of his sublime gesture from the pilots who survived the mission. His earlier behavior and the strange glow they had seen in his eyes as he prepared to take off had made them expect an act of that kind, though none of them had dared to express his presentiments.

Arima's pilots were deeply grieved by his death, but his exploits filled them with enthusiastic admiration. News of it quickly spread to all units stationed in the Philippines, and beyond. Radio Tokyo reported it as a patriotic act that had revealed a new spirit and demonstrated a way of causing irreparable enemy losses.

It was naturally discussed by all Japanese pilots. Some of them drew conclusions from it that determined their future conduct. Admiral Arima had had the courage and determination to do what many of them had already been considering for several months. He had showed them the way, and they were strongly influenced by his example.

Accelerating Developments

The men of the First Air Fleet had recently learned that they were going to have a new commander. The news was surprising and proved to be heavy with consequences for the future. Vice Admiral Kimpei Teraoka had taken command of the First Air Fleet on August 12, 1944, after the suicide of his predecessor, Rear Admiral Kakuji Kakuta. The fact that he was now being replaced less than two months after his appointment appeared to indicate that he had fallen into disfavor, and this seemed unjustified to all the men under his command. What were they to think of that unexpected change?

The name of their new commander, Vice Admiral Takijiro Onishi, was reassuring, since he was a famous aviation specialist, but did his appointment mean that Tokyo wanted to inaugurate some new and revolutionary kind of tactics in the Philippines? They all questioned each other in vain.

Admiral Onishi was an ardent partisan of aviation, he was a pilot himself, and he had been in charge of aircraft production in the Aviation Department of the Ministry of Munitions in Tokyo, so there was no doubt about his capability. His appointment dated from October 2 but he did not take command of the First Air Fleet until October 17, when his plane landed at Nichols Field, near Manila.

That same day, amphibious forces landed on the little island of Suluan, at the mouth of Leyte Gulf. The Americans apparently wanted to secure a local base of operations before launching their great invasion. A few hours after the landing began, a message announced that the defenders of Suluan, consisting of only a few dozen observers, were burning their documents and preparing to die for the emperor.

The Sho Plan was put into effect. The next day, Japanese naval forces began moving toward the Philippines for the great battle that was to decide the fate of Japan. On October 17 and the days following, concentrated American air raids against Japanese airfields in Luzon destroyed a large number of planes and installations. The loss of those precious planes gave still greater urgency to the plan that Admiral Onishi had been instructed to carry out.

Admiral Onishi soon decided to put his plan into immediate execution. Had his decision been made beforehand, or was it hastened by events? No one knows. One thing is certain: at 8:30 in the morning of October 19, only two days after his arrival, he learned that the American invasion fleet was in sight.

All through the morning, reconnaissance planes sent messages confirming the news and describing the composition of the invasion forces. Numerous enemy units were reported at distances of between 130 and 180 miles from Tacloban, on Leyte Island.

There was no longer any doubt about the Americans' intentions: the great invasion was about to begin. Admiral Onishi realized that it was urgent to coordinate naval and air operations within the framework of the Sho Plan and carry out the project that had been preoccupying him for several months.

Toward the end of the afternoon a car bearing the yellow pennant of a flag officer arrived at Mabalacat Airfield, about 50 miles from Manila. When it stopped, Admiral Onishi and his aide, Chikanori Moji, got out of it. An unannounced visit by an admiral at such a late hour was unusual. This, combined with the tense atmosphere of the current situation, made all the officers present feel a certain uneasiness.

The admiral returned their salutes and asked to be taken to the command post of the 201st Air Group. In the single room of the little building, he sat down and watched the intense activity on the base. Then, after a long silence, he announced that he would hold a conference at the headquarters of the unit, giving the officers to understand that he had a special question to ask them and wanted to know their opinion. They all got into cars and drove to the town of Mabalacat.

The three large Western-style houses in Mabalacat had been requisitioned by the Japanese for officers' billets, and the headquarters of the 201st Air Group were installed in one of them. Admiral Onishi and the officers he had assembled went to a room on the second floor and sat down around a large table. Besides the admiral and his aide, there were Commander Asaichi Tamai, executive officer of the 201st Air Group, Captain Rikihei Inoguchi, senior staff officer of the First Air Fleet, staff officer Chuichi Yoshioka of the 26th Air Flotilla, and lieutenants Ibusuki and Yokoyama, squadron leaders of the 201st Air Group.

Usually energetic and dynamic, Onishi was now obviously tired and dejected. In the light of the small bulb hanging overhead by a wire, he looked at the officers one by one, then said quietly:

As you know, the war situation is grave. The appearance of strong American forces in Leyte Gulf has been confirmed. The fate of the Empire depends upon the outcome of the Sho Operation, which Imperial General Headquarters has activated to hurl back the enemy assault on the Philippines. Our surface forces are already in motion. Vice Admiral Kurita's Second Fleet, containing our main battle strength, will advance to the Leyte area and annihilate the enemy invasion force. The mission of the First Air Fleet is to provide land-based air cover for Admiral Kurita's advance and make sure that enemy air attacks do not prevent him from reaching Leyte Gulf. To do this, we must hit the enemy's carriers and keep them neutralized for at least one week . . .

In my opinion, there is only one way of assuring that our meager strength will be effective to a maximum degree. That is to organize suicide attack units composed of Zero fighters armed with 550-pound bombs, with each plane to crash-dive into an enemy carrier . . . What do you think? [1]

The admiral stopped speaking to observe the reactions of his subordinates. The idea was not new to them, of course; they had all given some thought to it and knew that there had already been many individual cases of such suicide attacks, but they were surprised to hear an admiral proposing to make them an official operation.

Commander Tamai, who had the awesome honor of making the decision for his unit, asked Admiral Onishi to let him withdraw for a few moments with one of his squadron leaders, Lieutenant Ibusuki. After a brief conversation the two men came back into the room and Tamai said: "I share completely the opinions expressed by the Admiral. The 201st Air Group will carry out his proposal. May I ask that you leave to us the organization of our crash-dive unit?" [2]

Everyone present realized the gravity of the decision that

[1] The Divine Wind, *by Inoguchi, Nakajima and Pineau, pp. 5-7.*
[2] Ibid., *p. 8.*

had just been made. It was no longer a question of individual pilots deciding in the midst of combat to crash-dive an enemy target: from now on, a group of volunteers, fully conscious of what they were going to do, would consent to that sublime act several days, sometimes several weeks, in advance.

A Delicate Organizational Task

Commander Tamai had just assumed a very heavy responsibility. The other officers at the conference had all accepted the need for the new tactics, but he did not yet know how his men would react. That same night he summoned the 23 noncommissioned pilots of the 201st Air Group to a meeting at headquarters in Mabalacat. He gave them a brief summary of the war situation, stressed how important it was that the Sho Plan should succeed and finally described Admiral Onishi's proposal.

Every man raised both arms as a sign of enthusiastic approval. Tamai was proud of them, and overwhelmed by their response. He brought the meeting to an end, telling them to say nothing about what had been decided.

Later that night, he spoke with Captain Inoguchi, who had been present during the conference with Admiral Onishi, and told him about the meeting he had just had with his pilots.

"Inoguchi," he said, "they are so young. But though they cannot explain what is in their hearts, I shall never forget the firm resolution in their faces. Their eyes shone feverishly in the dimly lit room. Each must have been thinking of this as a chance to avenge comrades who had fallen recently in the fierce Marianas fighting and at Palau and Yap. Theirs was an enthusiasm that flames naturally in the hearts of youthful men." [3]

The two officers discussed the problem of choosing a man

[3] Ibid., *p.* 9.

to head the new unit. He would have to be an expert pilot with superior qualities of leadership. They considered several men and finally decided on Lieutenant Yukio Seki, who had shown remarkable fighting spirit and seemed capable of being an excellent leader.

But the most important question still had to be answered: would he volunteer? Neither Admiral Onishi nor the other officers had any thought of forcing anyone to join the new unit. It would be made up entirely of volunteers. Tamai and Inoguchi decided to ask Lieutenant Seki the terrible question without delay.

Awakened by an orderly, Seki quickly dressed and came to meet them. Tamai asked him to sit down. Paternally putting his hands on Seki's shoulders, he described Admiral Onishi's proposal and told him that because of his outstanding qualities he had thought of him to lead the new unit.

Seki closed his eyes and meditated for a long time with his head between his hands. Then he looked up and said firmly, "You absolutely must let me do it." [4]

Kamikaze!

Giving names to combat units and missions was a common practice in the armed forces of all nations during World War II. A single word could thus be used to designate something that might otherwise have required a long description. It was Captain Inoguchi who suggested the name "kamikaze," [5] which means "divine wind," for the new suicide unit.

Why that name? Because it recalled the legend of Ise, the wind god, who had saved Japan from an enemy invasion in ancient times. This legend was based on a real event. On

[4] Ibid., p. 11.
[5] *The word was first used in the form of "shinfu," the alternate pronunciation of the Japanese characters used to write it. (Although they may differ greatly phonetically, the two possible readings of a Japanese character have the same meaning.)*

神風

KAMI — KAZE
Shin — Fu

August 14 and 15, 1281, an imposing Sino-Mongol fleet of 3500 ships, under the command of the great despot Kublai Khan, left China with more than 100,000 warriors to invade Japan. Divided and torn by ceaseless internal wars, Japan was in no condition to turn back that colossal assault. Her people were expecting either death or slavery, when a violent typhoon destroyed most of the approaching fleet. The terrified survivors returned to China and never attempted another invasion. The Japanese gave thanks for the *kamikaze*, the "divine wind" that had saved their country.

Now that Japan was again facing the danger of invasion, the choice of "kamikaze" as the name of the force that was to destroy the enemy fleet seemed highly appropriate. It was adopted unanimously.

During that same night of October 19, so rich in events, Captain Inoguchi went to Admiral Onishi to inform him of what had been done.

The admiral had gone upstairs to bed immediately after his conference. Inoguchi knocked on the door and went in. Onishi was lying on a cot in the dark, but he had not been sleeping. He had been meditating on the fate of Japan, as well as the enormous responsibility that now rested on his shoulders. He knew that in the eyes of history he would be the man who, by his convictions and decisions, had systematically sent young men to a knowingly accepted death.

He sat up on his cot, turned on the light and listened to Inoguchi's detailed report. When it was finished, Onishi stood up, called in his aide and began dictating an official order creating the new corps.

Of the 26 planes available to the 201st Air Group, half would crash-dive against the enemy and half would be used as escorts. The 26 planes were divided into four sections that were given poetic names in keeping with Japanese custom: Yamazakura, Yamato, Asahi and Shikishima.[6]

The next day Admiral Onishi decided to speak to the volunteers, whom he did not yet know. At one o'clock in the afternoon, when they had assembled near their living quarters at the Mabalacat airfield, they saw his car arrive. He was pale and tense. The men stood at attention while he walked in front of them, looking at them intently. Then he began to speak:

> Japan is in grave danger. The salvation of our country is now beyond the power of the ministers of state, the General Staff, and lowly commanders like myself. It can come only from spirited young men such as you. Thus, on behalf of your hundred million countrymen, I ask of you this sacrifice, and pray for your success. You are already gods, without earthly desires. But one thing you want to know is that your own crash-dive is not in vain. Regrettably, we will not be able to tell you the results. But I shall watch your efforts to the end and report your deeds to the Throne. You may all rest assured on this point. I ask you all to do your best.[7]

[6] *Yamazakura: the wild cherry tree; Yamato: the ancient name of Japan; Asahi: the rising sun; Shikishima: a poetic name for Japan. These names are taken from a poem by the famous Noringa Motoori:* Shikishima no Yamato Gokoro wo hito towaba Asahi ni niu Yamazakura Bana: *"If I am asked what is the heart of Japan, I shall reply that it is the fragrance of the wild cherry tree in the rising sun."*

[7] The Divine Wind, *by Inoguchi, Nakajima and Pineau, p. 18.*

The Hour of Sacrifice Approaches

On the afternoon of October 20 the Yamato Unit of the new kamikaze corps, consisting of four Zeros carrying bombs, escorted by four other Zeros, took off from Mabalacat and landed at Cebu at about five o'clock. The creation of the corps was still a secret, but the personnel of the Cebu base would now have to be informed of it.

The situation was urgent. At ten o'clock that morning, American amphibious forces had landed on the east coast of Leyte Island and quickly established a front extending 19 miles northward to Tacloban. The offensive launched by General MacArthur's troops had powerful air and naval support.

Tadashi Nakajima, flight officer of the 201st Air Group, who had piloted one of the four escort fighters, assembled the personnel at Cebu, told them about the newly created kamikaze corps and announced that it would begin operations immediately. The men listened in astounded silence. Nakajima ended his speech by suggesting the formation of a suicide unit at Cebu, but he urged all men who did not feel fully ready for self-sacrifice, whether because of family reasons or other considerations, not to volunteer, because the number of available planes was severely limited.

That night the pilots wrote their answers on pieces of paper and put them into envelopes. A petty officer collected the envelopes and brought them to Nakajima, who opened them, not without emotion. The pilots had all volunteered.

Within the framework of the Sho Plan, the First Air Fleet, decimated by constant American bombings, was to be reinforced by the Second Air Fleet. As of October 21, the First Fleet had only about 30 Zeros and 50 bombers of various types. The transfer of the Second Fleet had been delayed only because of its pilots' inexperience. It had been created in Kyushu on June 15, 1944, and had first trained on Formosa, where it had received its baptism of fire during the American attacks of October 12-14.

On October 23, under orders from Admiral Soemu Toyoda, the 350 planes of the Second Air Fleet landed in the Philippines. Its commander, Vice Admiral Shigeru Fukudome, had been ordered to fight in close cooperation with the First Fleet.

Admiral Fukudome, former Chief of the Operations Bureau of the Naval General Staff, was still influenced by the great victories Japan had won at the beginning of the war, and therefore favored mass-formation air attacks. As soon as he arrived in the Philippines and was informed of the situation, he prepared to launch large-scale conventional raids. On October 24, the day after his arrival, he sent 250 planes to attack the American fleet. Bad weather and the great strength of the enemy's defenses made this raid ineffective. No ships were sunk and only five were damaged.

That same day, a ridiculously small detachment of 14 Zeros was sent to provide air cover for Admiral Kurita's naval force in the Sibuyan Sea. This was totally inadequate to ensure the safety of the ships, which had a vital role in the execution of the Sho Plan, and furthermore communications were so bad that when the Japanese gunners saw the Zeros they mistook them for American planes and opened fire, forcing them to withdraw.

Admiral Onishi persistently tried to convince his colleague Fukudome that he, too, should form kamikaze units. He explained his viewpoint several times, telling him that the situation no longer called for large conventional raids, but for attacks by small groups of suicide pilots who would have a better chance of getting through the enemy's formidable defenses. Fukudome remained deaf to Onishi's arguments.

Meanwhile four Japanese naval squadrons were converging on Leyte Gulf, where one of the greatest battles in history was to take place. On the evening of October 24 they reached the points assigned to them by the Sho Plan. We shall not describe the gigantic Battle of Leyte Gulf; we shall limit ourselves to the aerial aspect of the Sho Plan, and in particular the actions of the kamikaze groups.

On October 21 a message reached Cebu reporting that an American task force containing six carriers had been sighted 60 miles east of Suluan Island. The volunteer suicide pilots of the Yamato Unit were resting in the shade of some mango trees. Their planes had been placed under foliage 500 yards from the edge of the airfield to hide them from American raiders. At the alert signal, ground crews hurried to bring them out to the runway and the pilots went to the command post for their flight instructions. The attack group was to be composed of five Zeros: three suicide planes and two escorts.

When the Zeros had been readied for takeoff and the pilots were walking toward them, American Hellcats appeared above the other end of the airfield and began strafing the Japanese planes on the runway. Within a few minutes they hit all of them. Then some American bombers arrived to finish the job. When it was all over, the five Zeros were in flames.

Ground crews quickly brought out three more. Two attackers and one escort took off in a great cloud of sandy dust. At sundown, two of them returned. Their pilots reported that bad weather had prevented them from finding the enemy and they had lost sight of the plane flown by their leader, Lieutenant Kuno. He may have succeeded in locating a target; but if so he failed to hit it, because no American ship reported a suicide attack on October 21.

At Mabalacat that same day, the Shikishima Unit prepared to launch its first attack. The pilots lined up in front of the command post beside their leader, Lieutenant Seki. As a ritual libation, they received a goblet filled with water from a container that Admiral Onishi had left for that purpose. They drank solemnly, then sang a traditional warrior's song.

The motors had been warmed up by the mechanics. The pilots took off, waving farewell. But after a long, futile search

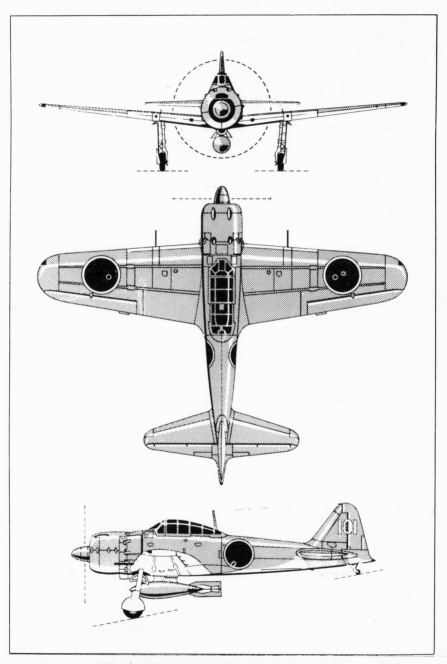

Mitsubishi A6M-7 Zero 63 ("Zeke"), kamikaze version.

for the American ships they had to return to Mabalacat, disappointed and gloomy, apologizing for having been unable to find the enemy.

The bad weather of October 21 continued through the next two days. Every kamikaze group that took off encountered the same difficulty and disappointment. Despite all their tenacity, not one of the pilots was able to crash-dive against an enemy target.

One might wonder why weather conditions handicapped the Japanese so severely while the Americans were able to continue their destructive air raids. The answer is that the American planes had radar and the Japanese planes did not. This was a disadvantage that the Japanese never overcame throughout the remainder of the war.

The Great Day

October 25 was the date of the Battle of Leyte Gulf, one of the most important turning points of the Pacific war. It was also the day when the kamikaze corps scored its first victories and entered history. And finally it was the day when the Japanese realized that they would not be able to dislodge the Americans from their beachhead on Leyte and that they could only try to destroy enough of their fleet to discourage them from advancing any closer to the Japanese home islands.

It should also be noted that on October 25 the Second Air Fleet launched another conventional mass-formation raid against the American fleet, again without significant results, despite a slight improvement in weather conditions. This failure, combined with Admiral Onishi's insistence, finally led Admiral Fukudome to authorize the creation of kamikaze units in his Second Air Fleet during the night of October 25. Then, for the sake of efficiency, the First and Second Air Fleets were given a unified command under Fukudome, who had greater seniority, with Onishi as his chief of staff.

The Yamato Unit

While sea fighting had been raging all around the Philippines since the early morning hours of October 25, a message from First Air Fleet headquarters urged the kamikaze units to attack without waiting until contact with the enemy had been established: there were so many American naval groups at sea that it should be possible to discover at least one of them.

Six planes took off from Cebu at sunrise and headed eastward. Their search for the enemy was not long. At 7:35 they reported contact with an American naval force that included several carriers. It was Taffy 1 (77-4-1),[8] consisting of four escort carriers and seven destroyers, under the command of Rear Admiral Thomas L. Sprague, cruising north of Mindanao, about 40 miles from Siargao Island.

At 7:40, when the Japanese planes were sighted, they were already very close, having taken advantage of heavy cloud cover to make their approach. They caught the American force so completely off guard that not one shot was fired from its antiaircraft guns.

One of the Zeros dived at the carrier *Santee* (CVE-29) with its guns blazing. While the American sailors watched in horrified fascination, it continued heading straight for the ship. There was a blinding flash when it struck the forward end of the flight deck, blasting out an opening 15 feet wide and 30 feet long. Fire broke out immediately and spread to the hangar deck. Flames were soon licking the eight 1000-pound bombs that were stored there. Fortunately they had not yet been fuzed, so they did not explode, which saved the *Santee* from certain catastrophe.

While the crew of the *Santee* were struggling against the fire on board, another kamikaze plane emerged from the clouds and dived. By now the gunners on the American

---

[8] *"Taffy" was the radio code designation of these escort carrier groups, and they were commonly referred to by that name.*

ships had begun firing. The suicide pilot seemed to have chosen the *Sangamon* (CVE-26) as his target, but the nearby *Suwanee* (CVE-27) scored a hit with one of its five-inch guns and the plane went into a spin. After taking another hit, it fell into the sea like a stone, 150 yards away from the *Suwanee*.

The Americans were now firing all their guns. When the third kamikaze swooped down toward its prey, the gunners of the *Petrof Bay* (CVE-80) were lucky enough to make a direct hit on it. It disintegrated in the air and blazing fragments fell into the water all around the ship.

At the same time, the *Suwanee*'s gunners shot down their second plane of the day. They were still cheering when they saw another Zero circling at an altitude of about 8000 feet, choosing a target. They opened up on it and obviously hit it, because it lurched and began trailing smoke. But just as they were thinking that the danger was over, they saw that the pilot had regained control of his plane and was coming straight at them.

It dived at prodigious speed. None of the ship's guns was able to deflect it. The *Suwanee* shuddered when the plane crashed into the flight deck a little forward of the stern elevator. High flames spurted out of a jagged hole about 25 feet across. The *Suwanee* appeared to have been gravely damaged.

The sixth Japanese plane disappeared in the clouds and no one ever knew what became of it.

The fire aboard the *Santee* was quickly brought under control, but 16 men had been killed and 27 wounded. Although flight operations were temporarily impossible, the *Santee* was able to remain in formation. As for the *Suwanee*, its damage was less serious than had been feared at first. Thanks to quick and efficient action by the crew, the fire had been extinguished. Several men had been killed and the elevator was unusable, but makeshift repairs made the flight deck operational again shortly after ten o'clock.

The Shikishima Unit

At 7:25 on the morning of October 25, a kamikaze group from the Shikishima Unit, led by Lieutenant Yukio Seki, left Mabalacat to attack some American ships that had been reported east of the airfield. This time the search was longer, because visibility was reduced by rain squalls. At 10:40 Seki radioed that he had spotted four carriers and six destroyers 90 miles east of Tacloban.

The formation he had found was Taffy 3 (77-4-3), commanded by Rear Admiral Clifton Sprague. It had originally contained six escort carriers and seven destroyers, but it had just suffered losses in the Battle of Samar.

At 10:50 the American ships had their first warning when a Zero, flying just above the water, roared past a few hundred yards ahead of the escort carrier *Kitkun Bay* (CVE-71). The kamikazes had gained the advantage of surprise by slipping in under the Americans' radar, which could not detect planes flying at such low altitude.

The Japanese abruptly climbed to about 5000 feet and began their dives. The first Zero headed for the *Kitkun Bay,* approaching from starboard and shooting at the men on the bridge. It was about to crash into the ship when it was deflected by a shellburst. Only its wing struck the island,[9] but the impact made its bomb fall out and strike the ship. Although the plane itself plunged into the sea, the explosion of the bomb caused great damage.

Two Zeros diving at the *Fanshaw Bay* (CVE-70) were shot down almost simultaneously. Two others dived at the *White Plains* (CVE-66), but the intense antiaircraft fire discouraged one of them and, trailing black smoke, it changed course and headed for the *St. Lo* (CVE-63).

The sky was filled with smoke from bursting shells, burn-

[9] *The island of an aircraft carrier is the superstructure above the flight deck, located on the extreme starboard side to leave as much space as possible for landings and takeoffs.*

ing ships and planes, and the stacks of all the ships in the formation, whose engines were racing at full speed. Under those conditions, it was hard for the American spotters to pick out the small, black, moving dots that could turn into lethal attackers at any moment. As a result, antiaircraft fire was disorderly and sometimes late.

This was the case aboard the *St. Lo*. The gunners were warned too late. They were able to fire only a few rounds at the attacking Zero, without effective coordination. It dived so fast and appeared so abruptly that some of the sailors did not even have time to throw themselves down on the deck. With an enormous explosion that shook the whole ship, the kamikaze crashed through the flight deck and spewed burning gasoline over the hangar deck below.

The fire exploded seven torpedoes. This gigantic blast blew the elevators, whole airplanes and large sections of the flight deck high into the air. Survivors later said they had the impression that the ship had been ripped in half like a piece of paper.

Other internal explosions finished devastating the *St. Lo*. It was soon transformed into a huge torch, giving off heat that could be felt from hundreds of yards away. Since everything on board had ceased to function, it was impossible to fight the fire. Captain MacKenna gave the order to abandon ship. At 11:25, not long after the evacuation of the crew had been completed, the *St. Lo* sank.

Admiral Onishi's Victory

The companion of the plane that struck the *St. Lo* continued diving at the *White Plains* but was hit several times by antiaircraft fire and began swerving erratically. To the sailors aboard the *White Plains* it was obvious that the pilot had been wounded and was struggling to regain control of his plane. It grazed the flight deck and exploded before it hit the water. Flying fragments damaged the side of the ship and wounded 11 men. Bits of wreckage, including pieces of the pilot's body, fell onto the deck.

If we have given the impression that these attacks occurred successively, it is because we have had to interrupt our account of the action to describe some of its details. The attacks were actually simultaneous, or nearly so.

At 11:10 a group of planes approached the *Kitkun Bay* from astern. Two of them dived: one at the *Kitkun Bay*, the other at the *Kalinin Bay* (CVE-68). The gunners of the *Kitkun Bay* opened fire a little late, but they were fortunate enough to make one shot that tore both wings off the attacking Zero. Its bomb was thrown clear and exploded 25 yards away from the carrier, causing only minor damage.

The other kamikaze pilot, ignoring the shells that were bursting all around him, continued his plunge toward the *Kalinin Bay*. His plane exploded against the flight deck, severely damaging it.

The crew of the *Kalinin Bay* were stunned by the nature and suddenness of the attack. Some of them were staring at the gaping hole in the deck and exchanging remarks on what had just happened when a spotter reported three more attackers. They were already very close before the gunners could open fire. The first one was deflected by a direct hit. It struck the carrier's stack and broke it off. Wreckage from the plane and the ship fell into the water at the same time.

The two other planes narrowly missed their target and crashed into the sea. The fire aboard the *Kalinin Bay* was put out and the ship was saved.

By 11:30 the sky was clear of planes. American sailors had undergone occasional suicide attacks since the beginning of the war, but on that day, October 25, 1944, they realized that something had changed. The Japanese seemed to be animated by an implacable fanaticism that went beyond anything conceivable to a Western mind and did not give an encouraging idea of what the rest of the war would be like.

These undeniable Japanese successes were a reward to Admiral Onishi and confirmed the soundness of his convictions.

A Success Heavy with Consequences

Rather than returning to Mabalacat, the three escort Zeros of the Shikishima Unit headed for the much nearer airfield at Cebu and landed there a little after noon. Out of the first plane came Hiroyoshi Nishizawa, the famous ace who had covered himself with glory in many air battles around Rabaul, in the Bismarck Islands. He went straight to the command post to report what he had just seen.

With great emotion, he described the first large and successful sortie of the kamikaze corps. The other pilots present all listened in attentive silence. Those who were waiting their turn to go on suicide missions added to their technical knowledge and received an answer to the question that had been worrying them most: whether, in the last few seconds of a crash-dive, the pilot could maintain enough lucidity to hit his target with precision.

This concern shows the nature of their feelings. They were undaunted by the thought of sacrificing themselves; their only fear was that their own reactions might betray them and lessen the effectiveness of their attacks. They were saddened by the deaths of Lieutenant Seki and the other men of the Shikishima Unit, but their grief was mingled with deep joy at the victory they had won. Now that the validity of Admiral Onishi's ideas had been so decisively demonstrated, hope that the kamikaze corps might reverse the military situation became much stronger.

The great naval battles which were fought that day all ended with the defeat and rout of the Japanese forces. The Sho Plan had failed. The Japanese had been unable not only to destroy the enemy fleet, but even to attain the essential goal of the Sho Plan: to stall the American invasion of the Philippines.

In their efforts to hide the extent of the disaster from the Japanese people, the high command seized on the news of the kamikaze victories as a diversion. Radio Tokyo repeatedly described them as a kind of divine vengeance. Imperial General Headquarters issued communiqués glorifying the kamikaze pilots, praising their exploits and proclaiming that they would save Japan from the threat of invasion.

This official enthusiasm had several consequences: it increased the already large number of kamikaze volunteers, it prompted Admiral Onishi to create more kamikaze units and extend their action, and it swept away Admiral Fukudome's reservations with regard to suicide tactics.

Useful Lessons

Admiral Onishi originally regarded the creation of kamikaze units as a temporary measure for a specific purpose: the successful defense of the Philippines. It was understood that once that goal had been achieved there would be a return to conventional warfare. Furthermore, there was to be only a small number of kamikaze units and their use was to be limited to specified targets, primarily enemy ships. Ordinary methods would continue to be used in other cases.

The idea of a limited, temporary effort was clearly understood by everyone, and was one reason for the large number of volunteers. If, from the beginning, the plan had been to transform the entire Imperial Navy Air Force into a kamikaze corps and use it as such throughout the rest of the war, there would probably have been fewer volunteers and the decision might have set off a reaction with unforeseeable consequences. Japanese pilots were fired with extraordinary patriotic zeal, but they were still men of flesh and blood, with normal human emotions.

In the critical plight of their country at the time, Japanese fighting men could not help thinking of the privations from which their families were already suffering and what their fate would be if Japan should lose the war. This intensified their concept of patriotic duty and favored their mystical predisposition toward self-sacrifice. We believe that Japanese suicide attacks must be viewed in this light. The kamikaze pilots provided a spectacular example of them, but the fact is that all branches of the Japanese armed forces made suicide attacks in particularly desperate situations.

Admiral Onishi created the kamikaze units only in the hope of restoring the lost effectiveness of the Japanese navy and using it in the execution of the Sho Plan. It was the surface fleet that was supposed to play the major part in that plan by dealing a crushing blow to the American navy on October 25. Air units were assigned a complementary role, mainly at the beginning and end of the action. The overall objective was a decisive weakening of the enemy.

Although he did not say so explicitly, it is probable that Onishi intended to limit suicide attacks to that single day of October 25, that he felt that their results would bring about a better balance of forces and make further use of such drastic methods unnecessary. Several officers close to him interpreted his viewpoint in this way. He died less than a year later without having clarified his thoughts on the matter.

Be that as it may, the Leyte disaster changed the whole situation. When the gigantic battle was over, the Japanese fleet had for all practical purposes been destroyed. Japan's fighting ability now lay solely in her land and air forces. And her air forces were in precarious condition: they suffered from shortages of planes, spare parts and fuel, and their pilots lacked training and experience.

In these circumstances, continuation of kamikaze operations seemed to be Japan's only hope. Within a few months they had almost completely replaced conventional air attacks. This marked a great departure from the spirit in which the first suicide units had been created.

Another lesson that could be drawn from that historic day of October 25 concerned the attitude of the Americans. With blind faith in their moral and spiritual superiority, many Japanese expected the kamikaze attacks to have an overwhelming psychological effect on the enemy: in the face of such sublime courage and fierce strength of will, the Americans would lose heart and give up their plan to carry the war to the Japanese homeland. This was a thoroughly naive conviction, but one cannot help marveling at the strength of the mystically patriotic fervor behind it.

The Americans disappointed Japanese expectations by maintaining a cool-headedness that could almost have been mistaken for indifference. With their usual practicality and admirable ability to adapt to changing circumstances, they reacted calmly but resolutely. There was no panic or discouragement aboard any of the ships that underwent kamikaze attacks on October 25. The new demonstration of Japanese fanaticism naturally made a strong impression on the American sailors, but it did not paralyze them with fear or produce the emotional shock that the Japanese had counted on.

Yet the Japanese did not give up their hope of demoralizing the enemy. They felt that relentless repetition of their kamikaze attacks might still succeed where the initial effect of surprise had failed.

CHAPTER

IV

From Experiment

to Generalization

The stinging defeat of the Imperial Navy in the Battle of
Leyte Gulf was a harsh blow to the pride of the Japanese but
they were not discouraged. Their immediate reaction was to
stiffen their will to resist still more. Since the navy had suffered such disastrous losses that it could no longer carry out
any coordinated action, they would have to fall back on the
only offensive weapon they had left: their air forces.

But, as already shown, aircraft production was seriously
limited by the shortage of raw materials and there was not
enough fuel to make it possible to train pilots properly.
Furthermore the qualitative difference between Japanese
and American planes was steadily growing. From 1943 on,
Japan was unable even to match the quality of the enemy's
planes, much less regain the clear superiority she had en-
joyed at the beginning of the war. Her aircraft industry
continued trying to improve existing types while the Americans were turning out new and increasingly superior models.
And finally, the effectiveness of the Japanese air forces had
been greatly reduced by the Americans' incessant bombings
of airfields.

Only radically new tactics would have any chance of making up for all these disadvantages. It took no speeches or
exhortations to convince Japanese commanders and pilots

that launching kamikaze raids on a much larger scale was the only logical thing to do.

The New Organization

The First Air Fleet had already undergone major losses, largely in earlier air battles and American bombings of airfields. The Japanese high command decided to reinforce it with the fighter groups of the Twelfth Air Fleet, then stationed at Chishima, in northern Japan. On October 26 these reinforcements landed at Clark Field, north of Manila. The men and planes were immediately incorporated into kamikaze units.

On the day after the creation of the kamikaze corps by Admiral Onishi, its members had begun discussing how they could best make use of the planes at their disposal. Considering the power and efficiency of the enemy's defenses, squadron leaders had suggested that raids be carried out by small groups which, they felt, would have a better chance of passing unnoticed and thus getting through to their targets.

It was finally decided that the groups would be composed of five planes each: three to attack and two to act as escorts. This number would not be rigidly fixed; it would be changed if circumstances required it. Judging from the attacks of October 25, it might sometimes take two or three impacts to damage a large ship decisively. As for the escort planes, two were regarded as the minimum: one above the attack planes and one below, to ward off enemy fighters.

There was another reason for limiting attacks to small groups. Because of the unremitting American air raids, Japanese planes at airfields in the Philippines had to be concealed under trees, sometimes at a great distance from the runway. Respites between raids were often so short that only a few planes could be brought out of hiding, readied for flight and sent into the air.

The escort pilots were instructed to stay with the attack

planes until they began their final plunge. On the way to the target, they were to avoid combat if possible and try to maneuver enemy fighters away from the kamikaze planes. Since this was an important job that required superior flying ability, the best pilots had to be reserved for escort duty and were therefore not accepted as suicide volunteers. But they were expected to sacrifice themselves when necessary to enable the attack planes to complete their mission.

On October 27, following Admiral Onishi's example, Admiral Fukudome formed four kamikaze units with men and planes from the 701st Air Group of the Second Air Fleet. They were placed under the command of Captain Tatsuhiko Kida and each unit was given a name: Chuyu, Seichu, Junchu and Giretsu.

Continued American Efforts

After their great victory in the Battle of Leyte Gulf, the American forces around the Philippines were more aggressive than ever. It was urgent for Japanese planes to destroy as many ships as possible to reduce enemy pressure and enable Japanese defenders to throw back General MacArthur's troops on land. In short, the air forces would have to take over the objectives that the surface fleet had failed to achieve.

Early on the morning of October 26, a reconnaissance plane reported American ships off Surigao. It was the same formation that had been attacked the day before by the Yamato Unit, which now prepared for another raid. At 8:15 two attack planes and an escort took off. They were never heard from again. Were they intercepted by enemy fighters? Did they reach their target without reporting it by radio? No one ever knew. There is no evidence that they made a successful attack, however; they simply vanished without a trace.

Another group—three attack planes and two escorts—took off at 10:30 and flew due east, toward the reported position of the American ships. An hour and a half later, a brief radio message was received at Cebu, announcing that the ships had been sighted about 90 miles east of Surigao.

The five Zeros succeeded in penetrating an intercepting force of no less than 60 Hellcats. The first two dived at the escort carriers *Sangamon* and *Petrof Bay* but missed them by a very close margin. Antiaircraft fire was intense; it is likely that the two pilots were either killed or wounded before they could strike their targets.

The third attack Zero took advantage of the general confusion to dive at the escort carrier *Suwanee*. The American gunners shifted their fire, but a little late. A Grumman Avenger had just landed on the carrier and been pushed to the forward elevator when the kamikaze struck. It crashed into the elevator, pulverizing the Avenger that was on the platform. The simultaneous explosion of both planes shook the whole ship and set off a large fire.

The flames raced toward the bow, where nine other Avengers were parked. They all caught fire but a veritable miracle saved the *Suwanee*. The Avengers were loaded with powerful depth charges. If they had also exploded, the ship would almost surely have sunk. But the depth charges did not explode; instead, they merely burned like flares.

The fire was hard to fight because it was raging in several different places but it was finally put out a few hours later. The attack had caused 245 casualties, including over 150 deaths. The *Suwanee* had to leave formation and go to a repair base.

Tactical Evolution

So far, kamikaze pilots had made American aircraft carriers their main targets. Admiral Onishi had stressed the fact that destroying them would prevent American carrier-based planes from continuing their devastating raids.

From the beginning of the war, air power had proven its

tactical and strategic preeminence. It had been the major
factor in most battles, and in many cases had alone decided
the outcome. The Americans had quickly realized that victory would hinge on the number of carriers each side had
and how well they were used. This was reflected in the
makeup of their task forces, composed of a core of one or
more carriers surrounded by accompanying ships (cruisers,
destroyers and sometimes battleships) intended more for
the defense of the core than for naval engagements in the
traditional sense.

One reason for the collapse of the Japanese navy was that
it was never able to obtain a sufficient number of carriers
manned by well-trained aviation personnel. Japanese ship-
yards could not compete with America's enormous industrial capacity and even the few carriers put into service after
the great turning point of Midway could not be given all the
equipment and expert personnel that they should have had.

The growing imbalance finally became so colossal that
there was no longer any possibility of reversing it. Japan
used 25 carriers in the whole course of the war; the United
States launched 125. These figures alone show how important
industrial capacity was in the war. They also make it easy
to understand why the Japanese air forces made such determined efforts to destroy American carriers, especially since
air raids by carrier-based planes did so much to paralyze
Japanese defensive action.

Carriers remained the number-one target of Japanese pilots
all through the American invasion of the Philippines, but
other types of vessels also became particularly important at
that time. Large numbers of transports and landing craft,
bringing reinforcements and supplies to the invading troops,
were constantly anchored or moving in Leyte Gulf. Japanese
air commanders decided to strike at these ships too, to support the ground forces defending Leyte. From October 27
on, kamikaze attacks were directed against both the American combat fleet at sea and the vessels of the amphibious
force in Leyte Gulf.

While ground fighting continued on Leyte Island, American planes kept up steady bombings of Japanese airfields, military installations and troop concentrations all over the Philippines. The Japanese lived in an oppressive atmosphere, unable to feel safe anywhere. Airfields, in particular, were constantly harassed. Bomb craters in the runways had to be hastily filled in before each takeoff, and then the planes were often attacked by the enemy before they were airborne. This climate of insecurity redoubled the Japanese pilots' determination to destroy the enemy at all cost, and thereby multiplied the number of kamikaze volunteers.

Small local successes occasionally lessened the pressure exerted by the enormous superiority of the omnipresent American forces. On October 27, 17 Zeros were transferred from Mabalacat to Cebu to reinforce the Yamato Unit. Cebu, 70 miles from Leyte, had become a vitally important operational base. During the flight, the Japanese planes, led by Lieutenant Kanno, ran into a formation of 16 Hellcats and a battle broke out immediately.

The Japanese threw themselves into the melee with a boldness that shook their opponents. A few minutes later, 12 of the Hellcats had fallen in flames and the four survivors were fleeing. Lieutenant Kanno's formation had lost only one plane. This one-sided victory, unhoped for in those difficult times, gave new confidence to Japanese airmen. That same day the kamikaze units of the Second Air Fleet went into action, substantially increasing the number of planes available for suicide attacks.

Yet it was also on October 27 that Admiral Onishi apparently experienced his first discouragement. Despite his justified reputation for buoyant vitality, he was melancholy that day. His faith in the kamikaze concept was still unshaken, but he was momentarily disheartened by Japan's disastrous plight, the recent heavy losses in the Philippines, and above all, no doubt, his brave fliers' deaths, for which he felt solely responsible. He could not hide his feelings from Rikihei Inoguchi, his senior staff officer. "The fact that we have to resort to a thing like this," he said to him, "shows how poor our strategy has been. This is certainly an unorthodox command." [1]

These bitter words are another proof that the kamikaze attacks were not a diabolical manifestation of blind fanaticism, but the result of a painful decision based on the realities of the war. The serene attitude of most of the volunteers after they had been accepted as kamikaze pilots shows that they had given careful thought to what they were going to do. They were not impelled by an explosion of anger, and certainly not by any kind of hysterical madness.

We can cite one significant incident that occurred at the Cebu airfield on October 27. Shortly after nightfall the men at the base heard the drone of an approaching plane. Knowing that it could be either an American raider or a Japanese plane from another base coming in for an emergency landing, they were relieved when they recognized it as an Aichi 99 dive bomber.

The pilot waited till the runway had been outlined by lights, then made a normal landing. He was a young officer from the 701st Air Group who had been promoted that morning to leader of the Junchu Unit of the Second Air Fleet's kamikaze corps. When he was shown to the command post, he reported that he and his men had left in the morning to attack American ships in Leyte Gulf, but that he had turned back and landed at Legaspi after discovering that the fuze of his bomb was jammed. It was late afternoon before he had finished repairing the fuze. He had taken off and flown on to Leyte Gulf, but by the time he arrived it was too dark to see anything, so he decided to spend the night at Cebu, then take off again at dawn.

He spoke calmly, as if he were describing a routine operation. His decision had been made, irrevocably, and his only concern now was to complete his mission as efficiently as possible. He spent part of the night writing his report, which included some recommendations to future kamikaze pilots. He urged them to remain patient until they found a good

[1] The Divine Wind, *by Inoguchi, Nakajima and Pineau, p. 63.*

target and make sure their bombs were armed before they attacked.

The base personnel felt that he had already left the world of the living and was acting with the sublime detachment that the Japanese attribute to the dead. His conduct toward the men around him was completely natural, but his spirit had already joined his valiant ancestors in eternity. On October 28, at sunrise, he took off and flew toward Leyte. He was never seen again.

The American Reaction

Although the Americans dealt with the first kamikaze attacks methodically and efficiently, without panic or terror, they were justifiably apprehensive. They were less concerned with the ideological and mystical aspects of the attacks than with their concrete results. On the whole, the American sailors had no desire to be self-sacrificing heroes, but they had the optimism that always comes from an awareness of being on the winning side, and it enabled them to overcome their natural fear.

Although they obviously did not feel like smiling when they saw a kamikaze plane heading straight toward them, their reaction was to defend themselves rather than shrink into paralyzed terror. They quickly learned the best methods of coping with the new menace, one of which was to set up a vast network of spotters and radar units to give them advance warning of approaching aircraft.

Antiaircraft defenses were strengthened both on ships and in the territory that had been reconquered by American ground forces. Larger and more numerous patrols of fighter planes were sent out to intercept the formidable kamikazes.

Within a few days these defensive measures had proven to be highly effective. While most of the Japanese pilots who had flown suicide missions on October 25 were able to dive at an American ship, the number of those who succeeded in getting through to their targets was now diminishing every day. By October 27, only 48 hours after the first systematic suicide raids, the attackers were suffering such heavy losses that whole kamikaze units were sometimes wiped out before they could even attempt a crash-dive. American antiaircraft fire from ships and shore batteries was so dense and accurate that the Japanese planes had to penetrate a veritable wall of steel.

Because the Zeros flown by the kamikaze pilots were made relatively slow and awkward by the heavy bombs they carried, it was often easy for American fighters to shoot them down. Many of those that escaped were destroyed by antiaircraft fire, sometimes at the last moment, when they had already begun their final plunge. Others missed their targets because of pilot error and crashed into the ocean.

During the month that followed the historic day of October 25, 1944, kamikaze attacks caused no serious American losses. Meanwhile the unending American bombing of the airfields from which the suicide planes took off continued to diminish Japanese air power by destroying aircraft on the ground and making runways difficult to use.

An Unchanged Mentality

Local Japanese commanders were fully aware of how efficiently the Americans had reacted but they were not alarmed. They felt that the use of kamikaze tactics was still in its initial phase and that lessons had to be drawn from experience. The pilots' determination was not shaken. Suicide missions were still carried out with enthusiasm, though always in small numbers.

During this period the organization of the kamikaze corps took on its final form. Its command structure was established and reinforcements were sent to the Philippines. Groups of planes, mostly Zeros, left from the Japanese home islands and flew to airfields on Luzon and Cebu via Kyushu and Formosa.

The number of volunteers continued to grow. Not all were accepted. The best and most experienced fliers had to be used as instructors and escort pilots.

The spirit of the kamikaze corps began to take on a certain lyrical aspect. Many of the pilots wrote poems in the grandiloquent style of medieval epics, exalting reverence for one's ancestors, the everlastingness of the Empire, absolute devotion to the emperor, the moral preeminence of the Japanese soul, and the courage of heroes who hurled themselves against the enemy for the glory of eternal Japan.

The surprising thing about this outpouring of romantic enthusiasm was that it came from below. Unlike most other countries going through a difficult period in a war, Japan never had to resort to the well-known means of propaganda and coercion to reinvigorate the fighting spirit of her armed forces. The principle of combat without survival, of sublime effort—in short, the kamikaze spirit—was a permanent norm that went into effect whenever circumstances required it. For most Japanese combatants it was an automatic reaction. Their commanders had no need to stimulate it.

In some cases, however, when the tactical situation was not clear to them, it was useful to inform and guide them. Officers often made speeches to their men before combat, usually to present information that would give meaning to their effort and, if necessary, to their sacrifice. Their determination and willingness to fight were never questioned. Sometimes they were asked to consider making the supreme sacrifice for their country and their emperor, but this was only a reminder of something they had already accepted in principle. They could always be counted on to give their lives if they were shown the need for it. This did not mean that they all wanted to die, or even that they did not hope to be saved or evacuated in time to avoid it. But when they found themselves in a situation where the only alternative to death was surrender, they fought with an implacable fury that was equivalent to deliberate suicide.

The idea of making crash-dive attacks against American ships was first expressed by the pilots themselves. The high command merely structured and coordinated their suggestions. That was why the idea spread spontaneously and attracted so many volunteers. If it had come from above, it might have aroused less enthusiasm.

As soon as volunteers were accepted into the kamikaze corps they began insisting that they be allowed to fly their one-way missions without delay. We must not misinterpret their impatience: it did not come from a desire to cut short their nervous tension, but from fear that the fighting might end before they had a chance to act.

Some of them even asked that the names "kamikaze corps" and "special attack units" be eliminated. They felt it was unfitting that they should be given any special distinction in circumstances where all Japanese pilots, whether kamikazes or not, were facing certain death.

Before taking off on his final mission, each volunteer wrote a farewell letter to his family, sealed an envelope to be sent after his death, usually containing fingernail clippings and a lock of hair, and distributed his money and the contents of his pockets among the friends he would leave behind. When he was seated in the cockpit of his plane he waved good-bye to the men who had gathered to watch his takeoff with an emotion that they were often scarcely able to restrain.

The suicide pilots exemplified the kamikaze spirit in its purest form, but the ground personnel were also deeply influenced by it. They responded by redoubling their efforts, sometimes working around the clock with no time off for sleep, and doing everything in their power to give the volunteers the best possible living conditions until their last takeoff. This was their offering, their way of expressing their gratitude to the selfless heroes on whom all their hopes rested.

Kamikaze pilot in flight gear.

A Constant Quest for Efficiency

There were so many kamikaze raids in the Philippines that we must limit ourselves to describing only the most significant ones. But first it will be useful to summarize the military situation at the time.

On the ground, General MacArthur's troops were putting strong pressure on the Japanese defenders of Leyte. Starting from the east and south, the Americans had begun pushing toward the northwestern part of the island, but their advance was soon stopped by the fortified positions that the Japanese had built in the heights. American planes were very active, dividing their efforts between direct support of troops and attacks against military objectives, especially enemy airfields. In Leyte Gulf, vast numbers of ships supported the amphibious forces and brought them all the equipment and supplies they needed. Task forces of the American Third Fleet were constantly cruising nearby, their main function being to provide air cover.

Tacloban, the only airfield that the Americans had captured by the end of October, was so rain-soaked at first that only a few planes could be based there, but their number gradually grew until the field was an important factor in American air operations.

Things were different with the Japanese. Their decimated air units could not support the defenders directly: they devoted themselves entirely to attacking American ships. While his troops were digging into the heights of the island to stop the enemy's thrust, General Tomoyuki Yamashita, commander in chief of the Japanese forces in the Philippines, did everything possible to send reinforcements to Leyte. Lacking a navy, he used anything that would float—sampans, junks, rowboats, sailboats—to transport troops. It was a difficult operation and only a handful of men could be brought in at a time, but the number of Japanese troops on the island was raised from 22,000 on October 20 to 70,000 by mid-November. This reinforcement hampered the American advance considerably.

Kamikaze raids against ships became a daily occurrence that the Americans regarded almost as a routine. Their fighters and antiaircraft guns often downed all the attackers. For a time, suicide tactics were no longer a source of apprehension.

There was one exception, on October 30, when a kamikaze unit succeeded in slipping through American defenses and reaching a squadron of Task Force 38 cruising 40 miles southeast of Suluan Island. Antiaircraft fire was as heavy as usual but failed to stop the Japanese. Approaching in two groups of three from different directions and at different altitudes, they dived at the American ships. Two planes of the first group struck the fleet carrier *Franklin* almost at the same time, while the third attacked an escort carrier. A few minutes later the first plane of the second group also dived at the *Franklin* but missed it. The two others crashed into a battleship and another escort carrier.

For the third time in its career, the *Franklin* had been severely damaged. The other ships, however, were able to remain in formation.

It was clear to the kamikaze pilots that they would have to improve their methods of approach if significant numbers of them were to reach their targets with consistency. They eventually developed two main methods.

In the first, the pilot flew just above the surface of the ocean to escape early detection by American radar, whose range at that low altitude was only about ten miles. When he was close enough to his target, he climbed rapidly to 1500 or 2000 feet, then made his dive. Besides increasing the chances of taking the enemy by surprise, this method also hindered intercepting fighters because it was difficult for them to maneuver effectively so close to the water.

The other method involved an approach at high altitude (20,000 to 23,000 feet) in rarefied air that required the use of oxygen equipment. At that altitude, the danger from enemy antiaircraft guns and fighters was greatly reduced.

Defenders of the method claimed that the longer dive made it easier to choose a good target and strike it accurately. The drawbacks were that the pilots had to be skilled in instrument flying and that the planes had to have oxygen equipment.

Each method had points in its favor, and both were used. Sometimes, when the number of planes permitted it, they were used simultaneously. This had the advantage of dispersing American defenses so that more planes could penetrate them.

The hope attached to kamikaze tactics was so great that some officers were already thinking of aircraft specially designed for the purpose. They imagined whole fleets of efficient new planes destroying vast numbers of American ships and restoring Japan's chances of victory. Some of these officers worked on their own to design such planes. Finally the research departments of Japanese aircraft manufacturers began to take an interest in the problem.

The kamikaze volunteers gathered often to discuss approach methods and aiming points. They wanted to be sure they knew the most vulnerable and vital parts of each type of vessel, so that their crash-dives would be as destructive as possible. They spoke of all this with a serene detachment that sometimes led them to joke about it. An Occidental might be inclined to interpret this aspect of their attitude as a kind of morbid cynicism, but it was simply an imperturbable resignation that they preferred to take with a smile rather than with tears.

"Demigods" of the Twentieth Century

It must be understood that each volunteer felt that his suicide would be an honorable death only because it gave him the possibility of inflicting destruction on the enemy. In the midst of the general feeling of uncertainty and constant danger, the idea of a futile death was intolerable.

The ground personnel of Japanese air bases were haunted by the same dread of dying uselessly. They could only devote themselves body and soul to those who were able to make the glorious sacrifice. They often went without sleep or food to make their modest contribution. Nothing was too good for the volunteers. Everything was done with that in mind, whether it was a matter of touchingly thoughtful gestures, giving gifts, working relentlessly to keep the planes in flying condition and repair bomb damage to the runways, or making little improvements in the conditions of the fliers' day-to-day lives. Already humiliated by the fact that they could not volunteer, the ground personnel felt that giving the kamikaze pilots anything less than total devotion would be as infamous as desertion.

Despite pressing requests for planes from other sectors, the Japanese high command gave priority to the Philippines. The dominant role of air power in the defense of the islands, as well as its new "special" character, were decisive arguments. Admiral Onishi's trip to Tokyo to state his case was also influential.

About 150 planes were taken from training bases all over the home islands and transferred, along with their crews, to Formosa for a final ten-day training period before being sent to the Philippines.

It was not a simple operation, because most of the young pilots had not been trained beyond an elementary level. Furthermore the transfer had to be made in many stages, all at night, to avoid being intercepted by American planes. The different groups flew south, by way of Okinawa or Amami O Shima. Many of the pilots lost their way and fell into the sea, or crashed on landing. These losses reduced the number of planes that reached Taichu and Tainan, the two main airfields on Formosa.

The accidents were caused mainly by the pilots' lack of training, but also by the bad condition of the planes, most of which had been worn out by students in accelerated flying schools. Although some groups reached Formosa intact, others were drastically diminished on the way. One group, originally composed of 15 Zeros, had so many accidents and difficulties that only five of them arrived in Manila after the training period on Formosa, and of these five, two had accidents when they landed. The planes were mostly Zeros, with a smaller number of two-man Suisei dive bombers.

The instructors on Formosa had a difficult task. In only ten days they had to transform novices into fliers capable of navigating by dead reckoning and successfully carrying out a suicide attack. Instructions had to be limited to essentials. The young pilots were all filled with the ardent kamikaze spirit, but that did not replace the great skill of their elders at the beginning of the war.

Independently of this main contingent, many small groups of planes left the home islands to join kamikaze units in the Philippines. The Japanese were able to keep the number of aircraft in operation more or less unchanged till the middle of December, while reserving as many as possible for the great effort they expected to make when the Americans landed on Luzon, the largest island of the Philippines.

Meanwhile, no day went by without one or more kamikaze raids. There was no shortage of targets; to attack all the American naval groups that they sighted, the Japanese would have needed from four to six times more planes than they had. From the middle of November, kamikaze assaults were directed mainly against the ships of the amphibious force in Leyte Gulf.

It was not rare during this period for several members of a single family to die in combat. There were countless cases of brothers, fathers and sons, or uncles and nephews who were killed within a short time of each other, sometimes in the same area. While these deaths naturally sorrowed those who knew the victims personally, they had a galvanizing effect on men about to go into combat. At no time was there any sign of discouragement or demoralization among the kamikaze volunteers. On the contrary, the heavy loss of life that Japan was suffering seemed to make them still more determined and aggressive.

A description of those "demigods" would be incomplete without some reference to their everyday life. Japanese fighting men had always been trained to be stoical and content themselves with a minimum of food and shelter. In other countries, pilots usually live more comfortably than other servicemen, but in Japan they were treated the same as everyone else.

Conditions in the Philippines were particularly bad. The Japanese high command had not foreseen very long in advance that the islands would be the scene of gigantic military operations, so nothing had been done to provide for lodging large numbers of men. The airfields had remained, for the most part, just as they had been when the Japanese captured them at the beginning of the war. The problems that arose from overcrowding were never adequately solved. Pilots were squeezed into cramped, uncomfortable and unhygienic quarters and their food left much to be desired.

All this remained essentially the same after the kamikaze units were formed. The volunteers' living conditions were still deplorable, despite all the efforts that the ground personnel made to improve them. Up to their last takeoff, they lived ascetically, with only the bare necessities. But they were already so detached from physical life that they sometimes joked among themselves about their future places in the Yasukuni Shrine.[2]

Recrudescence

A new phase in the history of the kamikazes began at the end of November. The first reinforcements that arrived from Formosa made it possible to intensify the suicide attacks. It had become clear to the Japanese that the enemy was re-

[2] *A shrine near Tokyo where heroes who died in battle are venerated.*

grouping his naval forces in preparation for a new major operation.

On November 25, 1944, at twilight, several kamikaze units discovered Vice Admiral Marc A. Mitscher's Task Force 38 off the coast of Leyte. Despite heavy antiaircraft fire and swarms of enemy fighters, some of the Japanese pilots were able to make their suicide attacks while many of their comrades fell in flames around them. They all dived at carriers, the biggest ships in the group. Some of them missed their targets, but others crashed into flight decks. The enormous flash produced by each impact was made all the more spectacular by the gathering darkness.

The assault lasted a little less than half an hour. When it was over, three fleet carriers were seriously damaged and on fire: the *Hancock* (CV-19), the *Essex* (CV-9) and the *Intrepid* (CV-11). Two light carriers were also burning: the *Cabot* (CVL-28) and the *Independence* (CVL-22). The situation did not become desperate aboard any of these ships, however, and the fires were all brought under control.

On November 26 there were several more attacks. The first one, at ten in the morning, was a failure, but in the evening a group of 25 kamikaze planes, the largest that had yet been assembled, attacked troop transports in Leyte Gulf. One of the pilots was unable to follow the others and began wandering in search of the enemy, without success. He then flew west in the hope of finding his base, but became lost. Exhausted, with his fuel running low, he managed to land on an emergency field, intending to take off the next day and make an attack. He had had only two weeks of flying instruction in Japan and ten days of practice on Formosa, which was insufficient to teach a pilot to find his way alone. This was not an isolated case; it shows how rudimentary the training of young Japanese fliers was at that crucial stage of the war.

One of the most powerful kamikaze raids of the Philippines campaign took place on November 27. About 30 Japa-

nese planes left their base at 9:30 in the morning and succeeded in getting past the American fighters that went to
intercept them. By 10:50 they were within striking distance
of the ships of the Seventh Fleet, commanded by Admiral
Robert Hayler. They had been picked up by radar and American fighters had done their best to stop them, but their
unusually large number and new approach tactics enabled
them to get through. The 20 ships were steaming in a circular formation at full speed, throwing up a formidable wall
of antiaircraft fire.

The Japanese attacked shortly before eleven o'clock, from
several directions at once. Before the American gunners could
single out individual targets, they saw a black dot moving
with terrifying speed toward one of the ships in the formation.
A moment later there was a bright flash from the bow of the
light cruiser *St. Louis* (CL-49) and its crew immediately had
to struggle against a violent fire. The planes began diving one
by one, firing their guns until the final impact. The American
sailors had to protect themselves from that murderous fire and
try at the same time to avoid being hit by falling fragments of
their own antiaircraft shells.

The light cruiser *Montpelier* (CL-57) was struck by three
suicide planes in quick succession. Miraculously they did not
explode, but their impacts were still destructive. A fourth
plane was already making its dive when one of its wings was
shot off and it crashed into the water. Its bombs exploded and
sprayed fragments onto the ship. Then a fifth plane dived and
could not be deflected. It struck one of the five-inch mounts,
broke through the armor and wounded some of the men inside. A sixth plane crashed into a 40-millimeter mount but did
not explode. Two more planes barely missed the ship, both
exploding in the water. It was hard for the gunners of the
Montpelier to deal with all the attackers. They had to concentrate on the most pressing danger at the moment, constantly
pivoting their guns to shoot at the nearest enemy.

All the ships of the task force were attacked. It is likely that
the Japanese sent in new groups of planes during the engagement.

For two very long hours, the crew of the *Montpelier* thought that their ship would not be able to withstand such a relentless assault. Only when it had finally stopped could they take stock of the damage. They threw the wreckage overboard and sprayed the deck with powerful fire hoses. In some places the water was reddened by blood. Pieces of the kamikaze pilots' bodies were found: a tongue, a scalp, brains, a knee. One man cut a finger off a hand to take a ring from it. Still in the grip of the emotions aroused by the attack, the crew ignored the horror of the scene and went on clearing the deck of their ship.

The raid was less destructive than was thought. The battleship *Colorado* (BB-45) and the light cruiser *St. Louis* were both damaged. They lost 19 and 14 men respectively, and many more were wounded. The *Montpelier* underwent the heaviest assault and suffered the most damage, but was still able to keep its place in formation.

Radio Tokyo announced that the kamikaze pilots had won a great victory which placed the American fleet in grave difficulty. This was false, but the attack had been incredibly ferocious.

The Harsh Day of November 29

On November 28 there were two suicide assaults against ships of the amphibious force near the coast of Leyte, but they did no serious damage.

The American sailors had now been undergoing kamikaze attacks for more than a month and were beginning to feel the effects of fatigue and nervous tension. Although few ships had been sunk, many had been damaged, some so severely that they had remained afloat only by a miracle.

November 29 went by without incident until 4:30 in the afternoon, when the kamikaze raiders returned. All guns opened up and the whole sky seemed filled with fire and flying splinters of metal. The first plane began its dive as if it were invulnerable, heading straight for the battleship *Maryland* (BB-46), but it was rocked by the blast of an exploding shell and plunged into the ocean, sending up a huge spray of water more than 60 feet high. Two more planes were shot down. The others climbed and apparently flew away.

The American sailors were beginning to breathe more easily when, toward five o'clock, planes were sighted again. Were they the survivors of the first attack, or had others come to take their place? It made no difference. Every gun began firing at its maximum rate. One plane dived at the heavy cruiser *Portland* (CA-33) but the pilot incomprehensibly turned away from his perfect course and crashed into the nearby destroyer *Aulick* (DD-569). The impact was so violent that it altered the little ship's direction. Fire broke out but was quickly overcome. There was a mass of twisted, blackened metal in the middle of the ship and many men had been killed or wounded.

Another plane headed for the battleship *Maryland*. The crew were certain of what was going to happen. They were bracing themselves, expecting to feel the deck tremble under them, when they saw the plane pull out of its dive and continue climbing. No one understood why.

The plane returned and, incredibly, began putting on an exhibition of stunt flying: loops, chandelles and other acrobatics. The dumbfounded sailors could not help admiring the enemy pilot's skill and daring. Finally he went into a steep dive. Had his exhibition been a kind of defiance, or had he wanted to die with a flourish of virtuosity? Had he decided to prove his cool-headedness to himself before his final plunge? There was no time to think about it. The *Maryland* suddenly shook like a leaf. The plane had just crashed into one of the massive 16-inch turrets. A raging fire immediately broke out.

While this extraordinary attack was taking place, other Japanese planes were assailing the squadron. Several were shot down but one got through and began looking for a target. Unable to reach a big ship further away, probably because his controls had been damaged, the pilot crashed into the destroyer *Saufley* (DD-465), which was nearly broken in half by the enormous explosion. It did not sink, however, and was able to get to a repair base without assistance.

These examples show the excellent quality of the American ships. American shipyards were capable of producing all sorts of vessels at an amazing rate without sacrificing strength or fighting ability. It is not unreasonable to think that such violent impacts would have been fatal to most of the ships of other nations.

It should be remembered that a kamikaze attack had three different destructive effects. First, of course, was the explosion of the bomb. Second, the mass of the plane itself produced a tremendous shock that could rip open steel armor. Finally, the fuel in the plane's tanks spewed out, caught fire and flowed into the interior of the ship through the openings caused by the explosion. Added to all this was a psychological factor which, fortunately, had only a minor effect on the Americans.

Evolution of the Campaign

The Japanese continued their daily attacks, but on a smaller scale. Many of the Americans believed it was because they were running out of planes or having trouble finding volunteers. They were mistaken. The Japanese high command had decided to reduce the size of the attack groups for an entirely different reason. There had been clear indications that the Americans were preparing to launch more major operations. The Japanese felt that they had to hold planes and pilots in reserve for that new danger.

On December 3 several kamikaze planes attacked a small American formation cruising in Ormoc Bay, obviously in preparation for imminent operations. Two planes struck the Cooper (DD-695), one of a large and recent class of 2200-ton destroyers. The ship quivered from bow to stern and broke in half. It sank within a few minutes, with most of its crew. A nearby hospital ship was narrowly missed.

Because of the growing difficulties encountered by Mac-Arthur's troops in their advance across Leyte, the Americans had decided to make another landing in the enemy's rear. On December 7, the anniversary of the attack on Pearl Harbor, a small convoy steamed into Ormoc Bay and landed elements of the 77th Infantry Division four miles south of the town of Ormoc.

The Japanese sent a kamikaze unit to attack the ships of the new invasion force. The troops had already been put ashore when several planes dived at the anchored vessels. The destroyer *Mahan* (DD-364) took at least two hits and was sunk. The transport *Ward* (APD-16) was damaged so badly that it had to be scuttled.

Four days later, on December 11, a convoy of ships bringing supplies to the Ormoc beachhead was assailed by kamikazes. The destroyer *Reid* (DD-369), hit by at least two and perhaps even three suicide planes, was sunk. Another destroyer, the *Caldwell* (DD-605), was hit and seriously damaged, but not disabled.

It was obvious that the Japanese had improved their tactics. These recent results, achieved with a small number of planes, had several consequences. First, they encouraged the Japanese to pursue their suicide operations. Second, the number of kamikaze volunteers increased with each victory, until there were sometimes two or three times as many candidates as available planes. And finally, the Americans were forced to become even more vigilant and aggressive in their anti-aircraft defenses, which were already formidable.

The Japanese were apprehensive about the American forces entering the western Philippines. Not only might they cut communications among the various islands within a short time, but they were also a direct threat to Mindoro and Luzon. On the evening of December 13, several lookouts reported seeing a large enemy task force moving westward through Surigao Strait. This could only indicate a new American amphibious operation. The Japanese decided to launch a powerful aerial counteroffensive.

The next morning at dawn, 11 navy planes, including four

float bombers, were sent out to look for the enemy south of
Negros Island. Hours went by without any reported sighting.
But the threat was too serious to be ignored. The Japanese
quickly assembled a large though rather motley fleet of planes
to turn back the American incursion.

Two Saiun reconnaissance planes, 23 Shidens,[3] 30 Zeros
and six Gingas [4] took off from Mabalacat, and three Suisei
dive bombers, commanded by Ensign Yonosuke Iguchi, left
from a field nearby. This was the largest kamikaze group that
had ever been put into the air. Since there was still no further
information on the position of the American fleet that had
been sighted the night before, the group was instructed to fly
to the south coast of Negros Island, and then, if the enemy
was not yet found, to continue out over the Mindanao Sea.

The big formation was flying southward, 125 miles from its
point of departure, when it was intercepted by several patrols
of American Hellcat fighters. The Japanese had to scatter to
escape from their determined attackers. The weather was
rapidly deteriorating. Visibility was so poor that most of the
pilots abandoned their mission and headed for the nearest
airfields.

Ensign Iguchi's Suisei was the only plane that did not turn
back. At 11:50 he sent a radio message saying that he had not
yet sighted any enemy ships. He had thought of landing at
Cebu, but he had already armed his bomb and when he tried
to drop it he found that the release mechanism was jammed.
The live bomb would almost certainly have exploded if he
had tried to land with it. He reported by radio that he had
decided to fly to Leyte Gulf and look for a target there.

When he announced that he had reached Leyte Gulf without encountering any enemy fighters, the men gathered
around the radio receiver at Mabalacat closed their eyes in

[3] *The Shiden was the Japanese navy's newest fighter. Its performance was
excellent, superior in nearly every way to that of the Zero, but there had
not yet been time to test it thoroughly in combat and few pilots were capable of exploiting all its advantages.*
[4] *A new twin-engined plane, designed by the Yokosuka naval arsenal and
manufactured by Nakajima, that could be used for bombing, torpedo and
night-fighting missions. It was just beginning to be put into service at this
time.*

silence, realizing that even though he had not been intercepted by fighters he was surely in the midst of heavy antiaircraft fire. They were beginning to assume that he was
already dead when they heard him say that he was diving.
His last words were *"Tenno banzai!"* ("Long live the emperor!")

Imminent Invasion

Meanwhile other kamikaze groups had spotted an American
convoy in the Sulu Sea and attacked it. Following what was
now a proven method, the pilots dived at the ships one by
one. Several of them were shot down but the others got
through. One of them, diving at prodigious speed, struck the
flagship of the formation, the light cruiser *Nashville* (CL-43),
killing 133 men, wounding more than 190, and causing severe
damage. The *Nashville*, along with a destroyer that had also
been damaged by a suicide attack, had to turn back and go
to the provisional repair base at Leyte.

The invasion fleet continued on its way. On the morning of
December 15, 28,000 American troops landed on the south
coast of Mindoro. This island, halfway between Leyte and
Luzon, was an indispensable stepping-stone toward the reconquest of Luzon, the largest and most heavily defended of
all the Philippine Islands. During the day, kamikaze planes
appeared above the Mindoro beachhead and attacked the
landing craft there. Antiaircraft fire kept many of the raiders
from reaching their targets, but two landing ships were sunk
(LST-472 and LST-738) and a few others were damaged.

Three days later, on December 18, the American Third
Fleet was struck by a violent typhoon east of the Philippines.
Huge waves and unimaginably powerful winds shook even
the biggest ships and tossed them around as if they were
rowboats. The typhoon passed over as quickly as it had come,
but it left frightful destruction behind it.

The destroyers *Spence, Monaghan* and *Hull* had sunk and

many ships had suffered very heavy damage, including the light cruiser *Miami* and the carriers *Monterey, San Jacinto, Cowpens, Cabot, Altamaha, Nehenta Bay, Cap Esperance* and *Kwajalein*. About 800 men were either dead or injured and 186 planes lost. No battle of the war had wrought such devastation. The Third Fleet had to withdraw to Ulithi for repairs and was unable to carry out the operations that had been assigned to it.

Although the Americans enforced strict censorship to conceal the disaster, the Japanese soon had partial knowledge of what had happened. Some of them, perhaps more imaginative or mystical than the others, felt that the typhoon had been another "divine wind," like the one that had saved Japan from catastrophe in the thirteenth century by destroying an enemy fleet. The two situations would have been more similar if it had not been for the vast resources of the American navy.

Aside from what the typhoon had done, the list of losses from kamikaze attacks continued to grow. It was already long enough to make American commanders apprehensive about what might happen if the attacks were intensified.

On Leyte, the December 7 landing had radically altered the situation. American troops of the 77th Division had taken the town of Ormoc, broken through the Japanese lines and gone on to join the First Division. When the link was made on December 21, organized Japanese opposition collapsed, leaving only isolated but solid pockets of resistance. The conquest of the island was not yet finished, but most of the danger was over and the Americans could already begin planning other operations.

On Mindoro, American troops advanced without encountering any great difficulties. On December 21, however, there was a kamikaze raid against the landing ships cruising off the invasion coast. Two more LSTs (460 and 749) were sunk and a few others damaged. Meanwhile American forces, with the help of Philippine partisans, had gained control of the large island of Samar.

To counter the grave danger presented by the kamikaze attacks, Vice Admiral John S. MacCain, commander of Task Group 38-1 and second in command of Task Force 38, devised a new three-part defense. First, by intensive training, he increased the density and accuracy of shipboard antiaircraft fire. Second, he reduced the number of dive bombers on the carriers and added more fighters. Third, he kept fighters almost constantly in the air above Japanese airfields in the Philippines, especially those on Luzon. They prevented the Japanese from making large-scale kamikaze attacks and destroyed many planes on the ground: nearly 200 within the first few days. Some suicide planes did succeed in taking off from emergency fields or bases that were under less heavy attack, but they caused no important losses.

Knowing that an invasion of Luzon was imminent, the Japanese were doing everything they could to prepare for it, but their air power had been gravely depleted by the incessant American bombings as well as the many one-way missions flown by kamikaze pilots. Furthermore, American air and surface forces were tightening their blockade of the Philippines, preventing the arrival of reinforcements and supplies. Luzon had enough fuel and spare parts for only about ten days of operations. There were no more than 100 planes left, and about 20 of these were not in flying condition.

At sea, movements of American ships were more and more numerous. Whether to supply and support previous landings or prepare for new operations, hundreds of vessels of all types were steaming through the waters around the central Philippines.

On December 30 several kamikaze groups took off from Mabalacat and attacked one of the supply convoys off Mindoro. Four ships were sunk and four more damaged. Among those sunk were the tanker *Porcupine* (IX-126) and an ammunition transport that blew up with a monstrous flash more than 300 feet high, killing the entire crew. The next day, still off the coast of Mindoro, other transports were damaged and a cargo ship loaded with explosives blew up and simply vanished into the air.

The Reconquest of Luzon

On December 28, an English-language broadcast from Tokyo announced that the invasion of Luzon would begin on January 9. A premonition? A coincidence? Although the date proved to be exact, the Japanese were not certain of the place. Many officers were inclined to think that the first landing would be made in Lingayen Gulf, which had been used several times before in history, but it was not impossible that the Americans might land in the region of Aparri, at the northern end of Luzon, to take the Japanese troops from the rear.

American preparations were in full swing. Ships of the various fleets were loading their last supplies. On January 2, 1945, the first support fleet, composed of 164 vessels (6 old battleships, 12 escort carriers, 10 destroyers, 63 minesweepers, 73 auxiliary ships) under the command of Vice Admiral Jesse B. Oldendorf, put to sea and moved westward through the Surigao Strait. Late that afternoon, the presence of the fleet was reported by a Japanese spotter perched in the church steeple of a little village in northwestern Mindanao.

A small kamikaze group was sent out the next day. Shipboard antiaircraft fire was so prompt and efficient that only one suicide plane was able to make its dive. It exploded against a tanker, but surprisingly there was no fire and the ship continued on its way, having lost only two men.

From then on, the Japanese concentrated all their attention on Admiral Oldendorf's fleet. Reconnaissance planes watched it almost continuously as it steamed northwest, toward the South China Sea.

While it was rounding the southern tip of Panay Island on the afternoon of January 4, Japanese planes appeared. Several were shot down before they could begin their dives, but one penetrated the barrage and crashed into the flight deck of an escort carrier, the *Ommaney Bay* (CVE-79). A gigantic fire immediately broke out. The ship was shaken by internal explosions as the flames reached its magazines. The damage was so great that the captain had to give the order to abandon ship. A destroyer then finished off the *Ommaney Bay* so that what was left of it would not fall into the hands of the Japanese.

At Mabalacat, Lieutenant Shinichi Kanaya, who had recently brought in a reinforcement group of 13 Zeros from Formosa, quickly won everyone's esteem and admiration. He had tirelessly continued training his men, insisting on the greatest possible precision, speed and efficiency. Harsh with himself, showing remarkable uprightness and integrity, Kanaya was a warrior in the purest samurai style. Within a few days he had become a symbol of the kamikaze spirit, but although he had volunteered for every suicide mission, his request had always been turned down because of his important role in training the kamikaze units at Mabalacat.

His chance finally came on January 5, when all available planes of the First Air Fleet were ordered to attack. A reconnaissance plane had reported large enemy naval groups west of Mindoro, heading north. One of them contained no fewer than 700 vessels. Such an armada had never been seen in Philippine waters before.

Lieutenant Kanaya took off from Mabalacat with 15 attack Zeros and two escorts. He sighted the American fleet after a little less than an hour in the air, but at the same time he saw that it was being protected by a large formation of Hellcats. There was a brief air battle during which only one Japanese plane was shot down; the rest succeeded in eluding the enemy fighters and approaching the ships. As always, antiaircraft fire was heavy, but this time it could not prevent all the planes from carrying out their mission.

Five ships were hit: the escort carrier *Manila Bay* (CVE-61), the heavy cruiser *Louisville* (CA-28), a destroyer, an infantry landing ship and the Australian heavy cruiser *Australia*. Four planes narrowly missed their targets but damaged them when they struck the water and exploded. Several others were shot down.

This was the last large raid by the First Air Fleet in the Philippines. By the end of the day it no longer had any operational planes for suicide attacks.

Swan Song

That night, unknown to their superiors, mechanics of the First Air Fleet at Mabalacat began salvaging parts from wrecked planes that had been written off as beyond repair. They worked all night, without a moment's rest. By dawn they had succeeded in putting together five Zeros in flying condition. In their own way, the mechanics had shown the same enthusiasm and "kamikaze spirit" as the suicide volunteers.

Commander Nakajima assembled the 30 pilots of the base, told them the incredible news, announced that one last suicide mission could now be flown, and called for volunteers. All 30 men immediately raised their hands. Nakajima selected lieutenants Yuzo Nakano and Kunitane Nakao to command two units of three and two planes respectively.

American air raids were so frequent that there were nearly always enemy planes above the Mabalacat airfield. It was almost miraculous that none of the five resuscitated Zeros was destroyed by bombing or strafing. They began rolling along the runway at 4:45 in the afternoon, taking advantage of a lull between enemy raids. As they passed the command post, the pilots shouted their thanks to Commander Nakajima for having chosen them. They took off and flew toward Lingayen Gulf, where a large American naval formation had been reported.

On January 6, when Admiral Oldendorf's fleet entered Lingayen Gulf to make preparations for the imminent landing, the American sailors had a sense of foreboding, as if the clear sky and calm sea were hiding a storm. Covered by the big guns of the fleet, the minesweepers began their work of clearing broad channels through which the ships would move safely. It turned out that there were very few mines and underwater obstructions, and they were all eliminated.

The gunners were tense. They constantly checked the condition of their guns, made sure there was plenty of ammunition on hand, pivoted their mounts. They felt almost relieved when they learned that radar had picked up approaching enemy planes. At 11:45, several kamikaze units from the Japanese Second Air Fleet appeared above Lingayen Gulf. All the American guns opened up with a deafening roar. Within a few seconds the sky was no longer clear: it was filled with black smoke, bright flashes and streaks of fire.

The Japanese planes divided into groups that flew around the fleet, choosing the best angles for attack. The first kamikaze pilot made his dive shortly before noon and was followed by the others at intervals of several minutes. While they exploded against American ships one after another, more planes were arriving. The Japanese were throwing their last reserves into the battle, which they regarded as the final holocaust of the campaign. It was their swan song, and that was what the American sailors had sensed even before the attacks began. In war, combatants sometimes have strange presentiments that depend only remotely on logical reasoning.

The kamikaze pilots acted in small groups, leaving only short respites between attacks. Many of them were shot down, but their number and determination sometimes overwhelmed American defenses and several dozen were able to make their crash-dives.

The battleships *California* (BB-44) and *New Mexico* (BB-40) were each struck by at least two suicide planes. The light cruiser *Columbia* (CL-56), three destroyers and an aircraft tender received direct hits. The minesweeper *Long* (DMS-12) was hit twice and sunk. Another minesweeper, the *Hovey* (DMS-11), and the transport *Brooks* (APD-10) were so badly damaged that they sank a few hours later. The heavy cruisers *Australia* and *Louisville* were hit, each for the second time in its career.

The assaults broke off toward five o'clock. Half an hour later another kamikaze group reached Lingayen Gulf. It was the last five Zeros of the First Air Fleet which had left Mabalacat at 4:45. They plunged through the heavy antiaircraft fire and struck a cruiser, a battleship and three large transports. There were no more attacks that day.

This formidable kamikaze battle, the largest of the whole

Philippines campaign, had used up nearly all the available Japanese planes. Dozens of pilots had given their lives in the vain hope of stopping the inexorable American advance. In all, three ships were sunk and 11 suffered varying degrees of damage.

The Japanese now had only about 20 planes in the Philippines. Some of these were not operational, but thanks to the tireless work of the mechanics a few of them were put into flying condition. Pilots often had to wait for their planes to be repaired before they could take off. Operations were limited to attacks by small groups or single planes.

On January 7, while Rear Admiral Daniel E. Barbey's Seventh Amphibious Fleet was off the coast of Mindoro, heading for Lingayen Gulf, a Japanese plane succeeded in approaching undetected by radar and slipping past the American fighter patrols. It dived so quickly that the ships' guns were a little late in opening fire, but one shellburst was close enough to deflect it at the last moment and it exploded on the surface of the water, barely missing the light cruiser *Boise* (CL-47), which was carrying General MacArthur.

The fleet was attacked again that same day. A single plane came out of a cloud and dived at an LST. The impact produced a colossal explosion that was heard dozens of miles away. No one on the other ships expected to see the LST again. When the smoke cleared it reappeared, completely devastated but still afloat. It had to be towed to the nearest friendly port.

A little further north, over Lingayen Gulf, a kamikaze pilot in a hastily repaired Zero skillfully took advantage of small clouds to approach the American fleet. Swerving irregularly to throw off the gunners' aim, he chose his prey and dived into the minesweeper *Palmer* (DMS-5), which sank a few moments later.

On January 8, a Japanese pilot spotted Admiral Barbey's fleet 100 miles off Bataan and followed it for several minutes, staying just out of range. With remarkable calm, as if this were only a practice session, he picked out his target and began his approach. Miraculously escaping the concentrated fire directed against him, he dived at high speed and struck the escort carrier *Kadashan Bay* (CVE-76), damaging it so heavily that it was put out of combat.

A few minutes later a second plane crashed into a troop transport. To the surprise of everyone who saw the tremendous explosion, the ship remained afloat and was even able to continue on its way, with only moderate casualties among the soldiers and sailors it was carrying.

Several other kamikaze planes came over Lingayen Gulf that day. Most of them were shot down, but two were able to dive. They both crashed into the unfortunate cruiser *Australia,* which thus suffered its third and fourth suicide attacks in less than a week. Damage was extensive but the captain stubbornly refused to take his ship out of the combat zone, despite Admiral Oldendorf's urging.

Admiral Theodore S. Wilkinson's fleet of troop transports, then at the latitude of Manila, was also attacked on January 8. Just as the sun was setting, a Japanese plane came out of the shadows in the east and dived at the escort carrier *Kitkun Bay* (CVE-71). The explosion, particularly dazzling at that late hour, immediately set off a violent fire. The *Kitkun Bay* had to withdraw in a state of alarming devastation.

Before dawn on the morning of January 9, the date that had been so astonishingly predicted by Radio Tokyo, the huge American invasion fleet was assembled in Lingayen Gulf, ready to launch the great landing. In the pale moonlight, assault craft were lowered from transports to take the troops ashore. Further out at sea, the darkness was torn by the countless flashes of naval guns pounding the coast in preparation for the establishment of a beachhead. The sea was calm and the day promised to be clear.

A few minutes after sunrise, three Japanese planes were sighted. Coming from the southeast with the sun behind them, they had taken the Americans by surprise. The first one dived at a destroyer escort, missed it, but struck the mast in passing and exploded nearby on the surface of the water. The second one crashed into the cruiser *Columbia,* which had already been hit on January 6. This new attack left the *Columbia* with very serious damage. The third plane was stopped by a direct hit from a five-inch gun and its flaming debris flew in all directions.

The gigantic concentration of American naval forces in the narrow waters of Lingayen Gulf was an ideal target for the Japanese, but they no longer had any means of trying to stop the landing. The American soldiers went ashore without serious opposition. Within a few hours large numbers of troops and enormous quantities of equipment and supplies had been landed. The beachhead quickly became impregnable. Carrier planes and land-based army planes operating from the newly captured airfields on Mindoro supported the advance of the troops and protected the amphibious fleet.

In the afternoon, however, a small group of Japanese planes performed the amazing feat of getting past all the obstacles and reaching the ships. While several of them were falling in flames, two struck their targets. The battleship *Mississippi* (BB-41) was shaken by a violent explosion that killed or wounded nearly 100 men. And apparently marked by fate, the unlucky *Australia* took its fifth kamikaze hit. It was a very strong ship, but by now it was no longer recognizable as the proud cruiser it had once been.

That same day, January 9, the Americans learned from intelligence reports that the Japanese had extended the kamikaze principle to all forms of combat. American soldiers had already had many occasions to dread Japanese fanaticism, so this news was not a complete surprise to them. It did arouse a certain uneasiness in the navy, however. Since the Japanese fleet had been nearly wiped out, it was unlikely that American ships would be in any danger from large enemy surface vessels, but there were still submarines and small craft: in large numbers, they might inflict heavy damage. The Americans discussed the possibility without taking it very seriously.

Even so, special vigilance was ordered for the night of January 9 and a heavy smoke screen was laid down around the fleet of landing craft. The large ships went further out to sea, as they did every night. Many of the American sailors felt that the special security measures were unnecessary and ridiculous.

Shortly after midnight, radar screens began picking up little spots that were not airplanes. They could only be a multitude of small objects on the surface of the ocean. There was curiosity at first, then anxiety. The lookouts were alerted; they could see nothing.

Star shells were fired in the direction indicated by radar sightings. The lookouts were now able to see the source of the spots: less than five miles away, a Lilliputian fleet of about 70 motor boats was heading straight for the American ships. Each boat, powered by a car engine, carried a heavy explosive charge in the bow.

The Americans opened fire with all their guns. Most of the boats were sunk by direct hits or capsized by the huge columns of water thrown up by exploding shells, but a few were able to get through and ram their targets. There was a series of loud explosions. When silence had again settled over the dark ocean, it was found that four LSTs and two LCIs had been hit. One of the LCIs later sank. This was the first time the Japanese had used such "nautical kamikazes."

On January 10 more Japanese planes, each rebuilt with parts taken from several wrecked ones, flew to Lingayen Gulf and attacked the American fleet there. Two ships were struck and damaged. There was another attack on January 11 by a small group of planes. One of them crashed into the transport *Belknap* (APD-34) and damaged it so badly that it had to be scuttled.

The next day, January 12, a larger group reached Lingayen Gulf. Nine ships were hit; it was an impressive total, although damage was not serious in every case. On January 13, three more ships were hit. It was obvious that the Japanese were using up their last reserves. There were a few more isolated assaults, usually by a single plane and never by more than two, and then on January 15 the kamikaze attacks ceased completely.

It cannot be said that "the fighting stopped for lack of

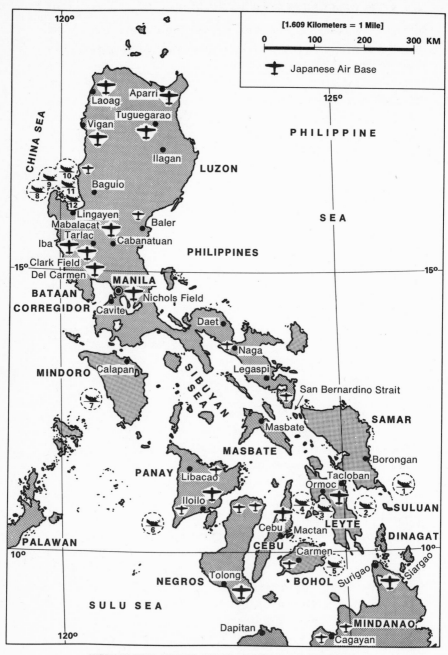

Scale bar: **[1.609 Kilometers = 1 Mile]**

0   100   200   300 KM

✈ Japanese Air Base

120°

CHINA SEA

Laoag
Aparri
Tuguegarao
Vigan
Ilagan
LUZON

9 10
8 11
12
Baguio

Lingayen
Baler
Mabalacat
Tarlac
Iba
Clark Field Cabanatuan
Del Carmen

PHILIPPINES

BATAAN
CORREGIDOR MANILA
Cavite Nichols Field

PHILIPPINE

125°

SEA

15°   15°

Daet

Naga
MINDORO Calapan Legaspi

SIBUYAN SEA

San Bernardino Strait

SAMAR

Masbate
MASBATE

7

PANAY Libacao
Iloilo
6
Cebu Mactan
Ormoc Tacloban
4 3
5 LEYTE
Borongan
1
2 SULUAN

DINAGAT

PALAWAN

10°   10°

NEGROS Tolong

CEBU Carmen
Surigao
Siargao
BOHOL

Dapitan
MINDANAO
Cagayan

SULU SEA

120°

AMERICAN SHIPS SUNK BY SUICIDE ATTACKS IN THE PHILIPPINES

fighters," because it was not suicide volunteers that were lacking, but planes. Japanese air power in the Philippines had ceased to exist. Defense of the islands was now entirely in the hands of the army, commanded by Marshal Terauchi and General Tomoyuki Yamashita.

AMERICAN SHIPS OF MORE THAN 1000 TONS SUNK BY KAMIKAZE
ATTACKS DURING THE PHILIPPINES CAMPAIGN

Type	Name	Date	Vicinity	*
1944				
Escort carrier	St. Lo (CVE-36)	Oct. 25	Leyte	2
Destroyer	Cooper (DD-695)	Dec. 3	Ormoc	3
Destroyer	Mahan (DD-364)	Dec. 7	Ormoc	4
Transport	Ward (APD-16)	Dec. 7	Ormoc	—
Destroyer	Reid (DD-369)	Dec. 11	Ormoc	5
Landing ship, tank	LST-472	Dec. 15	Mindoro	—
Landing ship, tank	LST-738	Dec. 15	Mindoro	—
Landing ship, tank	LST-460	Dec. 21	Mindoro	—
Landing ship, tank	LST-749	Dec. 21	Mindoro	—
Tanker	Porcupine (IX-126)	Dec. 30	Mindoro	7
1945				
Escort carrier	Ommaney Bay (CVE-79)	Jan. 4	Panay	6
Minesweeper	Hovey (DMS-11)	Jan. 6	Lingayen	8
Minesweeper	Long (DMS-12)	Jan. 6	Lingayen	9
Transport	Brooks (APD-10)	Jan. 6	Lingayen	10
Minesweeper	Palmer (DMS-5)	Jan. 7	Lingayen	11
Transport	Belknap (APD-34)	Jan. 11	Lingayen	12

* *Figures in this column refer to locations at which ships were sunk, indicated by corresponding figures on map on page 94.*

CHAPTER

V

Escalation

When Japanese aviation in the Philippines became non-existent, it was perhaps the first time in history that such a large segment of a country's armed forces had disappeared completely. From October 25, 1944, nearly all its planes had been used in kamikaze operations, with the varying results that we have seen. According to Japanese records, 424 aircraft of all types had taken part in suicide missions, and about 500 men had been killed in them.

To the Japanese high command, the number of enemy ships sunk, and especially the impressive number that had been forced to withdraw because of damage, were so encouraging that a continuation of kamikaze operations seemed clearly necessary. Important losses had been inflicted on the enemy with a relatively low expenditure of aircraft. No such results had been obtained in any of the conventional air-sea engagements that followed the Battle of the Coral Sea in May, 1942. And the Japanese still remembered the Marianas fighting in June, 1944, when a nearly equal number of planes was lost without causing any serious damage to the enemy.

Considering the overwhelming numerical and technical superiority of the American forces, it was certain that those 424 planes could never have accomplished what they did if they had been used in conventional attacks. The principle of kamikaze operations was therefore not brought into question; on the contrary, plans were made to extend it to all future campaigns.

Having been deprived of an effective navy since the disastrous Battle of Leyte Gulf, and now totally lacking air power, Japanese commanders in the Philippines had to make defensive plans based entirely on land operations. By the end of December, 1944, all their efforts were concentrated in that direction. Japanese sailors in the Philippines had already been incorporated into the ground forces. On December 24, while the last few planes were being used up, Admiral Onishi negotiated the transfer of his aviation personnel to ground units. Although the prospect of being turned into infantrymen made some of the pilots bitter, their resolution never weakened. In Admiral Onishi's view, which was shared by many Japanese, it was not necessary to fly an airplane in order to be a kamikaze. It was primarily a state of mind, no matter what the individual's specialty.

Speaking in their name, Onishi committed the men of the First Air Fleet to full participation in the land defense of Luzon. Rear Admiral Sugimoto, commander of the 26th Air Flotilla, and Captain Toshihiko Odawara, chief of staff of the First Air Fleet, worked out the details with army commanders. The defense plan specified that the bulk of the army would withdraw into the northeastern part of the island and that fortified positions would be built along a diagonal line running northwest to southeast. The sector reserved for the airmen-turned-infantrymen was a short distance from Bamban, where the headquarters of the First Air Fleet had already been established. Admiral Fukudome's Second Air Fleet, which at this time still had a certain number of planes, was not involved in these arrangements.

By early January, 1945, it was clear that the continued existence of Japanese aviation as an effective force in the Philippines was only a matter of days. Admiral Onishi knew this better than anyone else, but while he accepted the plan of having all the planes destroyed in suicide missions and then incorporating the remaining airmen into the army for the defense of Luzon, he insisted that the staff of the Second Air Fleet leave the Philippines in order to organize and train new units. The war was not over and there would undoubtedly be other battles to fight. The invaluable experience acquired in the Philippines could not be wasted.

During a conference on January 4, Onishi put pressure on the delegates of the Second Air Fleet to accept his plan. Admiral Fukudome hesitated to make a decision because he still had a few planes to throw into the fighting at Lingayen Gulf, but on January 6, at another conference, he gave his assent.

That evening Onishi, Fukudome and their staff officers gathered around a long table in the cellar-shelter of a house in Bamban. Over dishes of dried cuttlefish and glasses of sake, they bade each other farewell. Later that night, two Mitsubishi Type-1 bombers [1] landed at Clark Field. They had come from Formosa to evacuate the staff of the Second Air Fleet. Admiral Fukudome and his officers went from Bamban to Clark Field by car and boarded the planes. The two bombers took off immediately. Having escaped enemy fighters in the darkness, they landed at Tainan, Formosa, just before dawn.

The Transfer to Formosa

Admiral Onishi, his staff and the personnel of the First and Second Air Fleets remained behind to take part in the land defense of the Philippines. Onishi knew that they were all facing certain death. There could be no thought of evacuation, and it was expected that resistance to the invasion would end only when all Japanese forces in the Philippines had been annihilated. But Onishi did not want his personal records and all the reports of suicide operations, which constituted the whole history of the kamikaze corps he had created and developed, to disappear in the final catastrophe.

That same night, January 6, he summoned Commander Tadashi Nakajima to Bamban and told him to gather all the official documents as quickly as possible and take them to a

[1] These navy torpedo-bombers were nicknamed "Isshiki" by the Japanese and "Betty" by the Americans.

safe place, first in Formosa, then in Japan. Convinced of both their practical usefulness and their historical value as a message to mankind, he insisted not only that Nakajima preserve them, but also that he act as a personal witness to the deeds recorded in them, so that the Japanese people would be informed of the true kamikaze spirit.

Nakajima spent the next day assembling the documents and having a copy made of each one. The copies were given to Lieutenant Tadeshi Shimizu, one of the surviving kamikaze volunteers, and before dawn on January 8 the two men went to the Mabalacat airfield. Shimizu and his pilot boarded a Suisei bomber while another pilot and Nakajima, carrying the original documents, took their places in a second plane of the same type. To increase the chances that at least one set of the documents would get through, each plane took a different route. Nakajima's was slowed down by a mechanical difficulty. When he landed on Formosa, he learned that Shimizu's plane had encountered heavy fog and crashed into a mountain near Takao.

In the Philippines, Japanese aviation personnel, including a certain number of kamikaze volunteers, put on combat shoes and headed into the mountains, carrying weapons and supplies.

Then a surprising message came to Bamban from Combined Fleet headquarters. In it, Admiral Soemu Toyoda confirmed the transfer of most airmen to ground units, but ordered the staff, pilots and radio technicians of the First Air Fleet to withdraw to Formosa. Admiral Onishi could scarcely believe his eyes; he could not understand why headquarters had changed its recent decision. He did not want to abandon his men, but the new order left him no choice.

Although it was possible to take the staff members out by air, there were not enough planes for the other men. Those who had already begun their trek into the mountains were called back and ordered to go to Tuguegarao, in northern Luzon, and wait to be evacuated.

During the night of January 9 Admiral Onishi and his staff bade farewell to all the other officers in Bamban and went to

120°

CHINA

25° ——————————————————————————————————— 25°

Kirun

Taihoku

Giran

Yanaguni

Mount Tsugitaka

TAICHU ✳

Pescadores Islands
[Hoko Shoto
is the
Japanese name
for the
Pescadores]

Shoka

**FORMOSA
[TAIWAN]**

Kagi   Mount Niitaka
             ✳

Tai Sho

Shinko

TAINAN

CHINA SEA

Taito

TAKAO

Taibu

Koto Sho

Bashi Channel

120°

Batan Island

| 0 | 50 | 100 km |

[1.609 Kilometers = 1 Mile]

MAP OF FORMOSA

Clark Field. At 3:45 in the morning, January 10, they took off
in a large plane. They reached Formosa shortly after sunrise,
approaching through thick fog. As the pilot was looking for a
clear spot in which to make his descent, antiaircraft guns at
the Takao base opened fire on his plane. He flew away, came
back at low altitude and landed. The gunners were red-faced
with shame and embarrassment at their mistake. A few minutes later an American air raid ravaged the base and reminded Admiral Onishi, if he needed any reminding, that
Formosa was already in the thick of the war.

The island of Formosa (or Taiwan in Japanese) had been
the target of many American bombings in the past few days.
Under those conditions, forming new operational units was
no simple matter. Admiral Onishi installed his headquarters
in a shelter in the heights east of Takao and went to work.
The first thing to be done was to evacuate the men of the
First Air Fleet who were waiting at Tuguegarao and Aparri,
in the Philippines. This was a difficult task because of the
shortage of planes and the tight American blockade. The
pilots were transferred to Formosa but unfortunately the
radio technicians could not be evacuated.

Within a few days, Admiral Onishi formed a new kamikaze
unit composed of veterans who had already been suicide
volunteers and young pilots from the training centers in
Formosa.

Meanwhile the airmen left behind in the Philippines had
begun their fight against the American invaders. Their kamikaze spirit made up for their lack of experience in infantry
combat. They defended the terrain inch by inch and showed
as much heroism as their army comrades. But, sometimes
lacking ammunition and often food, they had to give way
before the enemy's increasing pressure. They began a long,
painful series of withdrawals and retreats.

In Formosa a new danger was added to the frequent raids
by American carrier-based planes: in mid-January, B-29

bombers [2] began making attacks from bases in free China. At first they came over only in small numbers and their aim was not good, but they flew at such great altitude that they were nearly invulnerable and they carried enormous bomb loads that sometimes caused heavy destruction.

In a ceremony to mark the creation of the first kamikaze unit in Formosa, its members were all assembled at the Tainan airfield. Admiral Onishi spoke to them personally, praising the volunteers who had given their lives in the Philippines and exhorting his men to prove themselves worthy of their valiant predecessors. The new group was officially designated as the Niitaka Unit, from the name of the highest peak in Formosa, Mount Niitaka.[3] The ceremony was followed by the traditional small meal. The cooks had managed to obtain such rare foods as corned beef and dried cuttlefish, plus locally grown vegetables and fruits. In those times of scarcity, this was a great treat. Despite the fact that the operations of the new unit would be a form of organized suicide, the atmosphere of the gathering was relaxed and cordial. Admiral Onishi, usually distant and haughty, was affable on this occasion and spoke to everyone. Toward the end of the afternoon he followed ancient custom by personally pouring a little glass of sake for each of the volunteers.

That evening they were given their final tactical instructions and the new pilots questioned the veterans, who were very little older, about the various attack methods that had been tested in the Philippines. They were eager to learn and to act. Admiral Onishi could be proud of his young heroes.

[2] *These giant four-engined planes, manufactured by Boeing, were specifically designed for bombing Japan.*
[3] *The name of this mountain had been used in the code message ordering the Pearl Harbor attack on December 7, 1941:* "Niitakayama nobore," *literally,* "Climb Mount Niitaka."

First Sortie

On the morning of January 21, when an American task force was reported to be moving toward Formosa, Admiral Onishi decided to put his new unit into action for the first time. He quickly formed three attack groups. The first was composed of two Suiseis and two Zeros as attackers, with two Zeros as escorts; the second was the same except that it had three Zero escorts; the third had two Suisei attackers and two Zero escorts.

It was a clear day with excellent visibility. A few little white clouds were floating at 3000 feet. On the Tainan airfield, ground crews were hurrying in all directions while the pilots gunned their engines to test them. Within a few minutes everything was ready and the 17 planes took off with a thunderous roar. The airfield became silent again, but everyone was now waiting for the arrival of the enemy raiders. Lookouts scattered all over the island were scanning the horizon and antiaircraft gun crews were at their posts, ready and impatient to act.

At sea, the task force from Admiral Halsey's Third Fleet continued its threatening advance. When it was 200 miles from Formosa, its carrier planes took off, assembled and headed for the island. There were several hundred planes in the air—dive bombers, torpedo-bombers, fighters—preparing to strike a terrible blow. According to reliable sources, the Americans believed they would take the enemy by surprise and considered it unlikely that their ships would be attacked.

The American planes approached Formosa from the southeast, across the Bashi Channel. The alert was sounded shortly before the lookouts at Takao saw countless black dots on the horizon. The planes split up into groups that flew to different targets. At Tainan, bombs rained down and added their fearful uproar to the thunder of Japanese antiaircraft guns. Ships at anchor were attacked. Ten of them (freighters and tankers) were sunk and several others damaged. On the airfields, about 60 Japanese planes were destroyed or damaged.

While this violent assault was taking place, the three Japanese kamikaze groups were in flight. Some of the attack planes were shot down by American Hellcats, but four of them, from the first and third groups, were able to make their dives. One crashed into the fleet carrier *Ticonderoga* (CV-14) and another struck the light carrier *Langley* (CVL-27) almost at the same time, causing very serious damage. A few moments later the *Ticonderoga* was hit again and the fire on board became a raging conflagration. The fourth suicide pilot missed the carrier he was aiming at and struck the nearby destroyer *Maddox* (DD-731).

Total damage was heavy. The fire on the *Langley* was quickly put out and the ship was able to remain in formation, but the *Ticonderoga* and the *Maddox* were so devastated that they had to withdraw to the American base at Ulithi. The first sortie of the Niitaka Unit had been a success.

More than three hours after their takeoff, six of the seven Zero escorts landed at Tainan. Their pilots, stirred by the heroism of their kamikaze comrades, made overly enthusiastic reports in which they exaggerated the extent of the damage inflicted and the number of ships put out of action.

Such exaggerations were not an exclusively Japanese failing. Plunged into the confusion of aerial combat, with their attention focused on pressing problems of attack and defense, pilots of every warring nation made similar errors of judgment in perfect good faith, especially since their offensive and defensive maneuvers often took them so far away from the target under attack that their observations became extremely dubious. And in a raid against ships, spectacularly large trails of smoke being blown across the surface of the ocean, seen from a certain altitude, could give the impression that fatal hits had been scored when actually the damage was insignificant.

The Overall Situation

This account of the air operations that were so prominent in the Philippines campaign has led us to neglect other developments in the Pacific war that were taking place at the same time. Although they are beyond the scope of this book, they must at least be mentioned because some of them directly affected the kamikaze corps.

On every front in southeast Asia, fighting was either in progress or about to break out. In the Philippines, China, Peleliu and Burma, Japanese forces were being compelled to withdraw or be wiped out. Despite frenzied propaganda efforts to conceal these defeats or disguise them as victories, most Japanese servicemen, even those who were not in combat, were at least partially aware of the true situation. By early 1945, many of them had come to doubt the final victory that was constantly being trumpeted by Radio Tokyo and the glowing communiqués of the high command. It should not be thought that a wind of defeatism was blowing over Japan, but there was undoubtedly a growing uneasiness.

Emperor Hirohito, whom most Japanese regarded as a semidivine being, was keenly interested in the course of the war. Kido, his Keeper of the Privy Seal and faithful friend, reported military developments to him, often several times a day, and certain jushins [4] with moderate views were received in the palace for the sole purpose of keeping the emperor informed. Hirohito was deeply concerned, but he had to exercise great caution because of the power wielded by the clique of militarists who were determined that there would be no surrender and that, if necessary, Japan would fight to the last man.

The emperor, however, had realized since the middle of 1944 that there could no longer be any doubt about the outcome of the war and that Japan was headed for a catastrophe

---

[4] *The jushins were high political dignitaries, often former prime ministers, who had access to the Imperial Palace.*

without precedent in her history. And by the end of that year he had become convinced, along with Kido and the moderate jushins, that the only sensible solution was to seek negotiations in order to save whatever could still be saved. The fanatical arguments of Prime Minister Kuniaki Koiso and the partisans of General Hideki Tojo, all prominent members of the militaristic clan, had failed to persuade him that the war had to be pursued at all cost.

Since executive power was in the hands of the militarists and their puppets, Hirohito could take no overt action. He surrounded himself with increasingly numerous supporters who helped him in his discreet efforts to find some way of opening peace discussions with the Americans. During this period he was reduced to adopting the role and behavior of a political opposition leader, and at the same time he headed the secret resistance to the militarists. This undercover power struggle lasted for long weeks and months before the peace movement was able to gain any influence. Meanwhile the war had not only continued, but had also taken a fanatical and horrible turn.

While one military disaster followed another, the war was being brought into the heart of Japan. Already, on June 15, 1944, B-29s based in China had bombed the Yawata factories in Kyushu, the southernmost of the Japanese home islands. This was only a prelude. On November 24 American planes took off from Saipan for the first raid on Tokyo. Under the command of General Curtis Le May, the 21st Bomber Command launched its great strategic air offensive. Relatively small and ineffective at first, these raids became larger, more frequent, and much more destructive.

This new aspect of the war had psychological and political consequences at least as important as those that followed the Japanese defeat in the Marianas in June, 1944. First of all, the enemy incursions into the Japanese homeland convinced Emperor Hirohito and his supporters that it was urgently necessary to bring the war to an end as soon as possible. For the moment, his task was still as difficult as ever, but the raids gave him an excellent new argument. The militarists, however, saw them only as one more reason for carrying on the war with even greater fanaticism. Knowing the conditions under which the Japanese were fighting at the time, one cannot help thinking that such extremism bordered on madness.

Japanese servicemen were strongly affected by the American air offensive. The destruction and loss of life, sometimes within their own families, aroused different reactions among them. Some felt an angry desire for vengeance that drove them to fight still more fiercely. Others were overwhelmed by what was happening to their country and realized that there was no longer any possibility of reversing the tragic situation into which it had fallen. To them, the endlessly repeated slogans of "final victory" and "unshakable faith in the destiny of Japan" were nothing but meaningless words, not even worthy of ironic comment. In other countries, such feelings would have generated pacifist movements, if not revolution, but Japan was a land of blind obedience where denunciation of dissenters was regarded as a patriotic duty, and even her most demoralized soldiers continued fighting with outstanding determination and heroism, simply to maintain their military traditions.

The American Air Offensive

The American strategic bombings gave Japanese civilians and servicemen one more demonstration of the enemy's enormous superiority. They reacted to the killing and destruction with feelings of horror, helplessness and injustice. Large numbers of civilian workers deserted their factories and workshops, preferring poverty in the country to suffering and death in the ravaged cities. This exodus had an adverse effect on war production, and therefore on the air units assigned to the defense of the homeland.

The B-29 bomber was very strongly built, it was defended by numerous well-placed guns, and it flew high and fast. Conventional fighter tactics were relatively ineffective against it. Japanese pilots soon began thinking of making suicide attacks against the aerial giants that came to devastate their country. During a raid on the large city of Sasebo, on November 21, 1944, a navy pilot, Lieutenant Mikihiko Sakamoto, deliberately collided with a B-29. Both planes exploded into fragments of flaming debris.

Army pilots began experimenting with an attack method that consisted of flying straight at a B-29, locking the controls, jumping out just before impact and floating to the ground with a parachute. The pilot had to wait until he was very close to his target, to make sure that neither plane would change direction at the last moment, so the method required a split-second timing that was hard to achieve. Sometimes the pilot jumped too soon and his plane flew past the B-29 without touching it, and sometimes he was killed by the explosion of the impact because he had jumped too late. On December 3, 1944, two B-29s were destroyed in this way over Tokyo, with both Japanese pilots reaching the ground safely.

The procedure was never organized or even recommended by the Japanese high command. Ramming attacks, whether the pilot tried to escape or not, remained a matter of individual initiative, perhaps because the high command, knowing that sooner or later the Americans would land on Japanese soil, wanted to preserve as many planes as possible for the final engagement.

Strategic Option

By the beginning of February, 1945, the high command was certain that the Americans were about to take another step in their advance toward Japan. They now had control of the whole South Pacific, they had turned the Mariana and Palau Islands into bases, their conquest of the Philippines enabled them to put still more pressure on Japanese shipping, and their extraordinarily mobile task forces could strike wherever and whenever they chose. To the Japanese, all this meant that they could soon expect another major enemy landing. Where? The large island of Kyushu might be the objective, but it seemed too far away and too well protected by the Japanese forces on Okinawa and Iwo Jima. In all likelihood, the next attack would be against one of those two islands.

The Japanese felt powerless to prevent the enemy from launching his next amphibious assault but they were tempted to try a strategic operation which, if successful, might have important effects on the course of the war. They knew that the gigantic American fleet had established its forward base at Ulithi, an atoll group in the western Caroline Islands. Ulithi was the point of departure for even its longest missions, and it was there that its ships returned for repairs, supplies and rest for their crews. The idea of attacking the American fleet at anchor had taken root in the minds of many Japanese officers. The prospect of a "second Pearl Harbor" was so attractive that the plan gained enthusiastic support.

For months it was examined from every angle. Its execution was always prevented by a single obstacle: distance. A normal bombing raid was out of the question because no Japanese plane had enough range to make a round trip to the target and back. The distance was too great even for a one-way suicide mission. It was a very difficult problem, but the idea seemed so promising that it was tenaciously pursued.

On February 11 the high command ordered the formation of a new air fleet based in Kyushu. Its function would be to oppose any enemy moves in the vicinity of Okinawa and Iwo Jima, the most probable targets of the next offensive. The new Fifth Air Fleet immediately began considering an attack on Ulithi. Only a suicide mission would be possible, and then only if an adequate type of plane could be found.

Admiral Kimpei Teraoka instructed Captain Riichi Sugiyama, commander of the 601st Air Group, to form a new kamikaze unit. Sugiyama completed its organization on February 18, and the next day Admiral Teraoka named it Mitate Unit No. 2. Commanded by Lieutenant Iroshi Murakawa, it was divided into five groups with a total of 32 planes. As in other kamikaze units, there were attack planes of various types and fighter escorts.

On February 16, however, it became necessary to abandon the idea of an attack on Ulithi for the time being, because on that day heavy enemy air activity over Iwo Jima and Japan had made it clear that a large operation was imminent. Three days later, American amphibious forces landed on Iwo Jima. This was now the most pressing problem the Japanese had to face, so the Mitate Unit made its first sortie against the countless American ships cruising off Iwo Jima.

On the morning of February 21, all five groups of the unit took off from Katori, refueled at Hachijo Island and then flew east toward Iwo Jima. After a long flight, they sighted the island late in the afternoon. From the air, it was partly hidden under the smoke and dust sent up by bombings, naval bombardments and ground fighting. Visibility was limited by low clouds and the first shadows of dusk were already appearing on the horizon.

Although the Americans were by now thoroughly familiar with kamikaze raids, they were taken by surprise. Perhaps because of the bad weather or the lateness of the hour, they no longer expected an attack that day. The Japanese planes came out of the clouds and began their dives before the anti-aircraft gunners could react effectively. It was about five o'clock when the fleet carrier Saratoga (CV-3) was shaken by the impact of the first suicide plane. The crew had not yet had time to deal with the damage when another plane struck the big ship at the waterline and opened a broad hole in its side.

As the sky continued to darken, the other kamikaze pilots wheeled in search of a target. Two of them hit the escort carrier Bismarck Sea (CVE-95) only a few seconds apart. The flashes of the two explosions were so bright that they momentarily blinded sailors on nearby ships. The Bismarck Sea was heavily damaged and fire spread rapidly.

Meanwhile a plane emerged from the clouds, streaked down at the escort carrier Lunga Point (CVE-94) and, failing to hit it squarely, skidded along its side and blew up at the waterline. The explosion smashed in the hull and riddled the whole ship with fragments. Another plane plunged at the *Saratoga,* which had already been hit, and crashed into the middle of the flight deck in a great ball of fire. Two other ships were hit but suffered no important damage. Having carried out their mission of protecting the attack planes, some of the escort pilots also dived at ships, apparently without success.

Of the three seriously damaged ships, only the *Lunga Point* was able to remain in formation. The *Saratoga* had taken three hits, two on the flight deck and one at the waterline. Fire had broken out in several places. A few hours after the attack, the flames were overcome and emergency repairs were begun. The *Saratoga* had lost more than 300 men, and was so devastated that it had to set off at reduced speed toward Pearl Harbor, where it remained out of action for over three months.

At first the *Bismarck Sea* did not appear to have been damaged as badly as the *Saratoga,* but fire soon began reaching the magazines. They blew up one by one, weakening the structure of the ship. When flames spread to the after magazine, there was an enormous explosion that tore off the stern. Two hours after the attack, the *Bismarck Sea,* devoured by fire and still shaken by internal explosions, began to list, then capsized and sank, taking about 350 men to their death.

The first mission of the Mitate Unit had scored an impressive victory.

Iwo Jima

The story of that mission has brought us to Iwo Jima, and it may be interesting to examine the way the Japanese pursued their policy of all-out war there. The fighting caused enormous bloodshed because they applied new tactics with the same kamikaze spirit that we have already come to know.

Iwo Jima is a volcanic island five and a half miles long and two and a half miles wide. Mount Suribachi, a volcano at its southeastern end, is its only mountain. The whole surface of the island is a mixture of lava and ash with a strong sulfurous smell. It has no drinkable water and almost no trees. Living conditions are difficult, nearly inhuman.

The Japanese had used their skill in building fortifications to make Iwo Jima a veritable fortress. Multitudes of underground shelters, caves, bunkers, small forts and artillery posts, interconnected by tunnels, had transformed the island into a gigantic labyrinth. On that bleak, sinister, inhospitable land, 21,000 invisibly entrenched Japanese were to inflict death and suffering on 24,000 American marines.

The commander in chief of the island, Lieutenant General Tadamichi Kuribayasha, a stern and merciless man, had not only built those fortifications but was also the fanatical moving spirit of Japanese resistance. A few days before the American invasion he had said in a speech to his men:

> We are here to defend this island to the limit of our strength. We must devote ourselves to that task entirely. Each of your shots must kill many Americans. We cannot allow ourselves to be captured by the enemy. If our positions are overrun, we will take bombs and grenades and throw ourselves under the tanks to destroy them. We will infiltrate the enemy's lines to exterminate him. No man must die until he has killed at least ten Americans. We will harass the enemy with guerilla actions until the last of us has perished. Long live the emperor!

These orders were followed to the letter. The implacable ferocity of the Japanese soldiers made the 26-day struggle one of the most terrible of the war. They all knew they would be killed. Evacuation was out of the question, and the idea of surrender was so odious and dishonorable to them that they never considered it.

Although the fighting did not differ essentially from earlier battles such as Tarawa, the Marianas or Peleliu, it was on a larger scale, bloodier and even more savage. The Japanese soldiers on Iwo Jima, and elsewhere, fought with the same spirit as the suicide pilots; in that sense they were true kamikazes.

The Tan *Operation*

The suicide attack of February 21 against the American fleet off Iwo Jima was not followed by any others. Despite its success, Japanese commanders felt that the distance and fuel consumption involved were too great to warrant a repetition of it. The same objection could have been raised two weeks later, when the idea of attacking Ulithi was again taken up, because the distance was even greater. But more important results could be expected from an attack on Ulithi than on any American force at sea.

On March 7 the Japanese received information which seemed to indicate that the American fleet, having completed its mission of supporting the landing on Iwo Jima, had returned to its base at Ulithi. Confirmation came two days later from a reconnaissance plane that had taken off from Truk, in the central Caroline Islands, and flown over Ulithi. This was the opportunity that the Fifth Air Fleet had been waiting for, especially since some new long-range planes had arrived at Kyushu a few days earlier. Within 24 hours, everything was ready. The attack group was named the Azusa Unit and the raid was known as the *Tan* Operation. Preceded by nine reconnaissance planes serving as guides, 24 twin-engined Ginga bombers, each carrying a 1760-pound bomb, took off on the morning of March 10.

Then came a series of mixups. First, a message from Truk was misinterpreted as saying that there was only one American carrier at Ulithi. Since this was not enough to justify such a large raid, all the planes were called back to the airfield. After they had landed, another message from Truk, clearer and more complete, stated that eight large carriers and seven escort carriers were anchored in the lagoon at Ulithi.

The attack was postponed to the next day. On March 11 the Azusa Unit took off again. Several planes developed engine trouble and had to land at emergency fields. Clear weather enabled the others to make the first half of the long flight without incident, but when they were near the small island of Okinotori Shima the weather quickly turned stormy and they had to fly around many rain squalls. These detours increased the distance, which had already been close to the maximum range of the Gingas. The weather became so bad that the pilots lost their bearings. At 6:30 the guide planes, useless now, separated from the Gingas and returned to Kyushu, according to plan.

The Ginga pilots continued to wander, using up their precious fuel, until they spotted an island that they recognized as Yap. They were now able to correct their course and head for Ulithi.

Since takeoff, 13 Gingas had been forced down. The remaining 11, flying at reduced speed to conserve fuel, had been in the air for the exceptionally long period of 12 hours when, in the thickening darkness, their pilots saw lights straight ahead. It was Ulithi.

The Americans had transformed the atoll into a gigantic base for repairs, maintenance and rest, with a stock of millions of tons of equipment and supplies. It was considered to be far beyond the reach of enemy raiders. Everyone felt so safe that there was no blackout: maintenance crews were working under powerful spotlights, the ships at anchor in the lagoon were brightly lighted and many of them were showing open-air movies topside. No one could have imagined that enemy planes might come to disturb that haven of peace so far away from the war, and yet . . .

The Japanese fliers were straining desperately toward their goal, but the engines of some of the planes had already begun to sputter. To stretch their last few drops of gasoline as far as possible, they were flying barely fast enough to stay in the air. Ulithi was now so close that the halo of light above it was beginning to dazzle the pilots.

Shortly after seven o'clock the first Ginga plunged toward

one of the carriers anchored in the big lagoon. No one had heard the planes approaching, and even the sound of the attacker's dive went unnoticed.

Aboard the fleet carrier *Randolph* (CV-15), most of the crew were gathered on the hangar deck, under the flight deck, watching a detective movie. The atmosphere was calm and relaxed. Everyone was caught up in the plot of the film. Suddenly the enormous steel carcass of the carrier quivered and there was a tremendous explosion. The men all leapt to their feet, bewildered, while the actors on the screen continued their dialogue unperturbed.

The explosion alerted the whole base. All lights were immediately turned off. Now that the lagoon was completely dark, the other Japanese planes were unable to find targets. As they used up the last of their fuel, they fell into the water one by one.

The plane that crashed into the *Randolph* had so little fuel in its tanks that it did not burst into flame, as usually happened in a kamikaze attack. The explosion of its bomb ignited some inflammable material aboard the carrier, but the fire was quickly put out. The damage was repaired within a few days.

One might wonder why the Americans had not heard the Japanese planes approaching. The answer is probably that the drone of their engines was drowned out by the din of the air hammers being used by repair crews.

The *Tan* Operation was a failure. The Japanese became aware of this the following day when photographs taken by a Saiun [5] from Truk showed that no American ships were missing from the lagoon. No further attempts were made to attack the American fleet at Ulithi.

[5] *The Nakajima C6N Saiun (nicknamed "Myrt" by the Americans) was a fast reconnaissance plane with graceful lines. Its exceptional speed often enabled it to escape interception by even the fastest American fighters.*

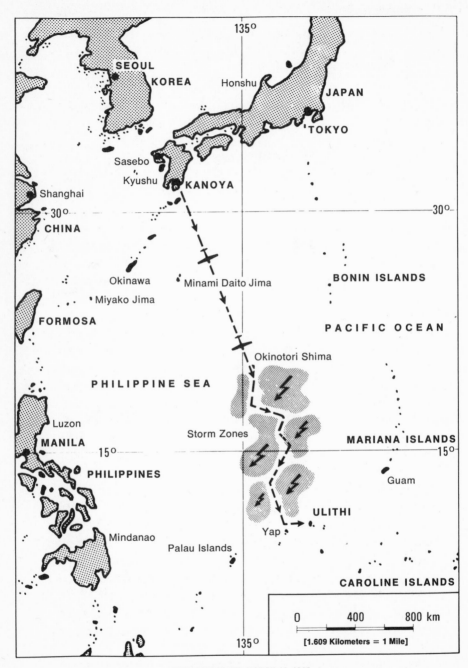

TAN OPERATION, MARCH 11, 1945

Under Pressure of Events

At the end of February the Japanese high command realized that the desperate struggle on Iwo Jima would not stop the Americans for long and that the next stage of their advance toward Japan would probably begin very soon. The vise was tightening and the whole Japanese people knew it, despite the lying propaganda that was constantly fed to them. There was alarming evidence that no one could ignore, such as the growing frequency and intensity of air raids and the enemy fleets that ventured into Japanese territorial waters more and more often.

Although badly informed, the Japanese people realized that their armed forces were incapable of turning back the tidal wave of destruction. The Japanese navy, once the pride of the nation, was no longer anything but a memory. The few ships it had left were either damaged or unable to operate effectively for lack of fuel. Japanese ground forces, though still numerous and resolute, could not struggle alone against the American steamroller. There remained the air forces, now weakened by colossal losses and dependent on an exhausted aircraft industry, but still fighting to stave off the inevitable.

High-ranking army officers had no illusions about what they could expect their troops to accomplish. They had abandoned the idea that the invader could be thrown back into the sea. Since Tarawa, in November, 1943, they had known that nothing could stop the American amphibious forces, and despite all the wild claims they made for propaganda purposes, they were now trying only to use the loyalty and fanaticism of their troops to slow down the enemy's advance, since it could not be stopped. In short, the whole Japanese army was expected to do nothing more than fight a delaying action.

Army general headquarters had repeatedly put pressure on the navy to use its last ships in suicide missions coordinated with ground operations. Navy commanders were reluctant to see what was left of the Imperial Fleet destroyed in actions that were doomed to failure from the start, so they declined the proposals put forward, often ironically, by the army. They felt that their last seaworthy ships should be reserved for the climax of the war, which would begin when the Americans made their first landing on Japanese soil. Furthermore they felt that the navy was already heavily engaged in the fighting, since nearly all its aircraft were in use. And, as we have seen, it was navy pilots who developed the principle of suicide tactics and formed the first kamikaze corps.

As the defense zone narrowed and the final struggle appeared to be approaching rapidly, the navy decided to reorganize its air fleets to make them more numerous and efficient. Thus on March 1, 1945, the Tenth Air Fleet was born. It incorporated the 11th, 12th and 13th air groups, which were still in training, and was intended to provide reserves for the newly created Fifth Air Fleet. The units composing the Tenth remained at their training bases, but contingents were to be drawn from them as they were needed.

By early March, naval air forces were distributed as follows: the reorganized and reinforced First Air Fleet had 300 planes in Formosa; the Third had 800 based at many different airfields in the eastern half of Japan; the Fifth covered the western half of the country with its 600 planes; and finally the Tenth, with 400, was scattered all over the home territory. This total of 2100 planes was small compared with the thousands of excellent aircraft that the Americans had at their disposal. Aside from the weaknesses that we have already discussed, the Japanese air forces were handicapped by the fact that they had to use a mixed collection of many different types of planes.

So far, only Admiral Onishi's First Air Fleet, in Formosa, was entirely devoted to suicide missions, but it was now obvious that because of the relatively small number of planes available and the mediocrity of the pilots' training conventional attacks no longer had much chance of achieving any important results. The high command had been strongly influenced by the success of the kamikaze raids made by the First and Second air fleets in the Philippines; it now appeared that there was almost no choice but to make such attacks the general rule. For the first time, headquarters of the Fifth and Tenth air fleets were invited to transform their units into kamikaze corps. The fact that they were invited, not ordered, probably made little if any difference in practice, but it was psychologically important.

When the unit leaders announced the "invitation," many of the pilots immediately volunteered for one-way missions without the slightest pressure having been put on them.

The New Units in Action

In early March, after having been concentrated around Iwo Jima for a time, the American forces began extending their activity again. Something was obviously in preparation. On the night of March 10 Tokyo underwent a horrible incendiary bombing that took many lives and caused great devastation. The Japanese people were enduring terrible suffering. Industries were being crushed one after another.

On March 16 the victorious American forces gained complete control of Iwo Jima. From then on the island served as a base for the strategic air offensive, as well as a source of supplies and protection for the future great amphibious operation.

As a prelude to the offensive, Vice Admiral Marc A. Mitscher's task forces left Ulithi in mid-March and headed for Japan. Their mission was to attack airfields for the purpose of reducing the threat from enemy air power. On March 18 hundreds of American planes took off from the carriers of Task Force 58 and flew toward Kyushu.

Japanese reconnaissance planes, which constantly patrolled the ocean, spotted the American ships and reported their approach. Here was a chance to strike a great blow and test the new kamikaze units of the Fifth Air Fleet. A group of 50 suicide planes took off, accompanied by escort fighters. The Japanese and American air groups passed without seeing each other. For several hours the Americans attacked the Kyushu airfields, destroying dozens of planes on the ground. Meanwhile the Japanese were approaching the American fleet.

As always, the kamikaze pilots chose carriers as their prime targets. They began their dives while their escorts fought furiously against the Hellcats that were trying to shoot down the suicide planes. Within a few minutes the fleet carriers *Enterprise* (CV-6) and *Franklin* (CV-13) were hit and damaged, but not badly enough to force them to withdraw.

The next day, American planes raided the Kyushu airfields again. They also attacked Japanese shipping in the vicinity of the large ports of Kobe and Kure. It was the first time the main island of Honshu and the Inland Sea had been violated by American carrier planes.

Then the kamikaze units of the Tenth Air Fleet went into action. They sent several groups, including one composed of 20 Suisei bombers, to attack the American ships. Despite violent antiaircraft fire, they succeeded in damaging three fleet carriers: the *Essex* (CV-9), the *Wasp* (CV-18) and, for the second time in two days, the *Franklin*.

The *Franklin* was now in serious condition. Two planes had broken through the flight deck, exploded against the hangar deck below, and set off a huge fire. American planes loaded with fuel and bombs, ready to take off, had blown up, adding to the disaster. And "disaster" is not too strong a word, because more than 700 men were killed and it was only by a miracle that the surviving crewmen were able to extinguish the fires that had broken out in different places. Devastated and listing heavily to starboard, the *Franklin* had to withdraw and began steaming, unassisted, toward the United States.

Those two days of attacks had cost the American navy 116 planes. That, plus the damage inflicted on ships, gave the Japanese reason to feel that they had fought successfully. It should be noted that during the attack on Kobe and Kure,

The close relationship between Japanese religious and military principles was reflected in certain ceremonies. *(Top)* Lieutenant Kawasaki, about to lead his company into combat, takes leave of the gods, asking for their protection and assuring them that his men will conduct themselves heroically. *(Bottom)* A ceremony marking the opening of a mine whose ore was to be used in war production. (u.s.i.s. PHOTOGRAPHS.)

A Shinto priest, standing in a consecrated cedar tree, chants prayers outside a temple. (U.S. I.S. PHOTOGRAPH.)

Japanese generals and admirals were granted the privilege of declaring their fidelity to the emperor in person. (U.S.I.S. PHOTO-GRAPH.)

(*Top*) Cadets of the Japanese naval academy bow respectfully in the direction of the Imperial Palace. This was the second of the three ritual bows with which all Japanese soldiers began each day. The first was toward a Shinto altar (in the background), and the third, performed individually, paid homage to each man's family house. (*Bottom*) Civilians also began the day with prayers in the nearest temple or, more often, before one of the little altars that were located nearly everywhere. Here miners piously invoke their ancestors before going down into their mine. (U.S.I.S. PHOTO-GRAPHS.)

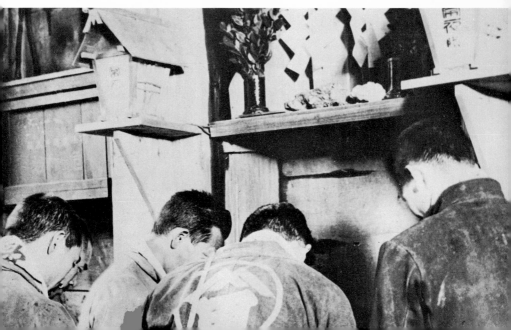

A Nakajima Tenzan B6N-2 torpedo-bomber tries to get through the terrible wall of fire thrown up by American antiaircraft guns. (U.S.I.S. PHOTOGRAPH.)

A Japanese suicide plane, disastrously damaged, is out of control and will not hit its target. (U.S.I.S. PHOTOGRAPH.)

The fleet carrier *Essex* (CV-9) has just been struck by a Japanese suicide plane. The picture shows the flame of the explosion, the large hole it has opened in the ship and the trail of smoke left by the plane just before it crashed. (OFFICIAL U.S. NAVY PHOTOGRAPH.)

(*Top*) A Japanese Yokosuka D4Y-2 Suisei dive bomber. It was in such a plane that Rear Admiral Masabumi Arima deliberately crashed into an American ship off the Philippines on October 15, 1944. (*Bottom*) The Mitsubishi A6M-5 Zero 52 fighter was the plane most often used in suicide attacks. It was the standard model for kamikaze units, especially in the Philippines. (PHOTOGRAPHS FROM THE AUTHOR'S COLLECTION.)

Vice Admiral Takijiro Onishi, the most ardent defender of the principle of suicide attacks, was the dynamic creator of the kamikaze units based in the Philippines. (AUTHOR'S COLLECTION.)

Rear Admiral Masabumi Arima, a true mystical hero, was the first flag officer to deliberately crash into an American ship. His act had far-reaching consequences. (AUTHOR'S COLLECTION.)

An American carrier, enveloped in the smoke of its antiaircraft guns, will not be able to stop the dive of the Japanese suicide plane (in the circle). (U.S.I.S. PHOTOGRAPH.)

(*Top*) This Zero has been hit in the wing and tail by antiaircraft fire. (*Bottom*) Deflected from the course of its suicide dive, it crashes into the water a short distance from its target. (U.S.I.S. PHOTOGRAPHS.)

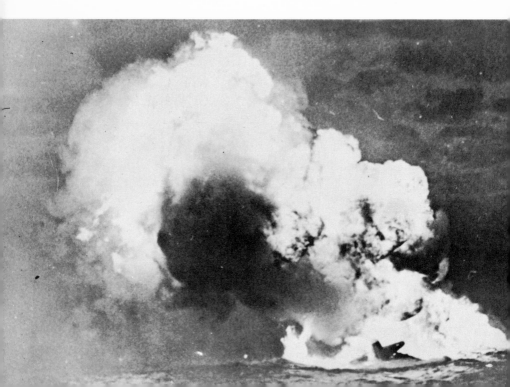

(Top) The fast twin-engined Yokosuka P1Y-1 Ginga was used in the *Tan* operation against the American anchorage at Ulithi. (AUTHOR'S COLLECTION.) *(Bottom)* The Fuji MXY-8 Ohka piloted bomb, of which several were discovered on Okinawa by American troops. (U.S.I.S. PHOTOGRAPH.)

Lieutenant General Tadamichi Kuri-
bayashi, commander of the Japanese
garrison on Iwo Jima, exhorted his men
to sacrifice their lives, following the
glorious example of the kamikaze
pilots. (U.S.I.S. PHOTOGRAPH.)

(Left) A twin-engined suicide plane goes down in flames not far from the American
escort carrier *Kitkun Bay* (CVE-71). (NAVY DEPARTMENT PHOTOGRAPH.)

(Below) The great American anchorage off the atoll of Ulithi was the target of
several suicide raids, by nautical craft as well as airplanes. In the foreground, the
carrier *Wasp* (CV-18). (NAVY DEPARTMENT PHOTOGRAPH.)

The carrier *Franklin* (CV-13) was probably hit more often than any other American ship. Here it has just been struck by another suicide plane. Fragments from the explosion are still in the air as crewmen run to take shelter. (NAVY DEPARTMENT PHOTOGRAPH.)

The *Franklin*, badly damaged, takes advantage of a calm to transfer the most seriously wounded men to a cruiser. The carrier's flight deck was buckled by the latest impact. (U.S.I.S. PHOTOGRAPH.)

A witness to the first suicide attack of the Pacific war, this Japanese A-2 ("Fly") midget submarine was grounded on a beach near Honolulu, where it was captured by American marines on December 8, 1941. (INTERCONAIR PHOTOGRAPH.)

(*Top*) This extraordinary photograph shows a Zero about to crash into the side of an American battleship. (*Bottom*) A disabled twin-engined Ginga just before it crashed into the water and exploded. (U.S.I.S. PHOTOGRAPHS.)

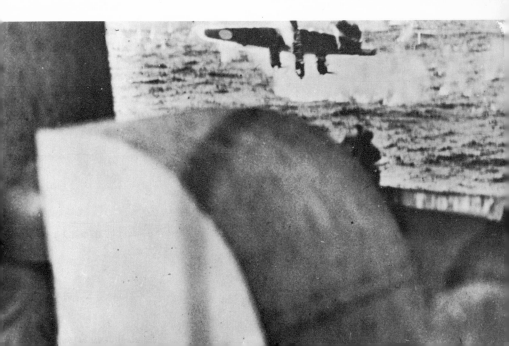

(*Top*) The pilot of this Ginga in flames has been killed. It is about to crash into the water. (U.S.I.S. PHOTOGRAPPH.) (*Bottom*) Japanese navy mechanics working on a Nakajima Kikka, the first Japanese jet, and also one of the first planes specially designed for suicide attacks. (PHOTOGRAPH: TADAO SHIBUSAWA.)

the American planes ran into serious opposition from Japanese fighters. The Matsuyama Wing, based on Shikoku Island, commanded by the famous Captain Minoru Genda and equipped with the new Shiden fighters, won an outstanding victory that day by shooting down more than two-thirds of the American planes lost during the attacks.

A Very Special Attack

On March 21 a Japanese reconnaissance plane reported several enemy carriers 320 miles southeast of Kyushu. Fearing a renewal of the American raids, Japanese air commanders prepared to act.

It was then that Vice Admiral Matome Ugaki intervened. He had recently come to Kyushu to take command of all air units there, including the Fifth Air Fleet. Formerly Admiral Yamamoto's chief of staff, Admiral Ugaki was noted for his decisive, forceful personality. He was a firm partisan of aviation, and in those difficult times he was determined more than ever to make air attacks as destructive as possible.

When a copy of the report from the reconnaissance plane was handed to him, he immediately decided to use the new Ohka,[6] feeling that this was a good chance to try it out. Captain Motoharu Okamura, leader of the Ohka unit, organized the raid. Okamura had supported the idea of the Ohka from the outset. He had made every effort to have it manufactured and put into use as quickly as possible. He believed it would revolutionize naval warfare and enable Japan to crush the enemy.

He wanted the bombers carrying the Ohkas to have a large escort of fighters so that the suicide pilots would have the greatest possible chance of reaching their targets, but there were only 55 fighters available that day. Okamura com-

---

[6] *The Ohka was a piloted bomb, designed to be carried close to the enemy by a twin-engined bomber, then released and guided to its target by a suicide volunteer. We will come back to it shortly.*

plained that this was insufficient: with such a small escort,
the bombers might not succeed in coming close enough to
the enemy to release the Ohkas.

Lieutenant Commander Goro Nonaka was placed in command of the group. He shared Okamura's misgivings, but he
yielded to Admiral Ugaki's insistence. Ugaki, determined to
act, swept away all objections and gave the order for departure. Dejected and bitter, Okamura did not want to let his
bomber crews go on such a hazardous mission without sharing their fate. He announced that he would lead the attack
group himself. Nonaka refused to yield his place, saying respectfully but firmly that fate had put him in charge of the
mission and that he would not let anything or anyone prevent
him from carrying it out. Okamura was disappointed but felt
he had no right to insist. The Ohka pilots and bomber crews
were already lining up on the runway to the sound of the
drumbeat that traditionally preceded the departure of heroes
going into battle.

At 11:35 in the morning, in the presence of Admiral Ugaki,
18 Type-1 bombers and their Zero escorts left the Kanoya
base and headed for the enemy's reported position. Some of
the fighters had not been in condition to take off and others
soon began dropping out because of engine trouble, reducing
the number of those in flight to 30. Only 16 of the bombers
were carrying Ohkas, the other two having been assigned to
take care of navigation and radio communication.

Toward two o'clock, when according to the navigators' cal-
culations they were within 50 miles of their objective, about
50 Hellcats suddenly came out of the clouds and streaked
toward the Japanese planes. The 30 Zeros broke away from
the bombers and went to meet the enemy.

Overwhelmed by superior numbers, but also by the ardor
of the American fliers, who had sensed that this unusual formation concealed an unknown but serious threat, the Japanese fighter pilots were not able to hold off their adversaries
for long. They were powerless to prevent the massacre of the
bombers. In the hope of escaping in the clouds, the bomber
pilots had lightened their planes by jettisoning the Ohkas

(which were not yet manned by the suicide volunteers) but 15 of them were shot down before they could reach conceal- ment. The remaining three succeeded in flying into the clouds, only to be caught and shot down later. About 15 Zeros were sent plummeting into the sea. Others, badly dam- aged, crashed on the way back to Kanoya.

The first Ohka raid had been a complete fiasco.

The Extraordinary Ohka

Although the Japanese manufactured other aircraft specifi- cally designed for suicide attacks, as we shall see later, only the Ohka was actually used. Because of its importance, we shall give a brief summary of its history.

Toward the end of 1943, when it was becoming apparent to Japanese pilots that American air superiority would con- tinue to grow and that their own chances of being able to take effective action were diminishing every day, some of them began dreaming of spectacular new aircraft capable of defying the enemy's defenses and inflicting irreparable dam- age on his ships. In most cases this was nothing but wishful thinking, but one man, Ensign Mitsuo Ota, put his ideas into concrete form and presented them to his superiors. Ota did not claim to have discovered a way to win the war overnight. His plan was based on a realistic appraisal of the current military situation and Japan's industrial limitations. That was probably why it was first received with a kind of benevolent indifference, rather than categorical rejection.

Ota knew that it was impossible to count on rapid develop- ment and production of aircraft superior to the enemy's. He also knew that Japanese air units were suffering greater and greater losses in raids that achieved only minor results or none at all. His idea was to build a big, gliding, piloted bomb that would be carried to the vicinity of its target by a twin- engined bomber. Not having to fly all the way to the target, the bomber would have a better chance of returning to its base for another mission. Once the winged bomb was released, its pilot would put it into a fast gliding dive and guide it toward an enemy ship. Its tremendous speed would make it almost impossible to shoot down, and its massive explosive charge would cause enormous damage when it struck.

Months went by, bringing new defeats and increasingly heavy losses. The Japanese could only choose between sending pilots out to be killed uselessly or leaving the planes on the ground to be destroyed by American raiders. Meanwhile Ensign Ota continued advocating his plan so enthusiastically and insistently that finally, in the spring of 1944, his superiors allowed him to go to Japan to present his ideas, which were still somewhat revolutionary at that time.

No one really believed in them, yet everyone felt that something had to be done. This was the attitude that young Ota encountered when he went to the Ministry of Industrial Production. His plan was not turned down but it had to make its way slowly through bureaucratic channels. It was eventually submitted to the aeronautical research department of the Imperial University, which drew up preliminary blueprints of the proposed craft and studied its tactical possibilities under the name of the Marudai Project.

Then the disastrous Marianas defeat of June, 1944, accelerated the process. The plans were presented to the navy's aeronautical research center at Yokosuka, which immediately took the whole idea very seriously and even gave it priority. By August, construction of the first prototypes was being completed in the greatest secrecy. No one but a handful of government officials, officers and specialists even knew of the existence of the Marudai Project. It is interesting to note that these flying bombs were designed and built before Admiral Onishi created the first kamikaze corps in the Philippines.

In September, Captain Motoharu Okamura was placed in command of a special unit to be trained in the use of the new weapon. Meanwhile the craft had come to be known by two different names, one poetic: Ohka ("cherry blossom" [7]), the

[7] *The cherry blossom, a symbol of purity, became the emblem of all kamikaze pilots shortly afterward.*

other more martial: Jinrai ("divine thunder"). The new unit was given the name Jinrai Butai ("Divine Thunder Corps"). It was composed of volunteers who had been discreetly recruited. They enthusiastically began the difficult task of learning to control the Ohka.

The Ohka had a fuselage 19.7 feet long, wings with a span of 16.4 feet, a horizontal stabilizer and two vertical stabilizers. The fuselage had a bullet-shaped nose section containing 2640 pounds of an explosive similar to TNT. This charge was enclosed in a thick casing, like that of an artillery shell, to produce a perforating explosion.

Next came a section located at the center of gravity. It contained the pilot's controls and detonators for the explosive charge. On its top side was the ring by which the Ohka was attached to the bomber that carried it. The cockpit was covered with a streamlined transparent bubble, with a sighting ring in front of it to help the pilot aim his craft. Flight instruments were rudimentary.

The last section contained rockets [8] to increase the Ohka's diving speed, so that it could elude enemy fighters and anti-aircraft fire. The powder that fueled them was stored behind the pilot's seat, with no protection. There were five of them: two at the base of the fuselage and three smaller ones above them, grouped in a single opening. They developed a thrust of 1800 pounds for nine seconds and could propel the Ohka at what was then an enormous speed: 575 to 650 miles an hour, depending on the angle of its dive.

Designed to be mass-produced, the Ohka was lightly constructed of wood and metal, and its strength was marginal. Because of its small wing area in relation to its weight, it was hard to control.

It was carried by a bomber to within about 20 miles of its objective and released at an altitude of between 20,000 and 26,000 feet. The first part of its flight was a shallow glide at a speed of slightly under 300 miles an hour. Then, when he had

[8] *These rockets were manufactured on the basis of information supplied by the German Walter firm, the leading authority on the subject at the time.*

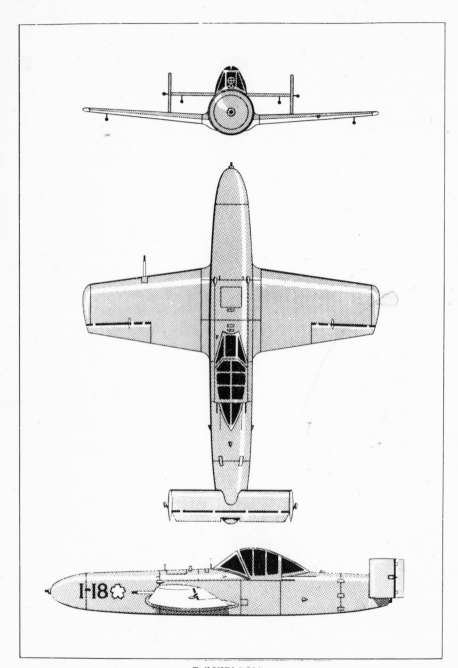

Fuji MXY-8 Ohka.

chosen his target, the pilot ignited the rockets and went into a dive at an angle of about 50 degrees.

Although many difficulties had been encountered in both the functioning of the Ohka and the training of pilots for it, its manufacture was assigned to several different factories in September, 1944, and production began soon afterward. The first mass-produced Ohkas, exactly the same as the prototypes, came off the assembly lines at the end of October under the designation of MXY-8 Ohka, Model 11.

At the same time a training version, without rockets or an explosive charge, was produced by the firm of Nihon Hikoki K.K. It had a wide skid under the fuselage that enabled it to be landed at the end of a training flight. Later, two prototypes of a two-seated version called the MXY-7 Kai were built, but this model was not put into production.

Several types of twin-engined bombers were considered for the role of carrier, or "mother plane." The requirements were that the plane would have to be capable of taking off with the 4700-pound load of the Ohka, and that its landing wheels would have to be far enough apart to allow the Ohka's wings to fit between them. Several bombers met these requirements, but the Mitsubishi G4M Type-1 was finally chosen because there were so many of them available.

The Mitsubishi firm made certain modifications in this bomber for the specific purpose of carrying the Ohka. The new version was known as the G4M 2E, Model 22. The Ohka was partially set into the bomb bay, whose doors had been removed. There was a telephone circuit for communication between the suicide pilot and the bomber crew before the Ohka was released. Finally, there was a small panel in the bomb bay, facing the cockpit of the Ohka, with red and green signal lights for transmitting orders from the bomber captain.

In theory, the distance between the release point and the target would allow the mother plane to avoid enemy interceptors and antiaircraft fire. Having dropped the Ohka, it would regain its top speed and have time to escape before enemy fighters could catch it. In practice, however, things

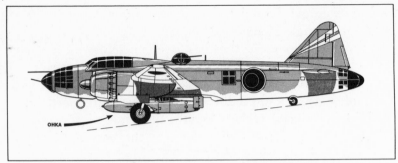

Mitsubishi G4M-2E Model 22 ("Betty") carrying an Ohka piloted bomb.

often turned out differently. Many mother planes were shot down, even after they had released their Ohkas.

The Ohka's tremendous speed and destructive power made it seem almost diabolical to the Americans. They had developed very effective defenses against "ordinary" kamikazes but they were nearly helpless against the Ohka unless they succeeded in shooting down the mother plane before it reached the release point. Once the Ohka was released, it was too fast to be stopped by fighters or antiaircraft fire.

We shall see later that during the Okinawa campaign the Ohka had a psychological effect that previous kamikaze attacks had never been able to produce. There was no paralyzing panic among the Americans, but they began to dread the worst. This was part of what the Japanese hoped to accomplish. They were counting on the Ohka not only to inflict terrible destruction on the enemy, but also to frighten him so much that he would stop his advance toward the Japanese homeland.

Because the Americans in their apprehension and anxiety regarded the Ohka as a manifestation of a kind of devilish Japanese insanity, they borrowed the word *baka*, meaning "stupid," from the Japanese language and nicknamed the new weapon the "baka bomb."

CHAPTER

VI

Nautical Kamikazes

In the preceding chapters we have been concerned mainly with the Japanese navy pilots who took the lead in developing the kamikaze concept, and we have also seen Japanese troops in terrible ground battles where they fought to the death even when they knew their situation was hopeless. So far we have said little about Japanese sailors, but they had the same spirit and their selfless patriotism was equally admirable. It is time to do them justice, especially since their suicide operations began earlier than those of the air and ground forces.

The midget submarines that took part in the Pearl Harbor attack on December 7, 1941, were engaged in a kamikaze mission before the term had been invented. Although the plan of the operation did not specify clearly that the men in these submarines were to be regarded as suicide volunteers, they knew that the provisions made for their rescue were only a theoretical gesture and they had no illusions about their fate. There was no doubt in their minds that they would be going on a one-way mission, yet they did not hesitate to undertake it. They were already kamikazes, or perhaps they were even more than kamikazes, because at that time Japan was triumphant and feared no one, so they were not driven by any kind of anxiety or despair when they went off to certain death.

Although the submarine operation at Pearl Harbor added nothing to the destruction caused by Japanese planes, the high command was still convinced that midget submarines could be a valuable weapon, because it had been proven that a very small submarine could penetrate a well-defended enemy harbor. Its small size enabled it to slip through obstructions and approach undetected.

The Japanese attached perhaps less importance to the strategic effects of midget-submarine attacks than to their spectacular nature. The idea was to create a feeling of insecurity and fear in the enemy by striking at targets far away from the theaters of operations. If, besides lowering enemy morale, the attacks could also achieve important strategic results, they would be extremely useful.

War in Miniature

For these reasons, more midget-submarine attacks were launched in the spring of 1942. The Japanese had been winning great victories; they decided to follow them up with psychological actions carried out by the valiant crews of the "flies," as Japanese sailors had come to call the midget submarines.

At this time the Allies had been driven from all their important positions in the Far East but they still had distant bases, so far unscathed, where they could concentrate forces for a counteroffensive. The Japanese feared that these bases might eventually be used as the departure points of an effort to reconquer the lost positions. Their fears were not ungrounded, because intelligence reports and reconnaissance flights over Sydney, Australia, and Diego-Suarez, Madagascar, indicated intense enemy activity in both places.

The high command decided to make simultaneous attacks against those two widely separated points. Part of the plan was obviously psychological: to show the omnipresence of the Imperial Fleet.

Under the direction of Rear Admiral Ishizaka, the Eighth Submarine Flotilla was organized and began its special training at the end of April. Each of the large submarines was equipped to carry a Type A two-man "fly." The attack was scheduled for the early hours of May 31, 1942.

The three submarines assigned to the attack, the I-16, I-18 and I-20, made one stop at Penang and another at a temporary base on the east coast of Burma, then headed for Madagascar. They were to use the same tactics that had been used at Pearl Harbor six months earlier. The large submarines would launch the midgets as close as possible to the entrance of the Diego-Suarez harbor. The "flies" would slip through the antisubmarine defenses and attack enemy ships at anchor. Then their crews would scuttle them.

Theoretically, as at Pearl Harbor, the two men in each "fly" were to return to their mother submarine, and again this aspect of the plan was nothing but an illusory gesture designed to relieve the high command of responsibility. Assuming that they escaped being killed by the enemy, the men would be exhausted after their difficult, nerve-racking mission, which would probably require them to dive and surface several times; it is hard to imagine how they could have been expected to destroy their craft, then swim nine or ten miles in darkness and reach the point where they were to be picked up.

At midnight, May 30, 1942, the three large submarines stopped ten miles north of the entrance to the harbor of Diego-Suarez. For security reasons, they could not come any closer.

The "fly" aboard the I-18 was the first to be launched. Its motor resisted all efforts to start it. The two others, from the I-16 and I-20, set off without difficulty, but when they were a few miles from the harbor entrance one of them suddenly began leaking and sank within a few minutes. The cause of the accident was never known.

The one remaining attacker continued moving toward its objective. The night was silent and the sea was calm. The little submarine, with only its periscope showing above the water, glided along the channel undetected. The British, who had just occupied Madagascar, were so far from thinking of an enemy incursion that they had not even bothered to reactivate the old cannons that had once defended the harbor.

The Japanese officer in command of the "fly" had carefully studied maps of the area, so he was able to keep his bearings by the coastal contours that he had memorized. He rounded a promontory and entered the harbor. He saw no ships at that point, contrary to what a reconnaissance plane had reported the day before. Undiscouraged, he headed for the indentations in the coast at the far end of the harbor.

When he had rounded a little cape and entered a bay, he discovered a big tanker less than 200 yards away. He could see its silhouette very clearly against the sky, but he knew that his own craft might be damaged if he fired a torpedo at such short range. He decided to fire one anyway. The torpedo took only about ten seconds to reach the tanker and strike it amidships with a blinding flash.

The explosion sent out a huge circular wave that tossed the little submarine like a cork and nearly capsized it. The two men inside it were thrown against its sides. The batteries began leaking. Toxic gas invaded the small cockpit and the output of the batteries dropped, weakening the motor. The officer did not want to die before he had used his second torpedo. He slowly guided his craft into another bay, where he saw the British battleship *Ramillies* about 2000 yards away, clearly visible in the light of the burning tanker. It was a perfect target.

He sent his torpedo on its way but he and his mechanic died soon afterward, asphyxiated by gas from the batteries. The little submarine surfaced and later drifted ashore.

The British battleship was hit but did not sink. It went to Durban, on the east coast of Africa, for repairs. As for the tanker, it burned like a torch and finally sank.

A Disappointing Weapon

At the same time, thousands of miles away, five other submarines of the Eighth Flotilla, the I-21, I-22, I-24, I-27 and I-29, commanded by Captain Sasaki, were approaching Sydney. The I-21 was carrying a collapsible float plane for reconnaissance, and to avoid hampering the plane's movements it did not have a midget submarine aboard.

At about 4:30 in the afternoon they stopped seven miles from Sydney. The "flies" were put into the water and began moving slowly toward shore. A little later, their pilots saw North Head, the promontory at the entrance to the harbor, in the bright moonlight.[1] As they approached the antisubmarine net, they saw that it was not closed. There was thus no obstacle to their entering the harbor, but one of the little craft strayed off course, collided with the net and became stuck fast. Determined efforts were made to free it, to no avail.

The three others continued on their way. Before long they were able to make out the high silhouettes of two heavy cruisers, the American *Chicago* and the Australian *Canberra*, and a little further on they saw a large supply ship. Everything was calm; they would have the advantage of complete surprise. They maneuvered to a good distance for firing their torpedoes.

The first attack was to be against the *Chicago*. The young Japanese ensign pressed the firing button. There was a bright flash and a huge column of foam and wreckage rose into the air, accompanied by a thunderous detonation that echoed from all sides of the harbor. The torpedo, probably either jammed or deteriorated, had exploded in its tube. The midget submarine was pulverized.

The warships at anchor reacted quickly. Their guns opened fire, first at random, then with greater precision. The commanders of the two other "flies," shaken by the unexpected explosion and the gunfire that followed, fired their torpedoes without taking time to aim them carefully. The water of the harbor was being churned by hundreds of projectiles. Eight-inch shells from the cruisers struck near the two remaining midget submarines and the explosions brought them up to

[1] *In the southern hemisphere, May 30 corresponds to September 30 in the northern hemisphere. The day is short and by 4:30 dusk has begun to fall.*

the surface, where they were soon cut to pieces. None of the torpedoes hit its target, but one of them continued on its course until it exploded against an innocent ferry and sank it. The raid against Sydney was a wretched failure.

Midget submarines were used several more times in the remaining years of the war, but always in small numbers and apparently with no better results than they had achieved at first. That was no doubt why their use was limited and finally discontinued. The last unit, composed of four "flies" based at Dumaguete, in the Philippines, was dissolved on March 20, 1945, when American troops were moving toward Davao. The little submarines were scuttled and their crews joined the defending ground forces.

The Imperial Navy underwent the same psychological and tactical changes as the other Japanese armed forces. At the beginning of the war, the navy won spectacular victories by conventional means, but later developments gradually forced it to resort to missions that achieved only minor results and offered little or no chance of survival to the men who carried them out.

Originally, however, there was nothing revolutionary about the Japanese midget submarines, and they were not unique: both the British and the Germans, for example, built and used such craft during World War II.

The Japanese had begun studying the possibility several years before the war. Their first two experimental models, called Type A, Nos. 1 and 2, were built at Kure in 1938. When their performance proved to be satisfactory, two other prototypes, Ha. 1 and Ha. 2, were built.

These little submarines carried two men, were 78.7 feet long and displaced 46 tons. They were capable of covering 80 miles at the reduced speed of two knots, or 20 miles at their top speed of 19 knots. They carried two 18-inch torpedoes in the bow. They had no generators, so their batteries had to be recharged either at a shore base or from a ship equipped for the purpose.

Production was begun with a series of 42, numbered Ha. 3 to Ha. 44, built at Urazaki, near Kure. Those that made the attacks at Pearl Harbor, Diego-Suarez and Sydney were from this series.

In the spring of 1942, the Japanese decided to use midget submarines for coastal defense. Sixteen more, numbered Ha. 46 to Ha. 61, were built in a modified version. Some of these were used in the Philippines in late 1944 and early 1945, particularly in the Surigao Strait and around Mindanao, again without significant results.

In October, 1942, another experimental model was launched. Called the Type B and numbered Ha. 45, it was 80.4 feet long and displaced 50 tons. Unlike the Type A, it was able to recharge its own batteries, which gave it greater range, and it carried a crew of three. It could cover 350 miles at 6 knots on the surface, or 120 miles at 4 knots when submerged.

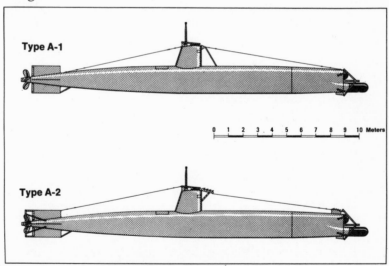

Japanese midget submarines ("flies").

These improvements prompted the navy to order a series of 15, identical to the prototype except that they carried only two men. They were called Type C and numbered Ha. 62 to Ha. 76. Construction of the whole series extended from the end of 1942 to the beginning of 1944. Since they were intended for coastal defense, there was no need for them to be carried by larger submarines. When necessary, they were to be transported by 1500-ton landing craft carrying two of them at a time.

The Koryu

Continuing their studies, Japanese naval engineers tried to improve the range and effectiveness of the Type C. Construction of a larger prototype, called Type D Ha. 77 and nicknamed Koryu, was begun in June, 1944, and finished in January, 1945. With a crew of five, a length of 86 feet and a displacement of 60 tons, it had a range of 1000 miles on the surface at 8 knots, or 320 miles at its top speed of 16 knots when submerged, and it could dive to a depth of 330 feet.

Its performance was so promising that the navy ordered 540 of them for the defense of Okinawa. But technical difficulties and shortages of materials slowed production so greatly that only 115 had been completed by the end of the war.

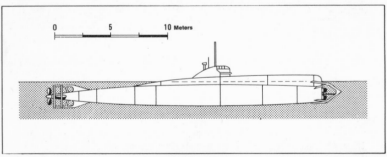

The Koryu submarine.

The koryus were designed to be launched either by means of rails installed on various types of ships or by cranes on shore. They were apparently not used in any great numbers, since no important destruction was attributed to them.

In the last months of the war, when there were not enough torpedoes to replace those that had been fired, the Koryu was modified: instead of its two torpedoes, it carried an added bow section filled with a heavy explosive charge. It was obviously intended to be rammed into an enemy ship, like a kamikaze plane. A few Koryus were set aside for training suicide crews. They were equipped with a second periscope and their conning towers were enlarged to make room for an instructor.

The Kairyu

At the end of 1943, an experimental version of the original Type A was built, the only change being the addition of horizontal fins on either side of the hull to increase stability and make the craft easier to trim when diving. In 1944 another modified version was built and extensively tested. It was the immediate ancestor of the Kairyu, an improved and even smaller version of the Type A.

The Kairyu was 55.8 feet long and displaced 19 tons. It had a range and speed of 450 miles and 5 knots on the surface, 36 miles and 3 knots submerged. It carried two 18-inch torpedoes extending below the hull, one on each side. Very strong for its size, the little two-man submarine could dive to 330 feet with its torpedoes and 480 feet without them. It was powered by an 85-horsepower Isuzu gasoline automobile engine on the surface and an 80-horsepower electric motor when submerged.

Production of the Kairyus began in February, 1945. They were made in three separate segments by different manufacturers, then assembled at Yokosuka. The first 20 were used for training and therefore had two periscopes and a larger conning tower.

As with the Koryu, the shortage of torpedoes led to a version of the Kairyu whose armament consisted of a forward section filled with 1320 pounds of TNT. The torpedoes were replaced by two long tubes, streamlined at each end, which could contain either ballast for trimming the craft or extra fuel to increase its range.

Study of another type of midget submarine, displacing 40 tons, was begun in 1945, but was not completed before the end of the war.

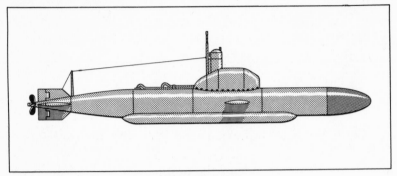

Kairyu 2 submarine.

The Kaiten Torpedo

The course taken by the war in its final phase drastically altered the action of the Japanese armed forces, including the navy. It was no longer a question of clever strategy, but of desperate efforts to maintain defenses that were constantly being threatened by enemy advances. As we have seen, the various models of midget submarines were originally conventional weapons—that is, they did not inevitably involve the death of their crews. But the worsening military situation, and also changes in the attitude of Japanese sailors, eventually led the navy to design and manufacture suicide craft. The first step in this direction was the transformation of the Koryus and Kairyus into explosive devices with the same function as kamikaze planes.

The shortage of torpedoes in the last months of the war was one reason for the radical change in the tactical use of midget submarines, but there was another reason, at least equally important. When the exploits of Admiral Onishi's kamikaze pilots in the Philippines became known, a kind of emotional tidal wave swept through all branches of the

Japanese armed forces. Many sailors wanted to follow the pilots' example of self-sacrifice. They could not understand why they were being spared at a time when they could do much for the defense of the Japanese homeland. They urged their superiors to create suicide units like the kamikaze corps in the Philippines. The modified versions of the Koryu and the Kairyu were a partial answer to these demands. Then Japanese engineers began reconsidering the technical problems involved and designing craft intended exclusively for suicide attacks.

This was what led to the creation of the famous Kaiten torpedo, or "human torpedo," as it was deprecatingly called all over the world. At this point we must correct a widespread mistake. It was commonly believed that the Japanese suicide volunteer straddled his "diabolical explosive cigar" and rode it like a horse. Although the Kaiten actually was a manned torpedo, the pilot was inside it and it was designed to strike its target without him, as we shall see shortly.

Based on the standard Type-93 torpedo, with the same explosive charge (3410 pounds of TNT), air chambers and motor, the Kaiten Type-1 was 48.2 feet long and 3.2 feet in diameter, with a displacement of 8.3 tons. Its range varied with its speed, going from 14 miles at 30 knots to 48 miles at 12 knots. Its propulsive power, on the order of 550 horsepower, was supplied by petroleum and oxygen.

The Kaiten Type-1 was thus a torpedo, except that the usual automatic directional equipment was replaced by a cockpit and a miniature conning tower surmounted by a short periscope. Furthermore, and this is important, under the cockpit was a hatch that the pilot could open by pressing a button, to escape from the torpedo when it was about 50 yards from its target. If it had not been for this possibility of survival, the navy probably would not have authorized study and construction of the Kaiten in February, 1944.

Although the Kaitens were originally intended for coastal defense, submarines were later adapted to carry four to six of them, depending on size. A submarine of the I-54 class, for example, carried five Kaitens on its deck, two forward and two aft.

The escape hatch in the bottom of the Kaiten allowed it to be used in a new way. The hatch was connected to the inside of the submarine by a tubular passageway equipped with a flooding chamber. This meant that the pilot could take his place in the Kaiten and set off toward his target while the submarine was submerged, which made the launching operation much more flexible and lessened the chances of detection.

In most cases where Kaitens were actually used, the pilots guided them all the way to the target. Very few even tried to use the escape mechanism that was "officially" provided. To be sure of a hit, they would have had to leave the torpedo a very short time before impact, at a distance where the shock wave of the explosion would be almost certain to kill them. For that reason, and because of the volunteers' frame of mind, the Kaitens were suicide torpedoes.

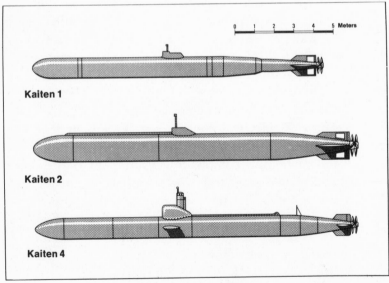

Kaiten piloted torpedoes.

The Kaiten Type-1 was mass-produced by various ship-yards, such as those at Yokosuka, Hikari, Maizuru, Kure and

Sasebo, and was by far the most commonly used model, perhaps even the only one used, because later models were not put into production until the war was nearly over and it is likely that only a small number of them were made.

These later models, called Types 2, 3 and 4, were larger, heavier and faster, with a length of 55 feet, a diameter of 5.5 feet, a weight of 18.3 tons and a top speed of 40 knots. Propelled by a hydrogen peroxide motor developing 1500 to 1800 horsepower, they carried an explosive charge of from 3300 to 3690 pounds of TNT, according to the model. Unlike the one-man Type-1, these later versions had a crew of two. Their conning tower was larger and they were equipped with horizontal fins. Their remarkable top speed could be reduced to increase their range.

The Kikumizu Unit

We cannot describe all the actions in which the Kaiten took part, but we shall relate some of them to show how it was used.

By late October, 1944, the Type-1 had been thoroughly tested and, despite numerous fatal accidents, methods of using it effectively and training pilots for it had been worked out. The naval high command then gave orders for the creation of the first operational unit. The Kikumizu Unit was formed on November 8, 1944, with three submarines, the I-36, I-37 and I-47, assigned to carry the Kaitens. Orders for its first mission were issued soon afterward. The I-36 and I-47 were to attack the great American base at Ulithi while, at the same time, the I-37 was to attack the American anchorage in the Kossol Channel in the Palau Islands.

The three submarines headed for their objectives. The Kaiten pilots shared the life of the crew on board. They seemed confident, determined and contemptuous of death. They were always courteous toward the crew, who treated them with great solicitude.

On the evening of November 19 the I-36 and the I-47 reached their assigned position off the coast of Ulithi. An aerial reconnaissance report, relayed from Tokyo, confirmed the presence of a large number of enemy ships lying at anchor.

At 4:30 the next morning, four Kaitens from the I-47 and one from the I-36 were launched. Just before their departure, the senior Kaiten pilot warmly thanked the captain of the I-47 for having brought him and his companions to the right place under the best conditions. He wished him long life and expressed the hope that future Kaiten pilots would obtain excellent results.

The five Kaitens moved along the channel and entered the big lagoon. A swirl on the surface of the water caught the attention of an American lookout who immediately sounded a general alarm. Guns opened fire and depth charges were launched, at first in great confusion, then with increasing accuracy. Within a few minutes, four Kaitens were sunk before they could attack.

Shells were making huge splashes all over the lagoon and its whole surface was swept by hundreds of searchlights. Probably because of this, the pilot of the last remaining Kaiten did not take time to approach an aircraft carrier as he had intended. Instead, he chose a rather large ship several hundred yards away as his target and headed straight for it.

There was an explosion that echoed across the entire atoll. The oiler *Mississinewa* (AO-59), transformed into a gigantic flaming torch, sank with 150 men of its crew. The Kaiten had scored its first victory.

The operation in the Palau Islands, however, was a total failure. The I-37 had reached its objective on the evening of November 19 and was preparing to launch its Kaitens when it was spotted by two American destroyer escorts. It dived in deep water but could not escape. Guided by sonar, the *McCoy Reynolds* (DE-440) and the *Conklin* (DE-439) dropped depth charges directly over the I-37. They exploded almost in contact with it. It broke open and sank.

Our account of the first Kaiten operation ends with an interesting sidelight of the attack at Ulithi. The American sailors had such confidence in their defensive precautions, consisting of vigilant watches, antisubmarine nets and constant patrols both inside and outside the lagoon, that some of them could not believe that Japanese submarines had been able to penetrate the harbor. To them, the only possible explanation for the attack was that the submarines must have been there since the conquest of the atoll, waiting under water for a chance to strike. Ulithi was conquered on September 23 and the attack took place on November 20; it is a little hard to imagine Japanese sailors remaining submerged in miniature submarines and patiently waiting eight weeks before they acted!

The Kongo Unit

Despite the semifailure of the November 20 operation, a new flotilla, the Kongo Unit, was formed in December. Six of the navy's newest submarines were assigned to it: the I-36, I-47, I-48, I-53, I-56 and I-58. As with the Kikumizu Unit, plans called for simultaneous attacks at different points, to produce a greater psychological effect. Ulithi, Hollandia, the Admiralty Islands, the Palau Islands and Guam were all to be attacked on the same day.

Preparations were begun in the second half of December and the operation was scheduled for January 11, 1945. On December 29 the submarines assembled to take aboard the suicide torpedoes and their pilots. Their departure was a festive occasion. A whole fleet of small craft swarmed all over the bay and accompanied the submarines when they put out to sea. Everyone in the boats chanted the names of the Kaiten pilots in chorus, repeating the list again and again, as a tribute to the men who would soon die and were already heroes.

Each pilot stood in the cockpit of his Kaiten with the upper part of his body showing above the conning tower, wearing a white scarf around his head as a symbol of patriotic purity and brandishing his saber in response to the cheers. Many of those who witnessed the scene could not hold back tears of deep emotion.

The submarines left the Inland Sea, passed through the Bungo Strait and entered the Pacific. They then separated and headed for their respective destinations. Certain clues picked up from monitored American radio transmissions seemed to indicate that the enemy knew about the existence of the Kaitens and, after the November 20 operation, was probably now on his guard, so the submarines maintained special vigilance and traveled under the surface most of the time.

The Kaiten pilots, all very young, were filled with calm courage and faith in victory. During the voyage they often offered to help the submarine crews and always met with a gentle refusal. They had already become legendary heroes, but with their cheerful, unfailing courtesy they could easily have been mistaken for a group of well-mannered students.

The I-58 was under orders to launch its Kaitens for an attack against Guam on January 11, and this was confirmed by a radio message on the 10th. But the approach was slowed by intense enemy air and surface activity. The captain decided to postpone the operation until early the following morning. That evening, January 11, he invited the volunteers to dinner and they bade each other farewell with the traditional glasses of sake.

At eleven o'clock, the pilots of Kaitens Nos. 2 and 3, wearing shorts, shook the captain's hand and climbed into the cockpits of their craft. The dark mass of Guam could be seen in the distance. The I-58 submerged and began moving toward the launch point. At two in the morning, January 12, the pilots of Kaitens Nos. 1 and 4 were also ordered to take their places. Since the I-58 was still submerged, they entered the Kaitens from underneath. When the watertight hatches had been closed, the captain remained in communication with the volunteers. Final preparations were made, and at three o'clock the captain gave the signal for the first departure. The pilot of Kaiten No. 1 shouted "Three cheers for the emperor!" into his telephone mouthpiece. Then there was silence; he was on his way and the telephone wire had been broken.

Kaiten No. 2 left a few minutes later, followed by Nos. 4 and 3. The I-58 remained submerged. Shortly after the last Kaiten had left, the crew of the submarine heard a powerful explosion. They surfaced but saw nothing. The Kaiten had apparently exploded accidentally. The I-58 cruised off the port of Apra, the Kaitens' objective, till eleven o'clock at night, vainly waiting to learn the results of the operation. It then headed back toward Japan.

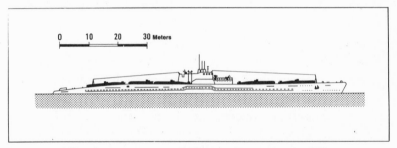

Carrying arrangement of Kaitens aboard submarine I-58.

Meanwhile most of the other submarines of the Kongo Unit had reached their destinations. The I-36 launched its Kaitens off Ulithi, but none of them hit an enemy ship. Four Kaitens had left the I-47 off the port of Hollandia, New Guinea, between 4:00 and 4:30 on the morning of January 12, but what happened to them remained unknown. The I-53 reached its objective in the Palau Islands and launched four Kaitens. Two of them sank shortly after departure; the two others continued in the direction of the enemy fleet. Here again, nothing was known about the outcome of the attack.

As for the I-56, it was stopped by enemy defenses in the vicinity of the Admiralty Islands. After its third unsuccessful attempt to break through, it had to give up and return to base. And finally the I-48, delayed by mechanical difficulties, launched its Kaitens toward Ulithi on January 20. It waited offshore to watch for explosions but saw nothing. On January

146 ·

23, as it was on its way back to Japan, it was attacked and sunk northeast of Yap Island by three American destroyer escorts, the *Corbesier* (DE-438), the *Raby* (DE-698) and the *Conklin* (DE-439).

During this period, no Allied losses were reported at any of the places involved. The Kongo Unit's entire operation had accomplished nothing.

The Kaitens at Iwo Jima

The results were discouraging, but the Japanese had no choice but to continue in the same direction because their surface fleet was no longer capable of taking significant action. The threat of an imminent invasion of Iwo Jima led the navy to form a new Kaiten group, the Chibaya Unit, with three submarines assigned to it: the I-44, I-368 and I-370. Preparations were speeded up on February 19, 1945, with the news that American forces had landed on the island. The three submarines left on February 22 and 23 and took up waiting positions off the coast of Iwo Jima.

On February 26 the I-370 was detected south of the island by the American destroyer escort *Finnegan* (DE-307) and subjected to a terrible depth-charge attack that sank it within a few minutes. The next day, the I-368 was spotted by an antisubmarine plane from the escort carrier *Anzio* (DVE-57) west of Iwo Jima. It quickly dived to escape, but its hull was split by a depth charge and it sank shortly afterward.

Just as the I-44 was reaching a good position to launch its Kaitens, it was seen by a destroyer escort. It was able to dive in time and was not attacked with depth charges, but it had to remain submerged nearly 48 hours because American patrol craft had been alerted and were now concentrating in the area. Conditions inside the submarine became unbearable. The whole crew turned livid from the heat, humidity and lack of oxygen. They were suffocating. Many were barely able to move, some lost consciousness and others were beginning to show signs of insanity.

The situation was so critical that the captain finally decided to abandon his mission and return to Japan. The I-44 moved far enough away from Iwo Jima to escape its pursuers, surfaced and renewed its air at last. Some of the men remained ill for several weeks after they were taken ashore.

To the admiral in command of the Japanese submarine fleet, the sufferings endured by the men of the I-44 did not justify its return without having accomplished its mission. He angrily denounced what he regarded as a desertion and relieved the captain of his command. This unjust punishment provides another illustration of what authority and obedience meant to the Japanese military hierarchy.

Despite the complete and disastrous failure of the Chibaya Unit, still another Kaiten group was formed: the Kamitake Unit, with the submarines I-36 and I-58. Iwo Jima was again the objective. The unit left Kure on March 1, 1945, after a great farewell ceremony, and its departure was accompanied by enthusiastic cheers.

By the night of March 3 the I-58 was nearing the coast of Iwo Jima. The presence of many enemy planes and ships made its approach difficult and dangerous. For the next three days it tried to come closer. Because of all the detours and emergency dives it had to make to avoid the enemy, it was not able to reach its assigned position until midnight, March 7. Half an hour later, while preparations were being made to launch the Kaitens, the captain received a radio message ordering him to abandon his mission and head for Okinawa. The I-58 was to serve as a radio relay in an operation scheduled for March 11.

The I-36 developed mechanical difficulties that forced it to return to Kure a short time after its departure.

These successive failures stopped neither the construction of Kaitens nor the enthusiasm of the volunteers. Operations were continued with the hope that a victory would soon be won.

More Mishaps

By the end of March it had become clear that the Americans would soon land on Okinawa. Many of their ships were cruising near the island and preliminary bombing had already begun. The Japanese decided to strike before the enemy had assembled all his forces. Three submarines, the I-8, Ro-41 and Ro-46, left for Okinawa on March 22 but ran into well-organized enemy defenses.

On March 23, still far from its destination, the Ro-41 was spotted and pursued by the American destroyer *Haggard* (DD-555), which sank it 320 miles from Okinawa.

The I-8 succeeded in coming close to the island but was stalled for days on end by enemy surface activity. Finally, at about 10:30 on the night of March 30, it was attacked by the destroyers *Stockton* (DD-646) and *Morrison* (DD-560). It dived immediately but exploding depth charges opened serious leaks in its hull. By the time it reached its maximum depth of 440 feet it was tilted at an angle of about 35 degrees and the invading sea water was accumulating in the stern. The situation was desperate because other damage was being worsened by the great pressure at that depth. The captain decided to surface [2] and fight the enemy with his 140-millimeter (5.5-inch) gun. The I-8 came up at an angle of 20 degrees. The gunners hurried to their battle stations but enemy shells began striking almost immediately. The conning tower was blown off and water began pouring in through the opening. The men on deck were cut down by machine-gun fire from the approaching destroyers. At 2:30 in the morning, March 31, the I-8 capsized and sank.

The third submarine in the operation, the Ro-46, was attacked and damaged before it could launch its Kaitens, but succeeded in returning to base.

Meanwhile the submarines I-44, I-47, I-56 and I-58 had

[2] *Surfacing, or simply reducing the depth of its dive so that pressure is diminished, generally enables a submarine to lessen the effects of any damage it has received. If it is leaking, for example, water penetrates at a lower rate.*

been grouped under the name of the Tatara Unit. The I-47 was the first to be ready. It left Kure on March 29. American planes began attacking it as soon as it emerged from the Bungo Strait. The next day it was spotted by destroyers and subjected to a depth-charge attack. Damage was minor, except for a fuel leak. The I-47 surfaced to repair it under cover of darkness, near Tanega Island. An American night patrol plane detected it by radar and dropped a bomb that exploded very close to it, worsening the fuel leak. Unable to dive, the I-47 returned to base.

The I-44 and the I-56 left port on April 3 and headed for Okinawa, carrying enough supplies for 30 days. Because enemy vigilance was so intense, they were under orders to cruise in the vicinity of the island and wait for a favorable opportunity. They spent two weeks unsuccessfully trying to find an opening in the American defenses. They were harassed by enemy planes and ships during this whole time, but escaped damage. Alarmed by the presence of Japanese submarines in the area, the Americans sent in still more ships and planes.

This extra effort soon paid off. On April 18, east of Okinawa, the I-56 was surrounded by five destroyers: the *Mertz* (DD-691), *McCord* (DD-534), *Collett* (DD-730), *Heermann* (DD-532) and *Uhlmann* (DD-687). Although devastated by countless depth-charge explosions, the I-56 succeeded in remaining submerged overnight, but was then sunk by a plane from the carrier *Bataan* (CVL-29).

The I-44 had also undergone many attacks. It had so far escaped major damage, but had still been unable to find a chance to act. On April 29, thinking that he was temporarily safe, the captain decided to resurface to recharge the batteries. The operation had scarcely begun when several planes, which no one had seen coming, dived at the submarine. One of them, from the carrier *Tulagi* (CVE-72), scored a direct hit on it just as it was making an emergency dive. The bomb exploded near the conning tower and opened a disastrous leak. The I-44 never came up.

The I-58 had left for Okinawa on April 2. It ran into so many enemy air and surface attacks that after four days it had gone no further than the island of Amami O Shima and had never been able to remain on the surface more than four hours at a time. It swung northward to throw off enemy patrols, then headed back toward Okinawa. By April 14 its supply of compressed air was getting dangerously low and it still had found no chance to attack. In the vicinity of Okinawa it was never able to stay on the surface more than an hour and a half, which was not long enough to recharge the batteries and replenish the reserves of compressed air. The Kaiten pilots aboard were losing hope of ever being able to attack. Since the submarine had to spend so much of its time submerged, it was impossible to give the Kaitens the maintenance they needed and they were gradually becoming unusable. Finally, on April 25, a radio message ordered the I-58 to return to base. It reached Kure on April 29, without having launched a single attack.

Other submarines carrying Kaitens had fallen victims to the implacable American patrols. The Ro-109, for example, had succeeded in approaching Okinawa, but on April 25 it was detected and sunk by the armed transport *Horace A. Bass* (APD-124).

Faced with a shortage of submarines, the navy decided to convert the large cargo submarine I-300 into a Kaiten carrier. It apparently was never actually used for that purpose, however, because Japanese records contain no mention of its having been sent on a Kaiten mission.

Still determined to make use of the Kaitens, the navy decided that since they had been unsuccessful in attacking ships at anchor, they would have to begin attacking them at sea. The Amatake Unit was created with this in mind. Its two submarines, the I-36 and I-47, each carried six Kaitens.

The I-47 put to sea on April 12, the I-36 on April 20. They both reached their assigned sectors near Okinawa and launched eight of their 12 Kaitens. Not one of them hit its target. After undergoing many attacks, the two submarines returned to base.

The I-367 left Kure on May 5, went to Okinawa and

launched two of its Kaitens with no better results than its predecessors had achieved. The I-361 left on May 23 and cruised east of Okinawa without finding a chance to attack. On its way back to Kure, it swung far south of the island to avoid American patrols. In spite of this precaution it was spotted on May 30 by a plane from the carrier *Anzio* 400 miles southeast of Okinawa. It dived in deep water but was sunk by a depth charge. The I-363 cruised in vain along the American sea lanes between Ulithi and Okinawa and returned without having launched any of its Kaitens.

On June 6 the I-36, by now a veteran of this type of operation, went to the vicinity of the Marianas, was attacked many times, launched several of its Kaitens without results, and finally came back to Kure on June 30 with such heavy damage that it was a long time before it could put to sea again.

The only successful Kaiten attack during this period occurred when an opportunity arose almost accidentally. In the second half of July, a Kaiten-carrying submarine was on its way to the Philippines to cruise off the northeastern coast of Luzon. As the captain was looking through the periscope on July 24, he saw an American destroyer escort in the distance. He slowly approached undetected and launched one of his Kaitens from about 1000 yards.

When the Kaiten had closed to within 200 yards, the American ship, the *Underhill* (DE-682) apparently spotted its wake, because it picked up speed and opened fire. A few shells exploded on the surface, too far away to do any damage. The *Underhill* tried to swing its bow toward the attacker but the Kaiten struck before it could complete the maneuver. The explosion blew an enormous hole in the destroyer escort's side. It sank immediately.

A New Orientation

Kaiten missions were still beginning with ceremonious departures. Each time a submarine put to sea with a load of human torpedoes, it was accompanied by a swarm of small craft for dozens of miles. The spectators cheered the valiant pilots, endlessly repeated their names and gave them their place in heroic legend while they were still alive. Flags and streamers bearing words that praised the suicide volunteers' courage and patriotic zeal flew from the masts of the boats.

Despite all the pilots' heroism, however, the Kaitens proved to be as disappointing as the midget submarines had been. Their meager results were not worth the price that had to be paid for them.

Japan's inability to produce enough new ships was the basic reason for the decision to employ that form of "miniature warfare." It might have been successful against any other opponent than the United States, but during the last year of the war, the American Pacific fleet, with its colossal size, the superior quality of its matériel, and its advanced technology, was obviously capable of defeating the entire navy of any other country in the world.

The leaders of the Japanese navy were not blinded by the patriotic fervor that rose from the ranks. They viewed the situation objectively and weighed their last chances. The overwhelming material superiority of the enemy made them willing to investigate any possibility, however unusual. They decided to add other suicide weapons to the midget submarines and piloted torpedoes already in existence. They realized the ineffectiveness of each of these weapons taken individually but they hoped that a combination of different forms of attack might ultimately be successful. And so two new means of action were offered to Japanese sailors in October, 1944.

At the end of that month, Captain Toshio Miyazaki, senior instructor of the torpedo school at Oppama, went to Kawatana, where a new torpedo boat school had been opened several months earlier.

The Japanese had previously neglected that type of craft, but as their situation worsened, and also when they had seen what American torpedo boats could do, they had opened the new school. No country in the world can make up for a technological lag overnight, and Japan was especially incapable of it at that time. Japanese manufacturers could not turn out torpedo boats fast and strong enough to do what was expected of them. Trial runs made in the course of instructing students were so disappointing that the officers were afraid to put the boats in operation. The school went on training crews for them nevertheless.

The concept of suicide tactics put the problem in a new light: although the navy's present torpedo boats were too slow to be used with much chance of success, smaller ones could be built, loaded with explosives and sent out to ram enemy ships. The plan was adopted, and it was for the purpose of explaining it to the students of the torpedo boat school that Captain Miyazaki had been sent to Kawatana.

On the morning after his arrival, the 400 students were assembled to listen to him. He described the new boats and the way in which they would be used. He also explained another method of attack that was being planned. Groups of frogmen wearing light diving gear would place delayed-action explosive charges under the hulls of enemy ships at anchor. The men would be brought close to the ships in small boats; they would then walk on the bottom of the sea, do their work and return to the boats.

There was no murmur among the students while Miyazaki spoke. His announcement was obviously a shock to them, but they were not terrified.

As soon as Miyazaki had finished, Captain Tameichi Hara, the officer in command of the school, spoke to the students:

I have no orders for you. You came here to prepare yourselves for conventional torpedo boats. You have just learned of two other weapons that have been authorized for study in this school. Starting tomorrow either of the three courses of study will be open to you. You have a free choice of which class you wish to attend, according to your own aptitude and inclination. I want your choice

to be made without compulsion or influence from anyone, according to the dictates of your own conscience.
This is my ruling. I will be in my office this afternoon
and evening, as long as is necessary. Each of you will
report to me personally on your choice. There will be
no questions asked or explanations required as to why
you make the choice you do. That is all.[3]

That afternoon the 400 students began coming to Hara's
office one by one. The last one did not leave until four o'clock
in the morning. Hara then gave Miyazaki the results of the
interviews. Half the students had elected to continue training for conventional torpedo boats, 150 had volunteered for
the suicide boats, and 50 had chosen to be frogmen. The new
training was begun immediately. The suicide boats were
soon named Shinyos ("Ocean Shakers"), and the frogmen
Fukuryus ("Crawling Dragons").

The Shinyo

When the idea of using small surface craft for suicide attacks
against enemy ships at anchor was first proposed, the navy
considered requisitioning civilian pleasure boats. This would
have made a certain number of boats available almost immediately, as soon as explosive charges could be installed in
them. But it would also have meant using boats of many different types, with great variations in performance and han-
dling characteristics, and that would have made it more
difficult to train the volunteers. The plan was therefore abandoned and three types of specially designed boats were put
into production.

The two most common types had a fragile wooden frame
covered with plywood. Their length varied from 16 to 17

[3] Japanese Destroyer Captain, by Tameichi Hara, with Fred Saito and Roger
Pineau, Ballantine Books, 1961, p. 268.

feet, their unloaded weight from 2470 to 3740 pounds. They were powered by an automobile engine that gave them a top speed of 26 knots. The explosive charge in the bow was composed of 3300 pounds of TNT.

The third main type of Shinyo was a little larger and had a steel frame covered with light metal. It was 18 feet long, weighed 4730 pounds empty, was powered by two automobile engines, had a top speed of 30 knots, and carried 4400 pounds of TNT or, in some models, two depth charges of equivalent explosive power.

In all three types, the pilot's cockpit, close to the stern, had a steering wheel, a throttle and a lever for arming the explosive charge just before impact.

The Shinyos were built by many different manufacturers. Several hundred of them were available by late 1944, and at the end of the war the impressive total of 6000 had been reached.

The new suicide boats were first used in the Philippines. Having arrived at Luzon in early January, 1945, the boats and their pilots were assembled on the northwestern coast to wait for the imminent American landing in Lingayen Gulf. As we saw in Chapter 4, 70 of them attacked the American invasion fleet on the night of January 9. Most were sunk by gunfire and a few turned back or became lost in the darkness, but six got through and attacked the first ships in sight. Two LCIs and four LSTs were hit. One of the LCIs sank during the night.

On January 31 another group of Shinyos attacked American auxiliary vessels. Defensive action was prompt, but one of the boats escaped the slaughter and sank a submarine chaser, the PC-1129.

On February 15 American amphibious forces landed on the Bataan Peninsula to take the Japanese troops from the rear and speed up the reconquest of Luzon. That evening three Shinyos managed to slip into the American supply fleet at twilight. Discovered at the last moment, they were fired at by hundreds of guns and two of them were quickly sunk. The third struck a ship and damaged it seriously.

As a preliminary to the invasion of Okinawa, the Americans had decided to occupy the Kerama Islands to obtain a base of operations only a short distance southwest of their main objective. Troops of the 77th Division landed on March 26 and eliminated all resistance within 48 hours. Taken by surprise, the Japanese were nearly all killed and did not have time to destroy their installations. The Americans discovered about 400 Shinyos hidden in coves, waiting to be used in attacks against the invasion fleet.

On Okinawa, the Japanese had installed two Shinyo bases: a rather large one in the Motobu Peninsula, in the northern half of the island, and another at Hagushi, in the center. The second one consisted only of a few hastily built wooden piers in the little estuary of the Bisha Gawa River. The Japanese intended to send out the Shinyos when the American invasion fleet was directly offshore, because they were certain that the enemy would land at Hagushi.

That was exactly what happened. While the first ships of the American amphibious force were approaching Hagushi on the night of March 31, the 50 Shinyo pilots were ordered to attack. The boats roared out of the estuary and into the sea, trailing phosphorescent wakes that glittered in the moonlight. The American ships quickly spotted them and opened fire. Most of the Shinyos were cut to pieces by direct hits and others were capsized by splashes from exploding shells. Apparently only one of them got through. The landing ship LSM-12 was shaken by a violent explosion. It came to a halt and the crew began working to stop up the hole in its side. The LSM-12 was kept afloat temporarily, but it finally sank on April 4.

These were the only Shinyo operations of the war. Although the results were disappointing, large numbers of Shinyos were concentrated at various points along the coastlines of the home islands for the great Japanese counteroffensive that never took place.

A Fatal Incapacity

With their midget submarines, their Kaiten piloted torpedoes, and finally their Shinyo suicide boats, the Japanese were unable to achieve the goal that had already proven to be beyond the capacity of their surface fleet: the destruction of the invincibly powerful American navy.

The very existence of such weapons was final proof that Japanese heavy industry was incapable of performing the task that had been set for it. They were by nature weapons of the weak, used as a last resort by a country that tried to make up for its inferiority in the major means of waging war by creating a multitude of minor ones. The Pacific war proved that nothing could counterbalance mastery of the sea and the air, and that without it nothing could be attempted with any chance of success.

Considered in themselves, the midget submarines, Kaitens and Shinyos, manned by pilots with extraordinary courage and devotion, might have seemed to justify the Japanese hope that they would cause enough destruction to be an important factor in reversing the military situation. But that hope was based on the assumption that they would be able to reach their targets. It thus failed to reckon with the Americans' control of the air and the sea, and their technological supremacy.

The use of those miniature weapons may not have resulted entirely from an underestimation of the enemy's defensive strength. The Japanese may also have been blinded by their faith in the power of their moral superiority.

Most of the suicide volunteers died before they could carry out their attacks. It is saddening to think of that great waste of admirable courage and patriotic fervor. And even if we are appalled by their calm determination to die, we must still recognize that those men were genuine heroes.

CHAPTER

VII

The Kikusuis of Okinawa

Imperial General Headquarters had known since the beginning of 1945 that the Americans would continue their advance toward the heart of the Japanese homeland by attacking the southern islands of the archipelago. Formosa, Iwo Jima and Okinawa were the most likely objectives. For a time the Japanese feared a major assault against Formosa. The invasion of Iwo Jima on February 19 showed that the enemy had a different plan.

After Iwo Jima, the next step could only be Okinawa. Because of its nearness to Japan and the time it would take to assemble the invasion forces, Japanese military leaders felt that Okinawa would probably not be invaded until June or perhaps even July, 1945. This would be the final test on which the future of Japan would depend. Everything possible had to be done to defend Okinawa; every inch of its soil was vital to the existence of the Empire of the Rising Sun.

This conviction, combined with the prevailing attitude of the Japanese armed forces, made it inevitable that the defense of Okinawa would be conceived in terms of a general holocaust. All preparations for it presupposed an acceptance of death. Since defeat was unthinkable, soldiers, sailors and airmen would all have to fight with an absolute determination that involved the possibility of deliberate self-sacrifice as a natural consequence. No provisions were made for evacuating troops from the island if they should fail to stop the enemy, and no conventional attacks were planned for sea and air units.

The ground force consisted of about 100,000 men of the 32nd Army, commanded by General Mitsuru Ushijima, with General Isamu Cho as his chief of staff. The Japanese adopted a new defensive strategy on Okinawa. The 32nd Army was ordered not to try to throw the invading troops back into the sea, but to immobilize them as long as possible, forcing the enemy to maintain large numbers of ships around the island thus exposing them to repeated suicide attacks by Japanese pilots. The goal was not only to defend Okinawa, but also to destroy American ships that would otherwise be used to support further invasions of Japanese territory.

The Kikusui Forces

Early in March, Vice Admiral Matome Ugaki was placed in command of all air units based in Kyushu and instructed to use them to defend Okinawa in close coordination with army operations. The Third, Fifth and Tenth air fleets were combined into a single air armada which, toward the end of March, became known as the Kikusui Forces.[1] Since all Kikusui pilots were suicide volunteers, Admiral Ugaki had a powerful and fanatically determined force at his disposal.

There were Kikusui units at many different airfields in Kyushu, but their main base was at Kanoya because it was furthest south and therefore nearest to Okinawa. Various subterfuges were used to prevent the planes from being spotted by American patrols and destroyed on the ground. They were concealed under trees or artificial foliage. Buildings housing the pilots and ground crews were dissimulated

[1] Kikusui *means "floating chrysanthemum." The chrysanthemum has always been regarded in Japan as a symbol of spiritual purity. Thus a floating chrysanthemum represented not only the moral grandeur of the suicide volunteers, but also the air-sea nature of their operations. A half-chrysanthemum floating on water became the emblem of all Japanese combatants who had deliberately accepted death to defend Okinawa.*

as much as possible by taking advantage of every irregularity in the terrain. Dummy planes were set out to make American raiders waste their bomb loads.

Admiral Ugaki knew that to defend Okinawa he would have to act on a much larger scale than Admiral Onishi had done in the Philippines. He also knew that Japanese aircraft production had not been keeping up with losses and that his younger pilots were inadequately trained. There would be other battles to fight; it was essential to save experienced pilots to instruct and lead inexperienced ones, and above all they had to be kept in reserve for the ultimate engagement that would take place when the Japanese homeland was invaded.

These considerations led Ugaki to plan mass-formation suicide attacks using the oldest planes of all types, flown by the least experienced pilots. "Herds" of novices would be protected and led to their targets by veteran pilots flying first-class fighters. As soon as the suicide planes began their attack, the veterans would return to base to escort another group. For this reason, many good pilots were never accepted into the Kikusui units even though they had volunteered.

Admiral Ugaki sent out a call for old planes of all kinds, anything that would fly. By the middle of March a motley assortment of aircraft had begun accumulating in Kyushu: outmoded fighters, float planes, twin-engined bombers, reconnaissance planes, even training biplanes.

Because of the fuel shortage, the young pilots were given very few hours of additional instruction. Some of them came straight from flying school and were sent on suicide missions without having made a single preparatory flight.

The Tokubetsu Units

So far we have mentioned only navy pilots. The army did not begin planning suicide air attacks until long after they had become common in the navy. The reason lay in the interservice rivalry that had plagued the Japanese armed forces for years.

Such rivalry has been a problem in many other countries, but in Japan it was so intense that it bordered on open hostility. If the navy made a decision, the army would oppose it automatically, even if important national interests were involved. And of course the navy did likewise. Their rivalry had already handicapped Japanese efforts many times, not only during World War II but in earlier conflicts as well. Despite joint missions and common interests, the two services had seldom been in agreement.

Their respective leaders had always vied with each other within the government, each trying to gain political supremacy over the other. The same animosity was expressed more directly by their enlisted men: violent and sometimes even bloody fighting between soldiers and sailors was so common that every effort was made to station them so that they would have no contact with each other. It was for this reason that some island outposts were defended by the army and others by the navy.

As Japan's position in the war became steadily worse, the two services were drawn closer together, more by force of circumstance than by a genuine reconciliation. The opposition remained, but it could not prevent the officers and men of the army from having the same preoccupations and emotions as their counterparts in the navy, and the urgency of the situation imposed a certain tacit agreement on them.

The army had already adopted the kamikaze principle in ground combat. Many soldiers had thrown themselves under Allied tanks with explosives strapped to their bodies, or made suicidal banzai charges, or killed themselves to avoid being captured by the enemy. But the army continued limiting its air force to conventional tactics.

In March, 1945, the desperate war situation and the imminence of major enemy moves forced army leaders to reconsider this policy. They could no longer tolerate the idea that their fliers were not making the same sacrifices that navy pilots had been making for months. They finally began form-

ing suicide squadrons, known as the Tokubetsu ("Special")
Units, modeled after those of the navy.

The Tokubetsu Units were placed within the framework of
the Kikusui operations for the defense of Okinawa. They
were commanded by General Miyoshi, who received his instructions from Admiral Ugaki. This dependency, which
would have been unthinkable a short time earlier, was accepted only because of the pressure of events.

Be that as it may, the army now began cooperating closely
with the navy. Army suicide volunteers were less numerous,
however, and while there was no difficulty in finding enough
of them for the first few weeks, recruitment later became a
problem.

The Invasion Begins

After their March 26 landing in the Kerama Islands, near
Okinawa, American forces quickly established bases that
would be useful to them in their main operation.

On March 31 a Japanese suicide plane, the first of a sinister
series, escaped the vigilance of American fighter pilots and
antiaircraft gunners and crashed into the heavy cruiser
Indianapolis (CA-35), flagship of Vice Admiral Raymond A.
Spruance. The bomb exploded inside the ship and blew two
holes in its hull. The *Indianapolis* had to withdraw to the
Keramas for emergency repairs before returning to the
United States. Admiral Spruance shifted his flag to the old
battleship *New Mexico* (BB-40).

The invasion of Okinawa began on April 1. Shortly after
8:30 in the morning, American amphibious forces landed on
the beach at Hagushi, near the Japanese airfields at Yontan
and Kadena.

The Americans expected fierce resistance. Incredibly, there
was none. They moved several miles inland without fighting.
A few sporadic shots were the only signs that there were
Japanese soldiers on the island. The American troops went

far beyond their immediate objectives. Artillery units and staff officers were landed ahead of schedule.

In the air, however, this first day of the invasion was marked by the opening of an important kamikaze offensive by the Kikusui Forces. In the evening a group of Japanese planes, coming from the north, attacked ships cruising off the beachhead. There were already many American antiaircraft guns ashore, but their gunners lacked experience. The kamikazes were able to make their approach with only light losses.

One plane crashed into the battleship *West Virginia* (BB-48), striking a turret and causing serious damage. Another hit the landing ship LST-884 amidships, killing 16 men, wounding 27, and setting off a violent fire that caused the magazines to explode. The ship was evacuated while damage-control parties continued to fight the fire. When it was finally put out, the rest of the crew came back aboard. A third plane hit the attack transport *Hinsdale* (APA-120). Disabled and swept by fire, the *Hinsdale* seemed doomed, but quick action by the crew saved it from total destruction. It was towed to a repair base.

For the first time in the Pacific war, a large British naval group was cooperating with the American forces. In accordance with an agreement between Prime Minister Churchill and President Roosevelt, Britain had sent a fleet into the Pacific composed of two battleships, four carriers, five cruisers and ten destroyers, commanded by Vice Admiral Sir Bernard Rawlings. Under the name of Task Force 57, it was given the mission of patrolling southwest of a line between Formosa and Okinawa, to cover the left flank of the American drive.

The British task force was also attacked on April 1, by suicide planes from Formosa. All but two of them were shot down or crashed into the sea. One struck a destroyer which, though badly damaged, kept its place in formation. The carrier *Indefatigable* took a hit in the middle of its flight deck, but, thanks to its strong construction, damage was only superficial.

On the whole, British carriers were not as well adapted to the specific conditions of the Pacific war as their American counterparts. They carried fewer planes and their maintenance facilities were less extensive. But they had armored flight decks, while those of American carriers were made of relatively light sheet metal covered with strips of wood. Because of its armored deck, a British carrier was much less vulnerable to kamikaze attacks. The impact usually resulted only in a pile of wreckage that could be simply "swept" overboard.

On April 2, American troops on Okinawa continued to advance as easily as they had done the day before. Many of them felt that the enemy's strange conduct concealed a trap, yet a solid beachhead had been established and a large area inland, including the Yontan and Kadena airfields, had already been occupied, all with only very light casualties. Any attempt by the Japanese to dislodge the American forces from Okinawa would now be futile.

That same day, a few kamikaze planes again attacked American ships off Hagushi. The only victim was the transport *Dickerson* (APD-21). It did not sink, but it was damaged beyond repair and had to be scuttled two days later.

The combination of suicide attacks in the air and lack of enemy resistance on the ground was making the Americans more perplexed and anxious than ever. Although losses from the suicide attacks had so far been light, there could be no doubt that the Japanese would make a great fanatical effort to defend Okinawa. The Americans were waiting apprehensively for it to begin.

Admiral Richmond Kelly Turner, in charge of the amphibious operations, had noticed that the Japanese planes always came from the north. He decided to set up an interception system to give advance warning of approaching suicide planes. He detached 15 destroyers, equipped with sky radar, from his own escort forces and stationed them in two arcs 35 and 75 miles north-northeast of Cape Bolo, also known as Cape Zampa, a few miles north of the Hagushi beachhead. The picket ships were to work in relays to maintain a constant vigil. This system proved to be a great asset. All through the campaign, the early warnings it provided made American defenses more effective.

A Massive Assault

As soon as news of the American invasion of Okinawa reached Kyushu, Admiral Ugaki and his staff prepared to make full use of the Kikusui Forces and immediately asked for reinforcements to replace the planes and pilots that would be sacrificed.

Ugaki planned to send suicide planes in such large groups that they would have a chance of overwhelming enemy defenses. The goal of his main operation would be to destroy an important part of the American fleet. The orders he issued contained these words: "You must sink or destroy 20 battleships or carriers to restore strategic equilibrium."

The size of the operation and the number of different units involved were so great that it could not be scheduled before April 8. It would deal the Americans a terrible blow, perhaps so terrible that they would lose all desire to pursue the war. Japanese leaders still had hopes of winning a position of strength that would bring them final victory or, failing that, an honorable peace settlement.

The one-week delay required for the opening of the great Japanese counteroffensive would be taken up with assembling more than 400 planes on airfields in southern Kyushu. Considering the shortages of spare parts, ammunition and fuel, and the precarious state of Japanese transportation facilities, one week was an incredibly short time in which to get everything done. Preparations were made still more difficult by the fact that the assembled aircraft had to be concealed as well as possible because enemy reconnaissance planes were flying over Kyushu almost constantly.

On April 4 several American reconnaissance pilots saw a large number of planes gathered on Kyushu airfields and noticed that they were of many different types. Such a strangely diverse collection could only be intended for use in kamikaze attacks. The pilots sent back urgent warnings. When Admiral Spruance was informed of what they had seen, he immediately realized the danger it represented and ordered air raids against Kyushu. On April 6, at dawn, hundreds of American carrier-based planes took off to attack all the Kyushu airfields.

As usual, the pilots exaggerated the results of their raids. They reported having destroyed more than 200 planes on the ground. Actually, because Japanese camouflage was excellent and the planes were scattered in many different hiding places, only a few dozen were destroyed or damaged. But the violence of the American raids and the likelihood that they would be repeated forced the Japanese to advance their schedule of operations. To avoid the possibility that all the laboriously assembled planes might be lost before they had even taken off, orders were given to launch the main attack without delay. Ground crews went into action, loading bombs, filling fuel tanks, wheeling planes out from under the concealing trees or camouflage nets.

The premature execution of the attack caused difficulties. First, not all of the fighter groups assigned to escort duty were able to reach their designated bases in time, which meant that the suicide planes would have less protection on the way to their targets. And there was no time for the traditional ceremonies that ordinarily preceded the departure of kamikaze units. This was more important than one might think. Having been deprived of the honors they had expected, many of the suicide pilots had a sense of frustration that affected their actions and weakened their determination.

Late in the morning of April 6, 355 planes, divided into two waves, took off from different airfields. The 195 navy planes included 80 kamikazes of various types, 8 Type-1 bombers carrying Ohkas and 107 escort fighters. They left from Kanoya and Shikoku. The army's Tokubetsu Units, with 160 planes, took off a little later, forming the bulk of the second wave.

In Kyushu, the Japanese officers were apprehensive. Despite all their hopes of success, they could not help wondering how effective American defenses would be. This was the first great kamikaze offensive of the war and its outcome would confirm or invalidate Admiral Ugaki's views. It was also only the second time that Ohkas had been used in an attack and no one could forget their failure on March 21. Wearing earphones, the officers waited for information from the planes.

North of Okinawa, aboard the American picket destroyers, lookouts and radar operators continued their vigilant search. They were all well aware that the fate of the whole fleet might depend on them. Having seen what kamikaze attacks could do, they were determined to do their best in their vital job as watchdogs.

At two in the afternoon a radar operator on the *Colhoun* (DD-801) picked up a multitude of spots on his screen. Other operators confirmed the contact shortly afterward. The destroyers increased their speed and began zigzagging. Patrolling American fighters headed for the enemy while other units took off.

Toward 2:30, pilots in the vanguard of the Japanese formation reported approaching enemy fighters. An aerial battle broke out a few moments later and trails of black smoke soon marked the fall of several Japanese planes, weighted down by their heavy bomb loads and unable to defend themselves efficiently.

The Japanese pilots quickly realized that it could only have been the picket destroyers that had alerted the American fighters. By eliminating the effect of surprise, they had endangered the success of the whole operation. The Japanese decided that some of their planes would attack them while the others tried to get through to the main body of the fleet.

No fewer than 40 planes headed for the destroyer *Bush*

(DD-529). It veered wildly to escape them, listing as much as 45 degrees in its abrupt turns, while its gunners desperately tried to ward off the attackers. But it was hit by one kamikaze plane that made it quiver like a leaf and lose speed. Then two more crashed into it.

The nearby *Colhoun* hurried to its assistance, but by the time it arrived the *Bush* was already sinking. The Japanese planes then went after the *Colhoun,* which shot down five of them before three struck and sank it.

Meanwhile fierce air fighting was still going on. The Japanese had suffered very heavy losses, including five of the eight Ohka-carrying bombers. But the American fighters could not attack all of them at once. Some were able to get through.

When this was reported by radio to Kyushu, the officers heaved a sigh of relief: the mission was not going to be a fiasco, as so many others had been. The ground crews had stopped working and gathered around loudspeakers broadcasting messages from the planes. They could hear sounds of the distant battle, mingled now and then with exclamations from the fliers. They listened intently, sometimes shuddering with anxiety, sometimes smiling when a victory was announced.

By now the fighting was spread over a larger area. The Japanese planes had split up into three main groups to attack different targets: the picket destroyers, the invasion fleet off Hagushi, and Admiral Spruance's task forces. In all three sectors the sky was dotted by explosions and dirtied by smoke from stricken aircraft.

The suicide planes, badly flown by inexperienced pilots and inadequately protected by an undersized contingent of escort fighters, were shot down in great numbers: about 135 of them fell during the first phase of the attack. Many of the pilots who got through to the American ships missed their targets because they were deflected, killed or wounded by antiaircraft fire while diving, or simply because they lacked the skill to control their planes properly. But, as Admiral Ugaki had hoped, their sheer number made it impossible for

American gunners and fighter pilots to cope with them all at once.

The minesweeper *Emmons* (DMS-22) was sent to the bottom; the attack transport *Logan Victory* (APA-196) was broken in half by the tremendous explosion of the ammunition it was carrying; the LST-447 was struck by at least two kamikazes and sank a short time later. Other ships were hit without being sunk: the fleet carrier *Hancock* (CV-19), the light carrier *San Jacinto* (CVL-30), 11 destroyers, 4 escort vessels and 5 minelayers. Among the more seriously damaged ships were the destroyers *Haynsworth* (DD-700) and *Taussig* (DD-746), each of which was disabled by at least two hits.

The attacks did not end until more than an hour after nightfall, at about eight o'clock. Besides the ships that had been sunk or put out of action by damage, others had to leave the fleet to escort those that withdrew for repairs.

An estimated 248 Japanese planes crashed or were shot down that day. It was hard to arrive at an exact figure because the attacks had been so numerous and spread over such large areas, but one thing is certain: only a few dozen escort fighters returned to Kyushu, and only one of the Ohka-carrying bombers landed at Kanoya. It had succeeded in escaping the slaughter by hiding in the clouds.

Although the Japanese air forces had been bled heavily, their leaders were encouraged by the results. They felt that nine or ten more attacks of that kind would force the Americans to withdraw their fleet from Okinawa and leave their troops on the island at the mercy of General Ushijima's valiant soldiers.

The gigantic raid had already had a psychological effect on the men of the American fleet. They had reacted to previous kamikaze attacks, never carried out by more than a few dozen planes at a time, with admirable confidence, courage and cool-headedness, but this massive assault made many of them wonder how far the enemy's patriotic frenzy would go, and how long they would be able to survive against it. Ship losses had been so numerous that they could no longer be regarded as normal or unimportant. A few American sailors were seized with horror, but the great majority continued to fight fiercely. There was, however, a growing anxiety that could not be stifled by the awareness that their forces were superior to the enemy's. This psychological climate was so obvious that, for the first time in the war, American communiqués began minimizing losses.

Such Beautiful Ships . . .

The capital importance of the defense of Okinawa, the disquieting idleness of the Imperial Fleet since the Battle of Leyte Gulf, and pressure from the army led the navy to commit what was left of its surface forces to the great Kikusui offensive at Okinawa. The decision was made on April 5.

It had been a painful decision for Admiral Soemu Toyoda, Commander in Chief of the Combined Fleet, and his chief of staff, Vice Admiral Ryunosoke Kusaka. They were about to sacrifice the last ships of the Imperial Fleet in fighting condition. To them, it meant the end, the collapse of Japan's dreams of grandeur. They were all the more bitter because they knew that the planned sortie, known as "Operation *Ten-go*," would be futile. It would be a sacrifice, pure and simple.

"Operation *Ten-go*" called for the ships of the Second Fleet [2] to head for Okinawa, fight their way through enemy defenses, deliberately run aground and continue firing their guns as long as they could. If they were too badly damaged to do this, their crews were to go ashore and kill as many of the enemy as they could before they themselves were killed. The ships would be given only enough fuel to reach Okinawa, since it was clearly understood that this was to be a one-way mission.

[2] See table, next page.

"OPERATION *TEN-GO*"—APRIL 7, 1945

Organization and Composition of the Japanese Second Fleet

COMMANDER IN CHIEF: Vice Admiral Seiichi Ito
FLAGSHIP: Battleship *Yamato*, Rear Admiral Kosaku Aruga

Destroyer Squadron 2, Rear Admiral Keizo Komura
FLAGSHIP: Light Cruiser *Yahagi*, Captain Tameichi Hara

Destroyer Division 17, Captain Kiichi Shintani

Isokaze, Commander Saneo Maeda
Hamakaze, Commander Isami Mukoi
Yukikaze, Commander Masamichi Terauchi

Destroyer Division 21, Captain Hisai Kotari

Asashimo, Commander Yoshiro Sugihara
Kasumi, Commander Hirao Yamana
Hatsushimo, Commander Masazao Sato

Destroyer Division 41, Captain Masayoshi Yoshida

Fuyutsuki, Commander Hidechika Sakuma
Suzutsuki, Commander Shigetaka Amano

The officers of the Second Fleet were overwhelmed to learn that the high command had decided to sacrifice its last ships, particularly the magnificent *Yamato*,[3] pride of the Japanese navy. They did not lack courage or willingness to die, but it was hard for them to accept the idea of losing the *Yamato*, the largest and most powerful battleship in the world. They had an almost religious reverence for it, and to many Japanese it was an integral part of Japan. It seemed

[3] *In 1937 the Japanese government decided to build two giant battleships, the* Yamato *and the* Musashi. *They were 863 feet long, had a displacement fully loaded of nearly 73,000 tons, and were armed with nine 18.1-inch guns, the largest ever carried by any ship. The* Musashi *was sunk by American carrier-based planes in the Sibuyan Sea on October 24, 1944.*

Construction of a third battleship of the same class, the Shinano, *was begun in 1939. The* Shinano *was converted into a carrier after the disastrous Battle of Midway in 1942. It was the largest carrier in the world at the time of its completion on November 19, 1944. It was sunk ten days later, during its first sortie, by the American submarine* Archerfish.

that if the *Yamato* were to disappear, an incurable wound would be opened in the vitals of the country.

Sublime Courage

On April 5 the Second Fleet was at anchor in Tokuyama Bay, in southwestern Honshu. At 11:30 Rear Admiral Keizo Komura summoned all division commanders and ship captains to a meeting at noon aboard the cruiser *Yahagi*. When they had assembled, he addressed them as follows:

> Gentlemen, you have all seen the signal that Operation *Ten-go* is now in force. Vice Admiral Ryunosuke Kusaka, the Combined Fleet chief of staff, has just come from Kanoya to confer with the flag-rank officers of our fleet.
>
> The operation formula proposed by Kusaka is an extraordinary one. The high command wants the Second Fleet to sortie for Okinawa, without air cover, with fuel enough for only a one-way trip. In short, the high command wants us to engage in a kamikaze mission.
>
> No, this is not even a kamikaze mission, for that implies the chance of chalking up a worthy target. I told Kusaka that our little fleet has no chance against the might of the enemy forces, and that such an operation would be a genuine suicide sortie. Aruga and Morishita agreed with me. Admiral Ito said nothing, so I do not know his opinion of the proposal.
>
> As you all know, I was chief of staff to Ozawa when he went on the decoy mission to the Philippines and lost four carriers. I have had to do with the killing of enough of our own men. I am not concerned with my death, but I do shrink from the wanton throwing of my men into a suicidal sortie. Accordingly, I asked Ito and Kusaka for a recess in order to get your opinions.[4]

[4] Japanese Destroyer Captain, by *Hara, Saito and Pineau, pp.* 275-76.

There were tears in Admiral Komura's eyes [5] as he waited for a response to what he had said. The atmosphere was almost explosively tense. One officer spoke up, then another. They condemned the mission as a senseless waste of men and ships and denounced the high command for having conceived it. Other officers expressed agreement. The Imperial Navy's rigid rule of blind obedience had lost its effect on them. Their conduct would have been unimaginable a year earlier.

They were not afraid of death; they had already accepted it. They expressed their disapproval because they did not want their sacrifice to be useless. Some of them proposed using the last ships of the fleet for missions that seemed to them more likely to be effective, such as individual attacks against American supply lines.

At one o'clock Admiral Komura left to report his subordinates' views to the high-ranking officers aboard the *Yamato*. When he returned to the *Yahagi* three hours later, his face was pale and drawn. He looked at each of the assembled division commanders and ship captains, then told them what had happened:

I spent a full hour in conveying your opinions and my concurrence in them. Kusaka and the others listened to me intently. When I finished, Kusaka explained that this sortie was a decoy mission. He emphasized that it was not his plan, but that it had been worked out during his visit at Kanoya. While enemy carriers are occupied in opposing our fleet, Kanoya, as the southernmost airfield on Kyushu, will fling hundreds of kamikaze planes at Okinawa. Kusaka assured me that this decoy sortie will not end in vain as did my last one.

Then he turned to Morishita and explained that the high command, and especially the Army members, had

[5] *It was not uncommon for Japanese officers and enlisted men to shed tears in public, as we have already seen several times in this book. While they might be interpreted in Western countries as a sign of cowardice or weak character, tears shed by men have no such meaning in Japan. They are regarded as a natural expression of intense emotion that is not at all incompatible with firm determination and self-control.*

been dismayed by *Yamato*'s breakoff at Leyte. Kusaka said that he felt it was not Morishita's fault, for he had worked a wonder in dodging all torpedoes, while *Musashi* fell victim to them. Yet he said that Tokyo was displeased that *Yamato* had returned without firing her 18.1-inch guns at the enemy. Morishita took these remarks very hard.

Kusaka said to Aruga that the whole nation would hate the Navy if the war should end with *Yamato* still intact. Through no fault of Aruga's, *Yamato* had been out of action for three years prior to Leyte, and was being spoken of as "a floating hotel for idle, inept admirals."

Ito broke his long silence at this point and said, "I think we are being given an appropriate chance to die. A samurai lives so that he is always prepared to die." That ended all argument. When Morishita and then Aruga finally gave in, I did too.[6]

One after another, the officers gathered aboard the *Yahagi* expressed their acceptance of the mission. They had yielded to a fundamental trait of the Japanese military character. Since their objections and counterproposals had been overridden, they felt that there was nothing more to be said and they were ready to obey what amounted to an order to commit suicide. That same afternoon, the ships of the Second Fleet took on fuel, water, ammunition and supplies.

The next morning, April 6, the crews continued preparing for action. Weapons and instruments were checked, all supplies that would not be needed on the mission were taken off the ships, cadets and invalids were put ashore.

By early afternoon, the Second Fleet was ready to put to sea.

[6] Ibid., *pp. 277-78.*

"Operation Ten-go"

The ships swung gently at anchor. It was a clear day and the sailors could see little fishing villages, terraced fields and countless blossoming cherry trees on shore.

At four o'clock the *Yamato* hoisted the signal to weigh anchor. The cruiser *Yahagi* led the way, followed by the *Yamato* and the eight destroyers. They headed southeast at 12 knots and entered the Bungo Strait, between the islands of Shikoku and Kyushu, at six o'clock. Because these waters were known to be mined special vigilance was maintained. When the ships emerged into the Pacific they increased their speed.

Soon afterward, two high-flying B-29s dropped a few bombs. They all missed, but the attack meant that the enemy had discovered the movement of the Second Fleet. It also reminded the Japanese of their weakness in radar. Only the *Yamato* and two of the destroyers had sky radar, and it was inferior in range and precision to that of the Americans. To the men of the Second Fleet, the brief air attack, though harmless, was a disquieting omen.

Their uneasy thoughts were interrupted when the crew of each ship was ordered to assemble to hear the captain read a message from Admiral Toyoda:

> The Imperial Navy is mounting a general offensive against the enemy at Okinawa by mustering in concert with the Army all of Japan's air, sea, and ground strength to render this operation a turning point of the war.
>
> Every unit and every man is expected to put up an inspiring fight and annihilate the enemy, thereby assuring the continuance of our Eternal Empire. The fate of our nation rests on this operation.[7]

Most of the captains added a few comments of their own after reading the admiral's message. Aboard the *Yahagi*, Captain Tameichi Hara said:

[7] Ibid., *p. 284.*

As you know, hundreds of our comrades have flown bomb-laden planes on one-way missions against the enemy. Thousands more of these flyers are standing by at every airfield. Hundreds of our comrades are ready in submarines to man one-way torpedoes. Thousands of others will drive explosive torpedo boats or crawl the bottom of the sea to fasten explosive charges against enemy ships.

Our job in this mission is part of the same pattern. Our mission appears suicidal and it is. But I wish to emphasize that suicide is not the objective. The objective is victory.

You are not sheep whipped to a sacrificial altar. We are lions released in the arena, to devour the enemy gladiators. You are not to be slain merely as sacrifices for the nation.

Do not hesitate to come back alive. We must force our way against any enemy effort to intercept our mission. But you must not give up your lives cheaply. Once this ship is crippled or sunk, do not hesitate to save yourselves for the next fight. There will be other battles. You are not to commit suicide. You are to beat the enemy! [8]

The fleet continued southward, carrying out a few exercises on the way. The ships practiced offensive and defensive maneuvers at top speed, then dropped back to cruising speed.

At about 2:45 in the morning, the American submarine *Hackleback* (SS-295) picked up the Japanese ships on radar, off the southeast coast of Kyushu. It moved closer until the captain was able to identify the massive shape of the *Yamato*. He immediately sent a contact message. Radiomen of the Second Fleet heard the message and knew it had come from a nearby enemy submarine, but no effort was made to hunt it down and it did not attack. Admiral Ito ordered a change of course that would bring the fleet nearer to land, so that its radar echoes would be mingled with those of the coast.

[8] Ibid., *p. 284.*

Aboard the flagship of the American Fifth Fleet, a radioman awakened Admiral Spruance in his cabin at three o'clock to tell him that the *Yamato* had left its base. Spruance glanced at a map showing the relative positions of the various American formations. An excellent tactician, he sized up the situation in an instant. Then, to the radioman's surprise, he instructed him to send Admiral Mitscher a message telling him to deal with the matter and calmly went back to bed.

During those first hours of April 7, while lookouts of the Japanese Second Fleet were scrutinizing the sky and the sea, the moon disappeared behind thick clouds, leaving everything in total darkness. The weather began deteriorating and the sea became rough. The fleet rounded the southeastern tip of Kyushu at a speed of 20 knots, moving in an irregular pattern of zigzags to evade enemy submarines. At four o'clock Admiral Ito ordered a change of course to west-northwest. This was a strategem. Believing that the Americans might very well be following the movements of the fleet, Ito wanted to give the impression that it was heading for the west coast of Kyushu, toward Sasebo. The detour would delay his approach, but it might deceive the enemy.

At seven o'clock he changed course again, this time to a southwesterly direction. The fleet now assumed a ring formation centered around the *Yamato*, increased its speed to 24 knots and resumed its zigzagging. The weather had not improved. Big, low-hanging clouds darkened the dawn sky. At eight o'clock a drizzling rain reduced visibility still more. A short time later, Japanese radiomen overheard conversations between American planes and ships which indicated that the Second Fleet was under observation by radar. Admiral Ito's feint had been futile. The Americans were not going to relax their vigilance.

American moves initiated during the night were now beginning to take effect. At four o'clock, Admiral Mitscher's carrier fleet had headed north-northeast to approach the enemy. Before sunrise, scout planes had taken off from the

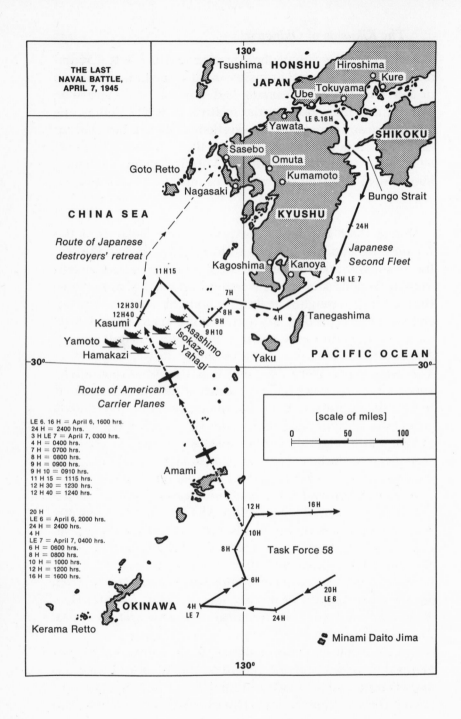

THE LAST NAVAL BATTLE, APRIL 7, 1945

130°

Tsushima **HONSHU** Hiroshima
JAPAN Kure
Tokuyama
Ube
LE 6.16H
SHIKOKU
Yawata
Sasebo
Omuta
Kumamoto
Goto Retto
Nagasaki
Bungo Strait

CHINA SEA
KYUSHU
24 H

Route of Japanese destroyers' retreat
Kagoshima Kanoya
Japanese Second Fleet
11 H 15
3H LE 7
7H
12 H 30
12 H 40
8 H
Kasumi
9 H
Asashimo
4 H
Tanegashima
Yamoto
Isokaze
9 H 10
Hamakazi
Yahagi
Yaku
PACIFIC OCEAN
-30°
30°-

Route of American Carrier Planes

LE 6. 16 H = April 6, 1600 hrs.
24 H = 2400 hrs.
3 H LE 7 = April 7, 0300 hrs.
4 H = 0400 hrs.
7 H = 0700 hrs.
8 H = 0800 hrs.
9 H = 0900 hrs.
9 H 10 = 0910 hrs.
11 H 15 = 1115 hrs.
12 H 30 = 1230 hrs.
12 H 40 = 1240 hrs.

[scale of miles]
0   50   100

Amami

20 H
LE 6 = April 6, 2000 hrs.
24 H = 2400 hrs.
4 H
LE 7 = April 7, 0400 hrs.
6 H = 0600 hrs.
8 H = 0800 hrs.
10 H = 1000 hrs.
12 H = 1200 hrs.
16 H = 1600 hrs.

12 H   16 H
10H
8 H
Task Force 58
6 H
20 H
LE 6
OKINAWA 4 H
LE 7
24 H
Kerama Retto
Minami Daito Jima

130°

carriers and also from the new base at Kerama Retto. Meanwhile Rear Admiral Morton Deyo's force of 16 battleships, 7 cruisers and 21 destroyers had been moving north-northwest to interpose itself between the enemy and the ships of the invasion fleet off Okinawa. Deyo was to attack if the planned air strikes were not successful.

The End of a Navy

It was a scout plane from the carrier *Essex* that made first radar contact with the Japanese ships at about eight o'clock. Half an hour later it reported that it had sighted them. From then on they were kept under constant observation. Admiral Mitscher, anticipating a spectacular victory, ordered all planes readied for takeoff. They totaled 386, divided into two attack waves.

Toward nine o'clock the Japanese destroyer *Asashimo* developed engine trouble that forced it to reduce speed. It gradually fell behind the rest of the fleet while its engine-room crew tried to clear up the difficulty. At 9:10 Admiral Ito shifted the fleet to a northwesterly course to help the *Asashimo* catch up, but the crippled destroyer finally dropped out of sight and never succeeded in resuming full speed.

At ten o'clock Admiral Mitscher's Task Force 58 reached the point where it was to launch its air attack, about 200 miles from the enemy. The first planes took off and within half an hour the first attack wave had been assembled. The huge formation headed for its target.

Japanese radiomen picked up more enemy messages. They showed that American observers were still following the fleet on its new course. At 11:15 it turned southward, toward its objective. Japanese lookouts were not surprised when, at 11:30, they saw an American float plane circling out of gun range. It had come from Kerama Retto and was transmitting reports on the enemy's movements.

Just then the Japanese fleet received a radio message announcing that lookouts on the island of Amami O Shima had seen 250 planes flying north. (Amami O Shima is halfway between Kyushu and Okinawa, thus was on the flight path of the American carrier planes.) They could be expected to arrive within an hour.

Admiral Ito ordered his ships to widen their formation until they were separated from each other by a distance of 5000 meters (3.1 miles). The Japanese sailors knew the probable outcome of the approaching attack, but they prepared for it with remarkable steadiness. At noon they ate lunch in an atmosphere of silent tension. They were all thinking about the imminent battle, realizing that for many of them it would be the last.

At 12:20 the *Yamato's* radar, which till now had been of little use, picked up the enemy planes 19 miles away. All ships increased their speed to maximum in anticipation of the attack. The sky was still overcast, with thick clouds at less than 5000 feet. When heavy rain suddenly began to fall, it would have been hard to imagine worse conditions for trying to repel an air attack.

A little later the Japanese saw planes begin emerging from the overcast. They circled just under the cloud ceiling at a safe distance, calmly picking out their targets. Japanese gunners were ordered to open fire at 12:32, but their efforts were useless. The planes seemed to be dancing a gigantic ballet in the sky while the ships below dashed forward at full speed, throwing up long wakes of white foam. It would have been a beautiful sight if it had not been a prelude to violent death.

At 12:34 the Hellcat fighters, Helldiver dive bombers and Avenger torpedo-bombers all attacked at once. Hampered by bad visibility and overwhelmed by the assailants' numbers, the Japanese gunners were unable to put up an effective barrage. The ships maneuvered frantically to avoid bombs and torpedoes. Hellcats strafed their bridges and decks, killing many men. Combined attacks by Helldivers and Avengers made evasive tactics almost futile: when a ship veered to escape a cluster of torpedoes, it placed itself in line with a dive bomber's approach, and vice versa. The *Yamato* was naturally the prime target, but all the other ships were attacked as well, even the destroyer *Asashimo*, 20 miles behind the rest of the fleet.

The *Yamato* was the first to be hit. At 12:40, two bombs exploded at the base of the conning tower, causing great damage and killing the crew of a machine-gun mount. A few minutes later, a torpedo blew a hole in the giant battleship's side. Dozens of planes kept after it relentlessly, piling up one hit after another.

By now several ships had been damaged so severely that they were doomed. The cruiser *Yahagi* had skillfully dodged a number of attacks, but at 12:45 a torpedo struck it amidships, below the waterline. Within minutes it came to a dead stop: its engines had been put out of operation. One bomb exploded on the bow, another on the stern. The handsome cruiser began listing. Motionless in the water, it was now an easy target. The exact number of bombs and torpedoes that struck the *Yahagi* is not known, but it was probably more than ten.

The *Yamato* was still under heavy attack. Listing to starboard, it had been reduced to an enormous mass of twisted, blackened metal. Many men had been killed, most of them mangled or blown to pieces. Bodies slid across the slanting deck, slippery with blood, and fell into the sea. It was in this condition that the second wave of American planes found the *Yamato*. More bombs and torpedoes found their mark. The ship listed still more, until one of its propellers was above water.

Admiral Ito gave the order to abandon ship at 2:05. The survivors jumped overboard, all except Admiral Ito and the *Yamato*'s captain, Admiral Aruga, who stayed behind to go down with the ship. At 2:17 the last of the 11 torpedoes that struck the *Yamato* opened another hole in its side. By 2:20 it was listing 20 degrees. It was the end. Internal explosions seemed to mark the devastated giant's last quiver of life. At 2:23 the *Yamato*, enveloped in a great shroud of smoke, plunged toward the bottom of the sea, creating a monstrous whirlpool whose powerful suction pulled down many survivors swimming nearby. In all, 2498 men, nearly the entire crew, either drowned or were killed during the attack.

By now the *Yahagi* had also gone down. The destroyers *Hamakaze* and *Asashimo* had been sunk. The *Isokaze* and the *Kasumi* were so badly damaged that they had to be scuttled. The *Fuyutsuki*, the *Suzutsuki* and the *Yukikaze* were also damaged, but they had succeeded in heading back toward Sasebo before the end of the attack. The *Suzutsuki,* with its bow blown off by a torpedo, had to move stern first to prevent water pressure from bursting the watertight compartments. Only the *Hatsushimo* had escaped direct hits. It stayed behind to rescue survivors and brought hundreds of them to Sasebo on April 8.

The last naval battle of the Pacific war was over. The Japanese Second Fleet had lost 3665 of its men without even being able to reach its objective, and with the sinking of the *Yamato,* the *Yahagi* and the four destroyers, the Imperial Navy ceased to exist.

By contrast, the Americans had won their great victory with the loss of only 12 men and 10 planes. Not all of the lost planes were shot down by Japanese antiaircraft fire: some crashed accidentally.

When the survivors of the sunken Japanese ships reached Sasebo aboard the *Hatsushimo,* a message from Admiral Toyoda was delivered to Admiral Komura. In it, Toyoda commended the Second Fleet for having made an heroic sacrifice that enabled aerial suicide units to achieve great results. Komura read the message and silently handed it to one of his subordinates with an expression that showed his bitterness and disenchantment.

It will be remembered that the sortie of the Second Fleet was to be accompanied by a massive kamikaze assault. Because of the heavy losses suffered the day before, only 114 planes, 60 of them escort fighters, could be assembled on April 7. They approached Okinawa toward the end of the afternoon. American fighter patrols, alerted and attacking under excellent conditions, intercepted the formation and cut it to pieces.

A few kamikaze planes succeeded in reaching the ships of Task Force 58. One of them crashed into the carrier *Hancock* (CV-19), killing 43 men and damaging the ship so severely that it had to withdraw to Ulithi for repairs. Another plane struck the battleship *Maryland* (BB-46), which suffered heavy damage and was swept by fire. It was kept afloat by emergency action, with assistance from several other ships, but it had to be sent back to the United States. At nightfall three other ships were damaged by suicide planes, including the destroyers *Gregory* (DD-802) and *Bennett* (DD-473). Nearly 100 Japanese planes were lost that day.

The attack of April 7 was not the gigantic, overwhelming air offensive that Japanese commanders had described, and its results were totally out of proportion to the sacrifice of the Second Fleet. It seems, in fact, that the alleged coordination between air and surface forces was only a pretext for sending out the fleet. This supposition is strengthened by the time gap between the two operations. Since the approximate position of Task Force 58 was known, it would have been easy to predict when it would launch its carrier planes against the Second Fleet, and the kamikaze raid could have been timed accordingly. The results might have been essentially the same, but at least there would have been genuine coordination, which would have made a great psychological difference to the men who carried out the operations.

In our opinion, Japanese naval leaders never believed that the Second Fleet's mission would accomplish anything and they brought their last remaining ships into action because they wanted to avoid having to scuttle them if the war ended unexpectedly. They may also have done it to silence the army's sarcastic remarks and appease the Japanese public, which had been increasingly upset about the navy's inactivity since the Battle of Leyte Gulf. If so, the mission was a sacrifice intended only to save the Imperial Fleet from dishonor after it had already become useless.

CHAPTER

VIII

The Holocaust

Meanwhile the ground fighting on Okinawa was changing. American troops had continued their disconcertingly easy advance with almost no casualties until April 4, when they began encountering pockets of resistance. From April 8 on, their casualties increased sharply in both the northern and southern parts of the island.

We have already seen that all this was deliberately planned by the Japanese. They intended to let the Americans become established on Okinawa, then hold them there while kamikaze attacks destroyed a major part of their navy. When American ground forces had been left without adequate naval support, General Ushijima's troops would be able to drive them into the sea. Such was the overall plan of the Japanese defense of Okinawa.

General Ushijima had therefore abandoned the whole center of the island, left only light forces in the north, and concentrated almost his entire army in the south, where the terrain favored a defense in depth. Most of his troops were in strongly fortified positions on several lines of hills. Understanding the situation and knowing what was at stake, they were all determined to die rather than yield a single inch. In short, they would defend Okinawa as other Japanese soldiers had defended Tarawa, Saipan, Peleliu and Iwo Jima.

The invasion of Okinawa proved to be hard and costly. For several days after their almost unopposed landing, the Americans had gone beyond their expected objectives, but then

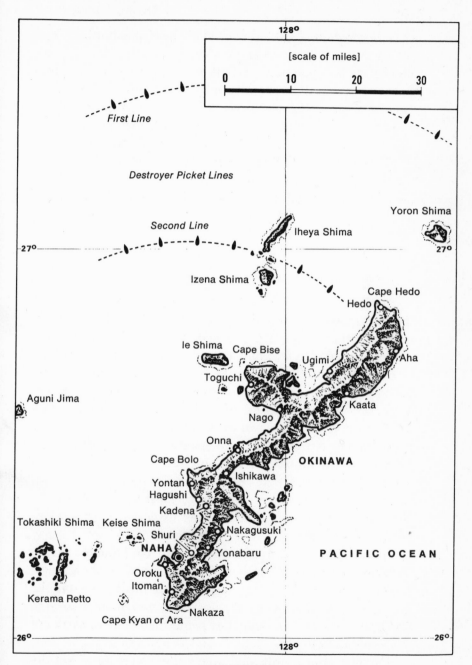

MAP OF OKINAWA

they began falling behind even their most pessimistic previous estimates. Their casualties became serious, sometimes alarming. The Japanese soldiers performed deeds of superhuman heroism that aroused a mixture of hatred and admiration in many of the Americans. They often slipped through the American lines at night to kill as many men or destroy as much matériel as possible before they met their own inevitable death. Many of them attached explosives to their bodies and threw themselves under American vehicles with a patriotic ardor that left no room for the instinct of self-preservation.

The Kikusui Assaults of April 12

Japanese losses in the suicide raids of April 6 and 7 had been so heavy that Admiral Ugaki had difficulty in forming new attack groups. He still had enough volunteer pilots, but he needed more planes. In answer to his urgent requests, the naval authorities sent him another large and motley collection. He could now begin planning a new massive attack against the American naval forces off Okinawa.

Beginning April 10, the Americans noticed a disturbing increase in the number of Japanese reconnaissance flights. It seemed to indicate that another aerial offensive was imminent. As a precautionary measure, most of the American ships moved further out to sea and dispersed over a wider area.

On the morning of April 12 more than 350 Japanese planes took off from bases in southern Kyushu, mainly from Kanoya. There were more than 100 navy kamikaze planes, 60 from the army, several Ohka-carrying bombers, and more than 150 escort fighters, plus a number of planes that were to carry out conventional attacks.

The first groups appeared above the American picket destroyers at about noon. A few planes dropped "chaff" [1] which hampered the enemy's defensive action. Efforts by American fighters to intercept the raiders were less efficient than usual.

The Japanese planes divided into groups that attacked Task Force 58, the ships of the invasion fleet, and the picket destroyers. There were two main assaults, but small groups continued to harass the American ships all through the afternoon. The attacks did not stop until nightfall.

The fleet carriers *Enterprise* (CV-6) and *Essex* (CV-9), the battleship *Missouri* (BB-63) and two destroyers were damaged. The destroyer *Kidd* (DD-661) was struck in the side by a kamikaze plane and the explosion opened a large hole that could not be closed up before it had put the ship in serious danger of sinking. Closer to Okinawa, the battleships *New Mexico* (BB-40), *Tennessee* (BB-43) and *Idaho* (BB-42) were hit and damaged by one suicide plane each. The light cruiser *Oakland* (CL-95), ten destroyers, three destroyer escorts, three minesweepers, two gunboats and one landing ship were so heavily damaged that they had to leave the combat zone.

It was an Ohka piloted bomb that caused the only sinking of the day. The crew of the destroyer *Mannert L. Abele* (DD-733) were preparing to open fire on an approaching Japanese bomber when they saw the Ohka drop away from it and dive toward them. Survivors later said that the attack took place with such incredible speed that the gunners could not shoot. The Ohka struck amidships with a tremendous explosion that broke the destroyer in half as if it were a dry twig. The *Mannert L. Abele* quickly sank.

About 330 Japanese planes were lost. New attacks were launched the next day, April 13, but they were smaller and unsuccessful: American gunners and fighter pilots were able to act in time.

[1] *"Chaff," also known as "window," consists of thin metal strips that produce a multitude of confusing radar signals as they fall to the ground and thus make detection of approaching aircraft more difficult. It was first used in 1943 by Allied bombers over Germany.*

Ushibuki

Minamata

Hitoyoshi

131°

Takanabe
Tsuma

130°

Okuchi

Honjo

Akune

32°

Kurino

Miyazaki

Miyanojo

Kami Koshiki Shima

Sendai

K   Y   U   S   H   U

Sato

Kamo

Kokubu

Miyakonojo

Shimo Koshiki Shima

Fukuyama

Ijuin

Koshiki Archipelago

KAGOSHIMA

Meitsu

Isaku

Tarumizu

Shibushi

KANOYA

Kiire

Makurazuki

Onejime

CHINA SEA

Yamagawa

31°

Cape Satano

31°

Osumi Kaikyo
Van Diemen Strait

PACIFIC OCEAN

Kuro Shima

Take Shima

Make Shima

Io Shima

Nishinoomote

*Direction
of Okinawa*

Tanegashima

Noma

Kuchinoerabu Shima

Yakushima

Osumi Gunto

Kamiyaku

131°

*Route followed by
Kamikaze units*

0	10	20	30

[scale of miles]

130°

LOCATION OF KIKUSUI FORCES IN SOUTHERN KYUSHU

American Alarm

Although American losses could not yet be called disastrous, the number of damaged ships forced to leave the theater of operations was increasing alarmingly, especially since each of them had to be accompanied by one and sometimes two undamaged ships.

Bombing the bases from which the suicide attacks were launched was a logical idea, but it was not as simple as it might seem. The Kyushu airfields were numerous, widely scattered, and defended by powerful antiaircraft batteries. Bombing raids would be costly to the Americans and might not always be successful, because of the excellent techniques of dispersion and camouflage employed by the Japanese. But the situation was so urgent that Admiral Spruance could not afford to hesitate. He moved his Task Force 58 northward. On April 15, hundreds of planes took off from its carriers and attacked airfields in southern Kyushu. The attacks were repeated the next day. Results were relatively slight: 55 Japanese planes destroyed on the ground. And the kamikaze raids were not stopped. On April 16 Admiral Ugaki, informed that American planes were returning for another strike, sent off a suicide squadron before it could be discovered.

About 155 planes, from both the army and the navy, attacked Task Force 58 and the ships anchored off Okinawa. The carrier *Intrepid* (CV-11) was struck by at least two planes. Disabled and ravaged by fire, it had to withdraw for repairs. The destroyer *Pringle* (DD-477) was sunk. The minesweeper *Harding* (DMS-28) was so badly damaged that it was given up as beyond repair. Three destroyers, two minesweepers, two gunboats and one tanker were also damaged.

There were more suicide attacks during the next ten days, but they were on a small scale, intended more to maintain the Americans' nervous tension and anxiety than to destroy large numbers of ships. Although other ships were hit, only one was lost: the minesweeper *Swallow* (AM-65) was so devastated on April 22 that it had to be scuttled.

At the end of April the Kikuṣui Forces launched a new offensive. It began on the night of the 27th with an attack by 115 planes, 50 of them from the army. In what had now become an established procedure, they attacked the Okinawa invasion fleet and Task Force 58. The first victim was the destroyer *Hutchins* (DD-476), which had to be abandoned by its crew. Then a cargo ship was sunk.

The attacks were continued on April 28 by small groups of planes that scored hits on five destroyers, one transport and several other ships. That night a kamikaze plane crashed into the hospital ship *Comfort* (AH-6), even though it was brightly lighted and clearly marked with the red cross that should have given it immunity. There were not many casualties, but the attack aroused angry indignation among the Americans.

Suicide groups pursued their attacks into the morning of April 29. The last victim was the destroyer *Haggard* (DD-555), which sank soon after it was hit. These assaults at the end of April had been carried out by about 200 planes.

The New Effort of May 4

During this time, American troops had been stopped by very strong Japanese defenses in the hilly terrain around Shuri, in southern Okinawa. Generals Ushijima and Cho decided to take advantage of the situation to launch a powerful counteroffensive. The operation was scheduled for May 4. Air attacks were to begin early on May 3 and continue all through the day, in preparation for the ground assault on the 4th.

Before dawn on May 3, Japanese planes bombed the airfield at Yontan, where a large number of American planes were based. Damage was light. At dawn, all available American fighters took off and flew to intercept more enemy aircraft that had just been reported by the picket destroyers.

The destroyers themselves were the first targets of the attackers. The Japanese wanted to be rid of those "informers." Four suicide planes struck the destroyer *Little* (DD-803). It was transformed into a smoking wreck and sank soon afterward. Two more planes hit the *Luce* (DD-522) and sent it to the bottom.

Closer to Okinawa, one ship of the invasion fleet, the LSMR-195, was sunk, and the minesweeper *Aaron Ward* (DM-34) was devastated by no fewer than six kamikaze hits. It was reduced to a shapeless mass of metal and its crew suffered heavy casualties. It did not sink, but it was beyond repair. Other ships, including a minelayer and an LCS, were damaged but not put out of action.

A little after midnight, a group of 60 conventional bombers released large amounts of "chaff" and then bombed the troops of the American Tenth Army. The bombs fell more or less at random and caused few casualties.

On May 4 at dawn, in coordination with the Japanese ground offensive, the suicide planes resumed their attacks. The destroyer *Morrison* (DD-560) took four hits in the space of a few minutes and sank. Two of the ships off the Hagushi beachhead, the LSMR-190 and the LSMR-194, were sunk almost simultaneously. The escort carrier *Sangamon* (CVE-26) was set afire and damaged beyond repair.

The minesweeper *Shea* (DM-30) was hit by an Ohka piloted bomb that caused enormous damage. Fire broke out immediately but was brought under control just as it was about to reach the magazine. The *Shea* had to withdraw; so did the cruiser *Birmingham* (CL-62), two destroyers, a minesweeper and an LCS.

In their air assaults of May 3 and 4, the Japanese had sent out a total of 305 planes: 75 kamikazes from the navy, 50 from the army, 120 escort fighters, and 60 conventional bombers. More than 280 were lost, either by crashing into their targets or being shot down.

The Cruel Month of May

Since Japanese air raids, mostly suicide attacks, were almost daily occurrences all through the terrible Okinawa campaign, we shall mention only the most important ones. As before, the Japanese continued to attack the picket destroyers before going on to the invasion fleet and Task Force 58.

On May 9 several dozen planes got through to the invasion fleet. Within a few minutes, the destroyer escorts *Oberrender* (DE-344) and *England* (DE-635) were so badly damaged that they were towed to Kerama Retto, where it was judged useless to try to repair them.

On May 11 the Japanese sent suicide groups against Task Force 58, the picket destroyers, and the British fleet off the Sakishima Islands. Admiral Mitscher's flagship, the fleet carrier *Bunker Hill* (CV-17), was gravely damaged by two planes. More than 400 of its men were killed, it began listing alarmingly, and it was swept by fire. Completely devastated, it had to withdraw. The battleship *New Mexico*, with damage from the attack of April 12 still unrepaired, was hit again. An LCS was narrowly saved from sinking by the determined efforts of its crew. The destroyers *Evans* (DD-552) and *Hugh W. Hadley* (DD-774) were smashed as though a giant steel fist had come down on them. They were towed to Kerama Retto in such hopeless condition that they could not be rebuilt. In the British fleet, the carriers *Victorious* and *Formidable* were hit, but, because of their armored flight decks, damage was insignificant.

After a respite, the suicide struggle was resumed on May 21, when a small group of planes slipped through the outer defenses but was unable to approach the big ships. One of them sank a submarine-chaser, the PC-1603.

During this time Admiral Ugaki was planning another large-scale operation. On the night of May 24 nearly 160 planes took off from bases in Kyushu and headed for Okinawa. In the early hours of May 25 they attacked with extraordinary ferocity. Searchlights, shellbursts and tracer bullets lit up the whole sky. Now and then a searchlight would catch a diving plane in its beam and a moment later there would be either a blinding flash from a stricken ship or, more often, a huge iridescent splash where the plane had plunged into the ocean.

The transport *Bates* (APD-47) and the LSM-135 were sunk. Eight other ships were damaged, including two—the transport *Barry* (APD-29) and the minesweeper *Butler* (DMS-29)—that were considered beyond repair. The *Barry* sank several hours later.

There were more kamikaze attacks during the days that followed, but they were small and sporadic. On May 27, however, a suicide plane crashed into the minesweeper *Forrest* (DMS-24) and damaged it beyond repair. The next day, the destroyer *Drexler* (DD-741) was sunk by two planes. And on May 29, the day when the marines of the 29th Regiment encircled Naha, the ruined capital of Okinawa, a few kamikazes attacked the picket destroyers. Most of them were shot down, but one dived at the *Shubrick* (DD-639). The whole ship was shaken by the impact. Its strong construction enabled it to remain afloat, but it was so devastated that it never saw action again.

The Demoralizing Effects

The almost daily repetition of suicide attacks did not lead the Americans and their allies to take them as a matter of routine. On the contrary, their anxiety continued to grow. Kamikaze raids had by now taken an alarming toll in lives and ships. Several hundred vessels had been either sunk or forced to withdraw from the combat zone, depriving the troops on Okinawa of their support and making the remaining ships still more vulnerable. Some officers estimated that if the raids continued at the same rate till the middle of June, the whole American fleet would have to withdraw. Repair facilities were numerous and well equipped, but they were desperately overburdened. The American navy had not been in such a critical situation since the beginning of the reconquest.

The psychological effect that the Japanese had tried so long to produce was becoming a reality. The American sailors had lost their usual self-assurance. They were now frightened and exhausted. Many expected death at any moment. Some, after hearing the shrill whines of diving suicide planes, feeling the jarring explosions of their impacts, and seeing men thrown into the air like broken puppets, were in such a state of emotional shock that they could not sleep and performed their duties like automatons. Those who worked in the engine rooms suffered as much as those on deck. When an attack was underway, they had to make strenuous efforts in overheated compartments to keep the engines running at full speed as the ships tried to dodge the oncoming planes. They were at the end of their physical and emotional strength. Some of them fainted from stress, fatigue and heat.

Added to all this was a deep feeling of helplessness. Despite the excellent efforts of their fighter pilots and the murderous density of their antiaircraft fire, the Americans knew that one or more kamikaze planes usually broke through, sometimes with fatal results. It was this relentless determination on the part of the enemy that strained their nerves to the breaking point.

A Profound Change

On the Japanese side, the psychological effects of the campaign were equally noticeable, though of a different nature. They were evident in the problem of recruiting suicide volunteers, the behavior of a certain number of those who had already volunteered, and the anguish of many pilots in the army's Tokubetsu Units.

The exploits and victories of kamikaze pilots in the Okinawa campaign were widely reported, to the accompaniment of glowing propaganda. They prompted other pilots to volunteer, but not in sufficient numbers. Nearly all the kamikaze units had been decimated. Replacements had to be found quickly and at a steady rate. The Japanese government finally decided to direct special efforts toward university students. There were fiery speeches and superpatriotic meetings designed to persuade them to enlist in the "special attack units." Many students responded to these appeals and volunteered.

There was then a selection which, though it may seem monstrous, was quite logical: mathematics and science students were assigned to factories and research centers where their knowledge could be put to use, while law and liberal arts students were immediately placed in flight schools for training as suicide pilots. They were volunteers, but they had been moved by a youthful surge of pure patriotic ardor, rather than by a clear awareness of military objectives to be attained. They were given only quick, summary training before being assigned to suicide units. Barely able to keep a plane in flight, they were incapable of navigating alone and there were many accidents during their practice sessions.

Many other young men enlisted on a sudden impulse or because of thinly disguised pressure. As a result, their behavior and frame of mind were quite different from those of their predecessors. They gave the impression of belonging to a herd being driven to slaughter.

They were nearly all stupefied when they fully realized what they were expected to do, but most of them soon overcame their initial reaction and selflessly accepted their responsibility. The ancient Japanese military psychology was stronger than their individual feeling. They became resolute men, convinced that they would make up for their lack of experience with unshakable faith.

Some of them continued to regret their decision, but, with their high regard for the principle of obedience, they did not try to go back on it. They drank to forget their fate, sang boisterous songs, or committed thefts or other unworthy acts, as if they felt outside of society and wanted to take revenge on it.

Most of these young volunteers did not have the dignity, the moral purity and the lofty consciousness of the ancient Japanese heritage that had made their elders seem like saints or even gods. There were extenuating circumstances. First, their lack of experience in life, the inadequacy of their training, and the weakness of their martial determination almost forced them to take refuge behind a kind of haughtiness that concealed their youthful unsteadiness. And second, the attitude of the public did not encourage their best instincts. The civilian population, saturated with propaganda and stories of victorious exploits of the heroes of the kamikaze units, adulated and pampered the young volunteers, overwhelmed them with gifts and attention, treated them with exaggerated deference, almost worshiped them. This was enough to make many of them vain, contemptuous and arrogant. But not all of them behaved like spoiled children. There were pure heroes among them, men whose uprightness and strength of soul made them worthy successors to Onishi's flying samurai in the Philippines.

We shall cite only one example, that of Ensign Tatsuya Ikariyama, who joined the Takuma Air Group in Shikoku on May 4, 1945. After the usual formalities of reporting to a new unit, he was informed that he would take part in a suicide attack the next day. Then he learned that three friends of his were at the base. He went to see them that evening. When they invited him to have a drink to celebrate their having met again, he refused. "Sorry," he said, "but I am going on a suicide attack tomorrow and want to be in top condition, so I do not care to drink." [2]

The next day, Ikariyama flew off toward Okinawa and was never seen again.

[2] The Divine Wind, *by Inoguchi, Nakajima and Pineau, p. 142.*

The Tragedy of the Tokubetsu Units

We have already mentioned that volunteers for the army's suicide units were less numerous than for the navy's. The first contingent was quickly lost in the almost daily missions that began with the Okinawa campaign. The problem of recruitment then became serious. Since the navy had already monopolized university students as a source of volunteers, the army was led to adopt more arbitrary methods. Beginning in May, army pilots were assigned to suicide units without having volunteered.

This was a violation of the fundamental principle of the kamikaze corps and its importance cannot be overstressed. Yet the dogma of blind obedience was so strong that none of the pilots assigned to the Tokubetsu Units rebelled or showed any insubordination, although one can imagine what their thoughts must have been.

General Miyoshi, commander of the army's suicide units in Kyushu, was shocked by the procedure and protested to General Sugiwara, commander in chief of the Tokubetsu Units. Sugiwara relayed his protests to Imperial General Headquarters but they were ignored.

Once their suicide missions were under way, the army's heroes under duress apparently performed as well as the volunteers, but on the ground their behavior was sometimes different. Some of them withdrew into themselves; they became taciturn and showed deep bitterness. Others threw themselves into drunken revelry, caused scandalous commotions and picked fights. A certain number of them were even drunk when they took off on their missions. These were not Onishi's inspired demigods, but desperate men trying to avoid thinking about their fate.

The Problem of Aircraft

The Japanese had lost an enormous number of planes, not
only in the suicide attacks themselves, but also among the
fighters that escorted the attackers to their targets. Supply
could not keep up with demand. By the end of May there
was a significant drop in the number of planes available for
suicide missions. Because of inadequate aircraft production,
allotments already made to conventional air units, and the
urgent need for reserves to counter the final invasion of Japan,
Admiral Ugaki could not be given as many planes as he
urgently requested. He had to diminish the size and frequency of his raids.

Japanese aircraft manufacturers, who had been studying
the problem of designing planes specifically for suicide attacks
since the fall of 1944, began producing variants of existing
models. Although there were not enough of them to have
significant effects, these planes had greater destructive power
and were better adapted to kamikaze missions. The Aichi-
Yokosuka D4Y-4 Model 43 Suisei Kai, for example, was faster
than the original model and carried double its bomb load.
Other firms were working on specially designed suicide planes
but most of them were not ready for production until the
summer of 1945, too late to alter the course of the war. We
shall return to them later.

In the Okinawa campaign, the Japanese continued to use
planes of every type available. This complicated the task of
the escort fighters and made the whole formation more vulnerable. The presence of such types as trainers and float planes
required a low cruising speed that gave American interceptors
an even better chance.

This handicap and the enormous risks it entailed were
accepted because there was no other way of increasing the
size of the raids. Admiral Ugaki was still convinced that
mass-formation attacks were the best guarantee of success.
He believed that a large number of planes in a single attack

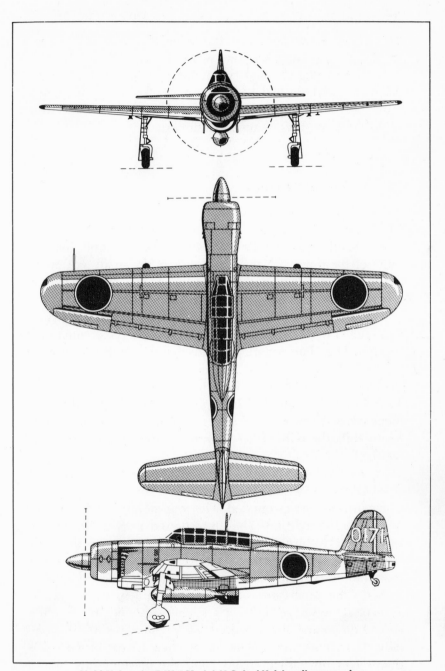

Aichi-Yokosuka D4Y-4 Model 43 Suisei Kai, kamikaze version.

could score more hits than the same number divided into smaller groups. His conviction was strengthened by what had happened during the first two months of the Okinawa campaign, when there had been many attacks by small groups. Most of them had failed completely because they were stopped before they reached their targets.

The End of Okinawa

By the beginning of June, the American advance on Okinawa had formed a front following an almost straight line just south of the town of Naha. On the map, the small part of the island that still remained in Japanese hands did not look as if it would be very hard to conquer, and yet . . .

First there was the Oroku (or Koroku) Peninsula, which was known to be held by naval troops under the command of Admiral Ota. The Americans considered not attacking it directly, but sooner or later it would have constituted a dangerous abscess in the right flank of the final drive to the south. Therefore on the night of June 3 marines of the Fourth Regiment crossed the Kokuba River and entered the peninsula. Meanwhile the bulk of the American forces advanced southward.

In the Oroku Peninsula, the Japanese fought fiercely till June 12, when white flags appeared above their positions. The marines were astounded. This was all but unprecedented in the Pacific fighting. They interpreted it as a sign of surrender but it turned out to be something quite different. Japanese spokesmen came forward to ask for a cease-fire so that they and their comrades could commit suicide undisturbed. The Americans suspected a trap at first, but finally agreed. They cautiously approached the edges of cliffs, looked down and saw hundreds of Japanese committing suicide in various ways. Some shot themselves, others blew themselves up with grenades, and the marines saw two of them sit on a case of explosives and detonate it.

Further south, in the Yaesu Dake hills, large numbers of Japanese had taken shelter in caves. Many of them were wounded or ill. Corpses that could be neither buried nor removed were decomposing in the caves. Each time the Japanese attempted a sortie, they were stopped by American infantry, artillery and aircraft, with heavy losses.

The fighting was murderous on both sides. The Japanese made the Americans pay dearly for each leap forward. It was during this period, on June 18, that General Simon Bolivar Buckner, commander of the Tenth Army, was killed while he was making an inspection.

In the caves and tunnels of the last Japanese stronghold, the situation was critical and in some places it reached the extreme limit of horror. The living stepped on the bodies of their dead comrades in a pervasive stench of decomposition. Medical supplies had been exhausted. Many soldiers were already killing themselves to avoid falling into the hands of the Americans. On June 22 a group of young girls from the island who had been enrolled as auxiliary nurses committed suicide by jumping from rocks overhanging the sea. A short time later, on a sheltered ledge, generals Ushijima and Cho carried out the seppuku suicide ritual in the purest samurai tradition. Each man knelt on a white cloth and thrust his saber into his abdomen; then, when he uttered a brief cry, his orderly cut off his head. Okinawa was conquered.

During the first three weeks of June, while the Japanese 32nd Army was dying, Admiral Ugaki did not remain inactive. He no longer had enough planes for massive suicide attacks, but he launched smaller ones day and night. Although they were more a form of harassment than a major offensive, they still resulted in enemy losses.

On June 3 a small group of planes succeeded in reaching the American beachhead and one of them damaged an LST. The next day, a cargo ship was disabled and had to be towed to the nearest repair base.

June 5 was a tragic day for the American navy. In the

first hours of the morning, kamikaze attacks seriously damaged the battleship *Mississippi* (BB-41), the heavy cruiser *Louisville* (CA-28), the destroyer *Anthony* (DD-515), and a minesweeper. Not long afterward, the fleet was struck by an incredibly violent typhoon. The battleships *Massachusetts* (BB-59), *Indiana* (BB-58) and *Alabama* (BB-60), the carriers *Hornet* (CV-12), *Bennington* (CV-20), *Windham Bay* (CVE-92) and *Salamaua* (CVE-96), the cruisers *Baltimore* (CA-68), *Duluth* (CL-87) and *Pittsburgh* (CA-72), 13 destroyers and a number of other ships suffered various degrees of damage. Most of them had to return to the United States for repairs. Since this disaster occurred after the Japanese fleet had been eliminated, it did not place the Americans in a vulnerable position, but it did affect the support they could give to ground operations, and this in turn affected the morale of their troops.

Admiral Ugaki soon learned of the destruction and decided to add to it as much as possible. The next day he launched a suicide raid with more planes than had become usual at this time. American defenses were still effective, however, and only one kamikaze got through to make its dive. It crashed into the minesweeper *J. William Ditter* (DM-31) and damaged it beyond repair. On June 7 a small group attacked Admiral Turner's support fleet. One plane hit the escort carrier *Natoma Bay* (CVE-62) and forced it to withdraw for repairs.

From this time on, Japanese suicide attacks became sporadic. The danger was not eliminated, but the Americans felt that the enemy was weakening. Between June 3 and 7, Admiral Ugaki had been able to send out a total of only 50 kamikaze planes.

There were no attacks on the 8th and 9th. On the 10th, a few planes appeared above the picket destroyers. One of them struck the *William D. Porter* (DD-579). There was an enormous explosion that hurled wreckage hundreds of yards away and sent the destroyer to the bottom. On June 16 there was an attack by kamikaze planes and twin-engined bombers carrying Ohka piloted bombs. Most of them were shot down by American Corsair fighters. By what must have been a coincidence, the only kamikaze and the only Ohka that succeeded in completing their dives both struck the same ship: the destroyer *Twiggs* (DD-591). It sank a few minutes after being devastated by the two explosions.

On June 21, the last day of fighting on Okinawa, a kamikaze escaped its pursuers by slipping from cloud to cloud, dived at a landing ship, the LSM-59, and sank it.

Epilogue

Thus ended the terrible Okinawa campaign. Except for that of Guadalcanal, which was different in many ways, the conquest of Okinawa was the longest, bloodiest and hardest of all the campaigns that made up the Pacific war.

The Americans had never suffered such heavy losses to take such a small piece of land. From the army 4500 men were killed and 18,000 wounded; from the marines, 2900 killed and 13,600 wounded; from the navy, 4900 killed and 4800 wounded. Total American losses were thus 12,300 dead and 36,400 wounded.

Most of the Japanese defenders carried through their fanatical determination to fight to the end. There were 130,000 dead, including a little more than 40,000 Okinawa civilians caught in the fire of both sides. But the Americans took the unusually large number of 3400 prisoners, most of them wounded. This was a noteworthy change. Even so, those who surrendered had done so either individually or in very small groups, often in the midst of a battle, so that they could slip away unnoticed, because they knew that their officers and even their fellow enlisted men would have executed them on the spot if their intentions had become known beforehand.

Japanese aircraft losses were enormous: approximately 7600, more than half of them suicide planes,[3] as compared

[3] *Japanese records mention the loss of 4615 fliers in suicide missions, 2630 from the navy and 1985 from the army.*

to 763 for the Americans. Forty American ships were either sunk or damaged beyond repair and 368 others were damaged to a lesser extent, though often seriously. It is significant that despite the ferocity of the ground fighting, the American navy lost more men than either the army or the marines.

For several days after effective Japanese resistance on Okinawa had collapsed, American troops continued mopping-up operations against enemy soldiers who refused to surrender and had still not been dislodged from positions that were sometimes almost inaccessible. Caves filled with corpses had to be sealed off or disinfected to avoid the risk of an epidemic because the American high command intended to make Okinawa an important base for the final conquest of the Japanese homeland. The airfields of Yontan, Kadena, Oruku and Ie Shima were to be enlarged and modernized, and the island itself transformed into a gigantic storehouse of equipment, munitions and supplies. Many American ships remained in the vicinity of Okinawa to help in the work of carrying out this plan.

Their presence did not escape Admiral Ugaki's attention. Meanwhile, because of the frequent American raids on airfields in southern Kyushu, the suicide units had withdrawn to bases in the northern part of the island and in Shikoku. This naturally increased the distance they had to fly to reach Okinawa and therefore reduced the number and size of their attacks. But Admiral Ugaki still wanted to strike blows against the enemy, if only to make him realize that he would have to pay a high price for an assault on the Japanese home islands.

All through July a certain number of Japanese raids continued to harass the American fleet off Okinawa, and at the same time suicide attacks were launched against the many American naval formations that were now cruising in Japanese waters. On July 19 the destroyer *Thatcher* (DD-514) was so badly damaged that attempts to repair it had to be abandoned. Finally, on July 28, a kamikaze group flew over an American squadron and succeeded, not without losses, in penetrating its defenses. One plane struck the destroyer

Callaghan (DD-792) with an explosion that sent up a great reddish-orange flash. The *Callaghan* went down a short time later. It was the last American ship to be sunk by a suicide plane in the Pacific war.

The Final Struggle

American ship losses in the Okinawa campaign were so heavy that we do not think any other country in the world could have borne them without losing its ability to carry on the war. The existence of the American navy was never in doubt, but the number of ships destroyed or forced to leave the combat zone was great enough to make the high command revise its schedule of operations.

The conquest of Japan was to be completed by two great amphibious operations, named "Olympic" (landing on Kyushu) and "Coronet" (landing on Honshu, largest of the four main Japanese islands). The dates of their planned execution had to be postponed several months, to November, 1945, and March, 1946, respectively. Because of political developments within Japan and the use of a revolutionary weapon by the Americans, these two operations never took place.

With the fall of Okinawa, all the bastions that had once shielded the home islands were now in the hands of the Americans. In Japan, ground forces were massing along the coast and all remaining aircraft were ready for action. The civilian population, armed and steeped in patriotic propaganda, prepared to fight and die.

Prime Minister Kantaro Suzuki's government sought contacts with the United States for the purpose of bringing the war to an end but was thwarted by the opposition of militarists fanatically determined to continue hostilities at any cost. Emperor Hirohito, taking an increasingly active part in the deliberations, was able to make only slow progress in winning support for the idea of surrender because he, too, had to struggle against the power of the militarists.

AMERICAN NAVAL LOSSES IN THE OKINAWA CAMPAIGN

This list includes only ships sunk or damaged beyond repair, although some of the 368 others that were damaged never saw action again because they were still undergoing repairs when the war ended.

Type	Name	Date (1945)	Remarks
Transport	Dickerson (APD-21)	April 2	Scuttled April 4
Destroyer	Bush (DD-529)	April 6	Sunk
Destroyer	Colhoun (DD-801)	April 6	Sunk
Destroyer	Leutze (DD-481)	April 6	Beyond repair
Destroyer	Morris (DD-417)	April 6	Beyond repair
Destroyer	Newcombe (DD-586)	April 6	Beyond repair
Minesweeper	Emmons (DMS-22)	April 6	Sunk
Landing ship	LST-447	April 6	Sunk
Attack transport	Logan Victory (APA-196)	April 6	Sunk
Destroyer	Mannert L. Abele (DD-733)	April 12	Sunk by Ohka bomb
Destroyer	Pringle (DD-477)	April 16	Sunk
Minesweeper	Harding (DMS-28)	April 16	Beyond repair
Minesweeper	Swallow (AM-65)	April 22	Beyond repair
Destroyer	Hutchins (DD-476)	April 27	Beyond repair
Destroyer	Haggard (DD-555)	April 29	Sunk
Destroyer	Little (DD-803)	May 3	Sunk
Destroyer	Luce (DD-522)	May 3	Sunk

Type	Name	Date (1945)	Remarks
Landing ship	LSMR-195	May 3	Sunk
Minesweeper	Aaron Ward (DM-34)	May 3	Beyond repair
Destroyer	Morrison (DD-560)	May 4	Sunk
Landing ship	LSMR-190	May 4	Sunk
Landing ship	LSMR-194	May 4	Sunk
Destroyer escort	Oberrender (DE-344)	May 9	Beyond repair
Destroyer escort	England (DE-635)	May 9	Beyond repair
Destroyer	Evans (DD-522)	May 11	Beyond repair
Destroyer	Hugh W. Hadley (DD-774)	May 11	Beyond repair
Submarine chaser	PC-1603	May 21	Sunk
Transport	Bates (APD-47)	May 25	Sunk
Transport	Barry (APD-29)	May 25	Beyond repair
Landing ship	LSM-135	May 25	Sunk
Minesweeper	Butler (DMS-29)	May 25	Beyond repair
Minesweeper	Forrest (DMS-24)	May 27	Beyond repair
Destroyer	Drexler (DD-741)	May 28	Sunk
Destroyer	Shubrick (DD-639)	May 29	Beyond repair
Minesweeper	J. William Ditter (DM-31)	June 6	Beyond repair
Destroyer	William D. Porter (DD-579)	June 10	Sunk
Destroyer	Twiggs (DD-591)	June 16	Sunk by Ohka bomb
Landing ship	LSM-59	June 21	Sunk
Destroyer	Thatcher (DD-514)	July 19	Beyond repair
Destroyer	Callaghan (DD-792)	July 28	Sunk

Peace efforts were also hampered by the ambiguous attitude of the Soviet Union, which had been chosen as a mediator. The Russians wanted to take over some Japanese
territory, but they had not been able to carry out their plans
while they were engaged in fighting Germany. After the fall
of the Third Reich, they had to regroup their forces and
transport them to the other end of their immense country.
This took time and delayed their intervention in Asia. Furthermore Stalin knew the suffering his people had undergone
and did not want to plunge them into another major war. He
preferred to wait until he could gain the greatest possible
advantage at the lowest possible cost, and for that reason he
retarded Japanese diplomatic moves.

Advocates of peace, led by Hirohito and Prime Minister
Suzuki, were thus stalled for long weeks while the war situation became still worse. Meanwhile General Korechika Anami, Minister of War and leader of the fanatical militarists,
was still convinced that final victory could be won by throwing all remaining Japanese forces into the fight. His opposition to any form of surrender was based on this argument,
and also on the fact that Japan had never been conquered in
the whole course of her long history. It was a matter of
principle and national pride. To Anami and his supporters,
any Japanese, even the emperor himself, who so much as considered the possibility of surrender was an ignoble traitor.

The Japanese army had such influence on the whole governmental structure that peace efforts remained ineffectual.
There was no change until August 6, 1945, when the first
atomic bomb devastated the city of Hiroshima, killing tens
of thousands of people. Yet even this terrible blow was not
decisive. Although it gave peace advocates a strong new
argument for ending the war, it failed to overcome the blind
fanaticism of the militarists.

Only when the second atomic bomb struck Nagasaki three
days later was it possible to override their resistance and take
the first steps toward peace negotiations. They were still so
determined to keep fighting that their opposition took on the
aspect of a direct rebellion against the emperor, but the

process that would lead to Japan's unconditional surrender, in accordance with the Allied ultimatum issued at the Potsdam Conference, was already under way. Grave political events and numerous suicides, including that of General Anami, were to mark the last days of the Empire of the Rising Sun.

CHAPTER

IX

Eternal Japan

Japanese industry was already operating at near maximum capacity in 1941, and all through the war, with few exceptions, it was unable to do anything more than maintain its level of production. Aircraft production had risen slightly by the middle of 1944 but from then on it declined rapidly. It was severely handicapped by the effects of submarine attacks on shipping and, later, by American strategic bombing. The acute fuel shortage affected the development of new models of aircraft. Experiments with certain prototypes had to be curtailed for the simple and pitiful reason that not enough gasoline was available for them.

It was this disastrous situation that led to the first kamikaze operations. We have seen that standard aircraft were used for suicide attacks in the Philippines, but that unit commanders, squadron leaders and the pilots themselves soon began asking for planes better adapted to such attacks. Japanese manufacturers set about producing them.

At first they simply modified existing models. This was the case, for example, with the Zero and the Aichi-Yokosuka D4Y-4.[1] The modifications consisted primarily in adapting the planes to carry heavier bomb loads without the usual release mechanism. These planes were not entirely satisfactory; they were only hybrid solutions. When the pilots continued their demands for something more efficient, the manufacturers began planning to produce planes that would be specifically

[1] See drawings of these planes on pages 47 and 199, respectively.

designed for suicide missions and could therefore not be used for anything else.

Development of the Ohka piloted bomb was completed in the summer of 1944. Although it was the only craft of its kind that was actually used in combat, various manufacturers submitted other radically new designs and some prototypes were flight-tested. We shall describe a few of the more important models. They were significant for what they revealed about the condition of the Japanese aircraft industry and the direction its thinking had taken.

The Tsurugi

The Nakajima firm, one of the largest in Japan after the Mitsubishi syndicate, proposed a suicide plane known as the Nakajima Ki. 115 Tsurugi ("Saber"). The fact that it was intended to be destroyed on its first mission, the metal shortage and the need for quick and easy construction, led the Nakajima engineers to choose wood as the material for the Tsurugi's frame and covering. It was designed so that its sections could be built in many different workshops by subcontractors. The sections could then be rapidly put together on an assembly line.

It was a low-winged monoplane powered by an engine that was already available in large numbers: the 1130-horsepower Nakajima Ha. 115 Sakae ("Prosperity"). It carried an 1100-pound bomb bolted into the fuselage and partly projecting below it. In flight, it gained the advantage of a retractable landing gear by what might be called a releasable takeoff gear: as soon as the plane was airborne, the pilot pushed a button to jettison the wheels and their supports, which were then retrieved from the ground to be used again.

Theoretical studies of the Tsurugi were finished in February, 1945, and construction of prototypes was begun immediately. A number of tentative production models came off the assembly line at the end of April. Final development was completed in June, when pilot training for the new plane was already well-advanced. Although the Tsurugi was easy to build, its performance proved to be mediocre. Its speed was disappointing and it had an unfortunate tendency toward instability. It was hard to fly, even though it had been designed for inexperienced pilots. Many fatal accidents delayed its operational use.

Additional lifting surfaces were installed but made no appreciable improvement in stability. The Tsurugi remained such a dangerous plane to fly that it caused the premature suicide, if we can use that term, of many kamikaze pilots. The Nakajima firm nevertheless continued building it. It was produced in two versions: the Ki. 115 A and the Ki. 115 B, which differed only in minor details.

The Tsurugi was intended to be flown by the suicide pilots of the army's Tokubetsu Units. Between March and August, 105 of them were built, but there is no evidence that any were ever used.

The navy became interested in the plane and tested a version of it equipped with a more powerful engine. Results were no more encouraging than those obtained by the army.

The Tsurugi had a wingspan of 28.2 feet, a length of 28 feet, an unloaded weight of 3718 pounds, a top speed of 340 miles an hour, and a range of 750 miles.

Nakajima began considering a new version, the Ki. 230, but had not gone beyond the stage of preliminary studies at the time of the Japanese surrender.

The Nakajima Kikka

This plane was the direct result of cooperation between the members of the Berlin-Tokyo Axis. Faithful to the spirit of the treaty, the Germans shared their technological secrets with their Far Eastern allies. Thus when the Japanese became interested in jet propulsion, they asked the Germans to supply them with plans and essential parts of their best proto-

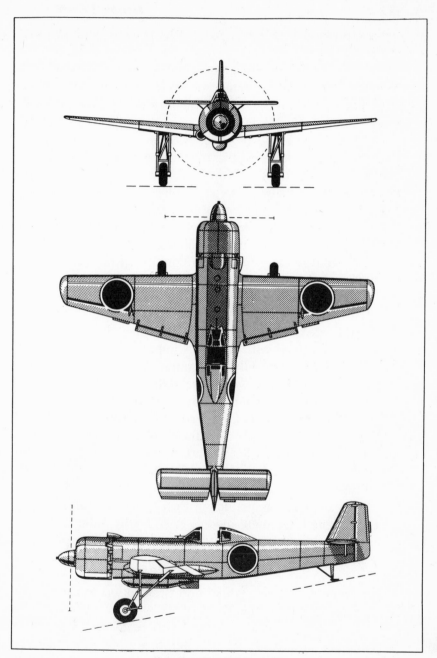

Nakajima Ki. 115 B Tsurugi.

types equipped with jet engines, which were revolutionary at the time.

The Messerschmitt Sturmvogel seemed particularly promising to the Japanese. They decided to modify it, however, because of production problems and their own special requirements: they were concerned mainly with suicide operations. At the end of 1944, Nakajima designed a twin-engined jet with lines similar to those of the Sturmvogel. It was named the Kikka ("Chrysanthemum") and was also known as the Kitsuka ("Orange Blossom"). It was to be capable of making both conventional and suicide attacks.

American bombing raids became so frequent that airstrips were being built near natural shelters, such as caves, which could be enlarged and made into bombproof hangars. Space in them was limited and storing planes was a serious problem. Navy carrier planes with folding wings could be stored more easily than other types. It was for that reason, and not because it was meant to be used aboard carriers, that the Kikka was designed with folding wings.

Work progressed rapidly. On January 28, 1945, a full-sized mock-up of the Kikka was presented to naval authorities. They decided to put it into production. But the problem of propulsion had not yet been solved. The Germans had obligingly sent several of their new BMW-003 jet engines. Japanese technicians took them apart to become familiar with them, then made a copy, the Ne. 12 (TR.12). Its 690-pound thrust was inadequate. An improved version, the Ne. 20, which developed 1045 pounds of thrust but was still inferior to the original German model, was finally adopted and mounted in a prototype assembled at the Nakajima plant at Koizumi, where it was given its first ground tests on June 30, 1945.

The plane was disassembled and transported to the naval base at Kisaragu, on the shore of Tokyo Bay. After being reassembled and checked over, it was ready to fly by the beginning of August. On the 7th, before a group of engineers and technicians, a Nakajima test pilot climbed into the cockpit and prepared to make the first Japanese jet flight. The

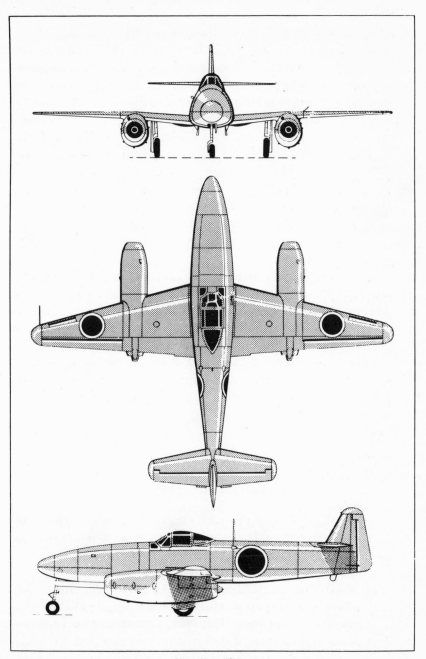

Nakajima Kikka.

plane taxied for a long time before picking up enough speed but finally took off. The flight lasted a little less than 20 minutes, at an altitude of 2000 feet. On the basis of the pilot's report, a few modifications were made in the prototype, including the addition of auxiliary takeoff rockets.

The second test flight took place on August 11, this time before naval authorities. The Kikka began rolling and the rockets ignited, making an enormous trail of white smoke, but it did not take off. When the rockets had burned out, the plane continued rolling and finally crashed beyond the end of the runway. Investigation showed that the reason was undoubtedly that the rockets had the wrong line of thrust. The second prototype was ready to fly when, four days later, Japan surrendered.

The main characteristics of the Kikka were: wingspan, 32.8 feet; length, 28.3 feet; height, 10 feet; weight empty, 5060 pounds; calculated top speed, 420 miles an hour; cruising speed, 345 miles an hour; landing speed, 98 miles an hour. It was capable of climbing to 6000 meters (19,680 feet) in 12 minutes and 6 seconds and had a ceiling of 10,700 meters (35,100 feet). Its range was a little over 550 miles. It could carry a bomb weighing from 1100 to 1760 pounds under the fuselage.

The Baika

In the last months of the war, the research departments of most Japanese aircraft manufacturers were busy trying to design suicide planes that would be cheap, reliable and easy to build. A multitude of plans was presented but none was considered ideal, partly because of the great difficulties from which Japanese aircraft production was suffering at the time.

Inspiration again came from the Germans. The Imperial Aeronautical Institute of Tokyo carefully studied the German "buzz bomb," the V-1, and especially its purely experimental piloted version, the V-4. It was powered by a new type of engine, the pulse-jet, which Japanese engineers hastened to copy. This engine had air-intake valves that opened and closed several times per second, producing a pulsating thrust by intermittent combustion.

In July, 1945, when professors Ichiro Tani and Taichiro Ogawa of the Aeronautical Institute had completed their preliminary studies, the Kawanashi firm prepared to build prototypes and work out the industrial problems involved. It was decided to mass-produce the plane by means of many different workshops employing relatively unskilled labor.

The final design, called the Baika or Baikwa ("Plum Blossom") was a small low-winged monoplane that closely resembled the German V-4. The pulse-jet engine was above the fuselage and behind the cockpit. The explosive charge, which could vary between 220 and 550 pounds, was placed in the pointed nose section of the plane. Production had not yet begun when the war ended.

The Strange Shinryu

Early in 1945, naval aeronautical engineers at Yokosuka designed a suicide glider for attacking enemy tanks when they landed on the home islands. A glider was considered adequate for this purpose because it would have to fly only a short distance.

The fuselage of the glider, called the Shinryu ("Divine Dragon"), had a rectangular cross section, its high wing had squared-off tips and the lines of its tail surfaces were almost entirely straight. Because of its simplicity, it could be mass-produced by a large number of small workshops without specialized machinery. The Mizuno firm was assigned to plan its production.

The Shinryu was to take off and gain sufficient altitude by means of a battery of rockets. The pilot, seated forward of the wing, could then glide toward an enemy tank and crash into it. There was a plan to increase the Shinryu's range by

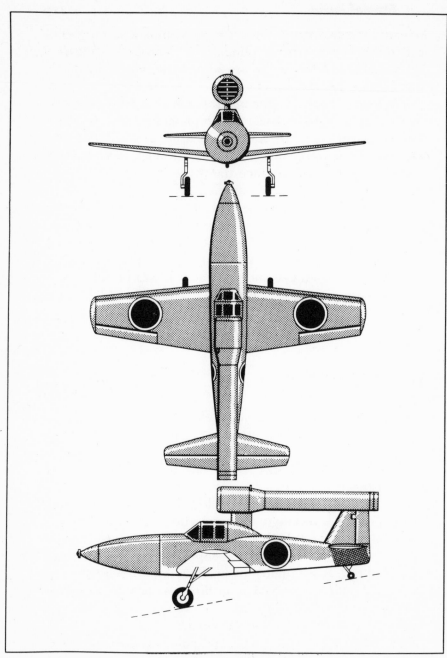

Kawanishi Baika.

having a Ginga bomber tow it to the vicinity of its target but this procedure was never tested. The light glider carried a 220-pound bomb inside the fuselage at the center of gravity, just behind the pilot's seat.

The first and only prototype was finished in July, 1945, and its single test flight took place at the Kasumigaura air base a few days before the Japanese surrender. The Shinryu took off and flew for several minutes. It was damaged in landing and there were no more tests.

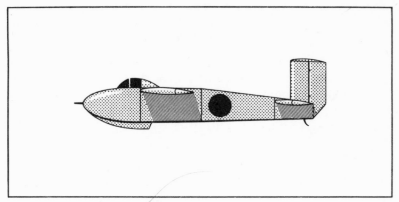

Yokosuka-Mizuno Shinryu.

Conclusions and Questions

The unsuccessful search for an ideal kamikaze plane points up some of the problems that the Japanese faced. First, it shows the weakness and lack of creativity of their technology. Their most promising attempts were based on work already done by the Germans; the others were particularly disappointing. The quest for simplification and decentralized manufacture illustrates the situation of the Japanese aircraft industry in the last months of the war.

The Japanese apparently gave little consideration to the idea of pilotless planes or missiles, at a time when other countries were already making great progress in that area.

Why did they continue to use suicide pilots rather than a system of remote control? Was it because they were unable to develop an efficient control system, or did the military authorities insist on using suicide volunteers even when other possibilities were open? The first explanation seems more plausible to us, because the Japanese had no reluctance to use technology when they could. But if an efficient control system were possible, would the high command still have wanted to pursue its suicide offensive in the hope that the enemy would be overwhelmed by that demonstration of Japanese moral superiority? One does not know, but the answer lies, perhaps, in the Japanese soul and the tenacious survival of ancient myths.

Nearly all kamikaze attacks were made with conventional aircraft, some modified, others not. Less than a hundred Ohka piloted bombs were used in operations and less than half of these reached their objectives. If the Japanese had been able to build a large fleet of sufficiently fast and stable suicide planes, events might have turned out differently because such planes would have been more difficult for the Americans to intercept and shoot down and a larger percentage of them would have struck their targets.

The Setting Sun

When the second atomic bomb was dropped on Nagasaki, the peace faction within the Japanese government gained many new supporters from among those who had still been hesitant. The fanatical militarists lost none of their determination, however, and they still had great power.

Emperor Hirohito, convinced that it was futile to continue the war and aware of the sufferings endured by his people, began taking steps to find a mediator other than the Soviet Union. Japanese forces were now being pressed back by the Americans in the south and by the Soviets in the northwest, in Manchuria and Korea. Industry was paralyzed by bombings and blockade, the whole nation was undernourished and civilian casualties were heavy.

Japanese peace overtures were transmitted to the Allies by way of Sweden and Switzerland. A violent political struggle immediately broke out in Tokyo between the two opposing factions within the government.

Most officers stationed in the home islands sensed that something important was taking place. It took no great discernment to realize that the war was lost and that the end was near. Some still hoped that Japan had not yet played her last card, others looked forward to official confirmation of their desire for peace. Generals and admirals were kept informed of the progress of negotiations. They were divided along the same lines as the two governmental factions, some recognizing that negotiation was the wisest course, others refusing to acknowledge the painful truth.

Opposition between the two viewpoints sometimes reached the point of open violence. Whole military units came to blows. On the night of August 14 there was murderous fighting even inside the Imperial Palace and the emperor feared for his life. Japan was like the mythological dragon that bit its tail in its death agony.

Some high civilian and military dignitaries, realizing the futility of prolonged war, committed suicide, either in public or in the privacy of their homes. Faithful to the ancestral Bushido code, these men felt that the war had to end in either victory or death.

In a radio broadcast on August 15 at noon, the emperor himself read the surrender proclamation. He announced to the Japanese people that he and his government had decided to end the hopeless conflict in order to spare the population still greater suffering. Millions of Japanese heard this message and most of them wept from deep emotion which included humiliation at the fact that their emperor had been led to read the proclamation in person.

The broadcast set off a veritable tidal wave of suicides. Thousands of Japanese, men and women, young and old, killed themselves to avoid living with the shame of the first defeat that Japan had known in centuries. Observing the ancient rites, civilians, officers and enlisted men took their own lives at home, at their bases, in the street, or in front of the Imperial Palace, as a sign of respectful submission.

Admiral Ugaki's Sacrifice

In the last hours of the night of August 14, Admiral Matome Ugaki ordered one of his officers to have planes prepared for an attack on Okinawa. His tone and attitude left no doubt about his intentions. Although he had not said so explicitly, it was clear that he planned to take part in the attack. When Captain Takashi Miyazaki, senior staff officer of the Fifth Air Fleet, was informed of this, he went to see the admiral.

Ugaki's living quarters were a small screened-off section of the cave that served as his headquarters. Miyazaki bowed when he came in, and said in a tone that revealed his anxiety, "The duty officer tells me that you have ordered preparations for a sortie of carrier bombers. May I ask your plans, sir?" [2]

Ugaki's expression had been stern, but his face relaxed when he replied, "I am going to accompany an attack. Go relay the order."

Although Miyazaki realized that his question had been insolent, he could not restrain himself from going further.

"I fully understand how you feel," he said, "but I beg you to reconsider, sir. It is my own opinion that such an action is not now practical."

Ugaki said firmly, "You have my order. Please carry it out."

Miyazaki could not bring himself to do it. He went to see Rear Admiral Toshiyuki Yokoi, Ugaki's chief of staff. Yokoi was ill and in bed, but as soon as he heard the news he got up, went to Ugaki and tried to make him change his mind. Ugaki's only response was to say calmly, "Please allow me the right to choose my own death."

[2] All quotations in this section are from The Divine Wind, by Inoguchi, Nakajima and Pineau, pp. 147-50.

Rear Admiral Takatsugu Jojima also tried to persuade him not to go on the mission. He, too, failed.

"This is my chance to die like a warrior," said Ugaki. "I must be permitted this chance. My successor has already been chosen and he can take care of things after I am gone."

Following Ugaki's orders, Lieutenant Tatsuo Nakatsuru had three dive bombers prepared for the raid. This took several hours, and at noon the surrender proclamation was broadcast by loudspeakers at the base. Ugaki did not change his decision. In the middle of the afternoon he went to the airfield with all insignia of rank removed from his uniform. When he arrived, he was surprised to see not three, but 11 dive bombers with their crews standing beside them.

Admiral Yokoi, who had accompanied Ugaki, said to Lieutenant Nakatsuru, "Did not the order call for only three planes?" Nakatsuru answered with obvious emotion, "Who could stand to see the attack limited to only three planes when our commander himself is going to lead in crash dives against the enemy? Every plane of my command will follow him."

Admiral Ugaki said to his men, "Are you all so willing to die with me?" All 22 men answered that they were.

Lieutenant Nakatsuru took his place at the controls of the lead plane and Ugaki sat behind him as his observer. At the last moment, Warrant Officer Akiyoshi Endo, who would normally have been Nakatsuru's observer, insisted that he be allowed to go on the mission. When Ugaki gently ordered him to stay behind, Endo shocked all the onlookers by refusing to obey: he climbed into the plane and sat on the seat beside the admiral.

Shortly after takeoff, four of the planes had to turn back because of engine trouble. The others continued on their way. Admiral Ugaki finally sent a radio message:

I alone am to blame for our failure to defend the homeland and destroy the arrogant enemy. The valiant efforts of all officers and men of my command during the past six months have been greatly appreciated.

I am going to make an attack at Okinawa where my men have fallen like cherry blossoms. There I will crash into and destroy the conceited enemy in the true spirit of Bushido, with firm conviction and faith in the eternity of Imperial Japan.

I trust that the members of all units under my command will understand my motives, will overcome all hardships of the future and will strive for the reconstruction of our great homeland that it may survive forever.

Long live His Imperial Majesty the Emperor!

A few moments later, another message announced that Ugaki's plane was about to dive, and similar messages soon followed from the six others.

Although it was never known if they had reachd Okinawa, no American ship reported a kamikaze attack that day. In any case Admiral Ugaki had lived and died as a samurai. His death was in accordance with his convictions and the kamikaze spirit that reflected the military heritage of his country.

Onishi's End

In the last months of the war, Admiral Takijiro Onishi, who had inaugurated suicide tactics in the Philippines, held the position of Vice Chief of the Naval General Staff. His great competence, perfect knowledge of operational problems and unshakable patriotic faith were recognized by everyone, and had led to his being given high responsibilities.

Onishi was an advocate of fighting to the end. In this he aligned himself with the militaristic faction within the government, but to him it was not a matter of personal pride or ambition. He was moved by the greatness of soul and lofty moral code of the samurai warriors. He used every means he could, from persuasion to threats, to make the government put off its decision to surrender. He struggled until the final moment, in vain.

On the afternoon of August 15, after the surrender had been announced, Onishi seemed to regain his calm. He invited several officers to his home. They drank and talked until midnight, when they left him. He went to his study and wrote a letter. He then knelt and thrust a sword into his abdomen. He was later found in his study, still conscious but dying. He refused all help and endured twelve hours of terrible suffering before he died. The letter he had written was then discovered:

> *I wish to express my deep appreciation to the souls of the brave special attackers. They fought and died valiantly with faith in our ultimate victory. In death I wish to atone for my part in the failure to achieve that victory and I apologize to the souls of these dead fliers and their bereaved families.*
>
> *I wish the young people of Japan to find a moral in my death. To be reckless is only to aid the enemy. You must abide by the spirit of the Emperor's decision with utmost perseverence. Do not forget your rightful pride in being Japanese.*
>
> *You are the treasure of the nation. With all the fervor of spirit of the special attackers, strive for the welfare of Japan and for peace throughout the world.*[3]

Before the Tribunal of History

Despite the intense and lyrical propaganda that glorified the kamikaze volunteers and their exploits, the Japanese people were not unanimously convinced that suicide tactics were necessary or justifiable. But it seems nearly certain that admirals Onishi and Ugaki did not commit suicide as a form of expiation, or even to avoid living in the shame of defeat, as

[3] The Divine Wind, *by Inoguchi, Nakajima and Pineau, p. 156.*

was the case with so many other Japanese. With them it was something quite different. They had launched the idea of kamikaze attacks and sent thousands of men to their death. Those who knew them believed that at every takeoff they felt torn, as if part of themselves were going with each volunteer. Their apparent insensitivity was only a pose required by the firmness of command. It is clear that they had always intended to join their men in death at the end of the war. Their feelings in this respect were independent of victory or defeat. They would probably have done the same if Japan had won.

No one in Japan was surprised to learn that they had committed suicide; the whole nation would have been shocked if they had remained alive. The spirit of the kamikaze corps was so lofty, so sublime, that the death of its leaders was regarded as the natural conclusion of its whole stirring epic.

The Men

All through that epic, for it can truly be called one, thousands of men followed one another down the runways; they all flew off toward death in the hope of destroying the enemy, but their feelings were not all the same. It is important to avoid the mistake of regarding them as fanatical robots devoid of meaningful personal reactions.

It would be impossible, of course, to study the temperament and behavior of each volunteer, but we can distinguish three main psychological types. First there were the spontaneous heroes, men who had been steeped in the Japanese martial tradition since childhood. They generally belonged either to the aristocracy, which was strongly nationalistic, or to the lower middle class, which was particularly devoted to militarism and included many families of samurai origin. To these men, the idea of patriotic duty dominated every other consideration and death was something that they had tacitly accepted in becoming members of the emperor's armed forces. It was men of this type who, early in the war, unknowingly laid the groundwork of the kamikaze corps by crashing their planes into enemy targets on their own initiative.

Next there was a category of men who, although they came from different social backgrounds, were alike in having strong religious principles, whether Shintoist, Buddhist or Confucian. The concept of unquestioning devotion to patriotic duty was less compelling to them, but their religious convictions made them receptive to the idea of self-sacrifice as a way of attaining spiritual elevation and joining their venerated ancestors.

These were also the men who were most responsive to example. They were stirred by stories of what kamikaze pilots had already done, the calm determination of those who would soon die in the same way, the inspiring speeches by their officers and the whole psychological climate created by the war. Their decision to volunteer was at least partly prompted by pride: they were ashamed to go on hesitating while others were doing noble deeds that covered them with glory and made them legendary heroes.

Finally there was a third category of men who volunteered for less subjective reasons. They judged kamikaze attacks in terms of their effectiveness and did not see suicide as a self-justifying act. They could almost be described, in contrast to the other two categories, as freethinkers who had nevertheless remained within the specific Japanese tradition. They were not completely insensitive to heroic example, but they were more strongly influenced by logical analysis.

Viewing the military situation clearly, without patriotic fanaticism or religious exaltation, the freethinkers were all the more distressed by it. It was obvious to them that conventional methods of attack had become useless, resulting only in terrible Japanese losses without significant harm to the enemy. Other methods would have to be used. The idea of a suicide attack inevitably presented itself to these men, not as a path to heroic immortality or spiritual transcendence, but as the only way to strike an effective blow at the enemy.

They were well aware that one suicide pilot could do more damage to an enemy ship than a conventional attack by a whole squadron. Their acceptance of suicide for that reason may seem alien to a Western mind, but not totally incomprehensible. It was the main reason for the decision of many kamikaze volunteers, probably even the majority of them.

As for the army pilots who were assigned to suicide units without having volunteered, it seems that most of them, after a period of perfectly understandable shock and anguish, adopted an outlook similar to that of the men described above.

Our psychological analysis of the kamikaze pilots is not a matter of pure speculation. Some of them wrote letters before they died and others survived because the war ended while they were still waiting to be sent on their suicide missions. The testimony of these survivors is valuable, but there is a special immediacy and poignancy in the letters of the men who were about to die. They were written mainly by reserve officers who had recently been university students; they are all the more significant because they express the thoughts and feelings of men who sacrificed themselves without blind fanaticism or excessive religious fervor.

We shall quote two of these letters. The first is from Ensign Susumu Kaijitsu, who went directly from Nagoya Technical College into navy flight training.

> Dear Father, Mother, brothers Hiroshi and Takeshi, and sister Eiko:
> I trust that this spring finds you all in fine health. I have never felt better and am now standing by, ready for action.
> The other day I flew over our home and bade a last farewell to our neighbors and to you. Thanks to Mr. Yamakawa I had a chance recently to have a last drink with father, and there now remains nothing but to await our call to duty.

My daily activities are quite ordinary. My greatest concern is not about death, but rather of how I can be sure of sinking an enemy carrier. Ensigns Miyazaki, Tanaka and Kimura, who will sortie as my wingmen, are calm and composed. Their behavior gives no indication that they are momentarily awaiting orders for their final crash-dive sortie. We spend our time in writing letters, playing cards and reading.

I am confident that my comrades will lead our divine Japan to victory.

Words cannot express my gratitude to the loving parents who reared and tended me to manhood that I might in some small manner reciprocate the grace which His Imperial Majesty has bestowed upon us.

Please watch for the results of my meager effort. If they prove good, think kindly of me and consider it my good fortune to have done something that may be praiseworthy. Most important of all, do not weep for me. Though my body departs, I will return home in spirit and remain with you forever. My thoughts and best regards are with you, our friends and neighbors. In concluding this letter, I pray for the well-being of my dear family.[4]

The other letter was written by Ensign Teruo Yamaguchi, who became a navy pilot after graduating from Kokugakuin University in Tokyo.

Dear Father:

As death approaches, my only regret is that I have never been able to do anything good for you in my life.

I was selected quite unexpectedly to be a special attack pilot and will be leaving for Okinawa today. Once the order was given for my one-way mission it became my sincere wish to achieve success in fulfilling this last duty. Even so, I cannot help feeling a strong attachment

[4] The Divine Wind, by Inoguchi, Nakajima and Pineau, p. 176.

to this beautiful land of Japan. Is that a weakness on my part?

On learning that my time had come I closed my eyes and saw visions of your face, mother's, grandmother's and the faces of my close friends. It was bracing and heartening to realize that each of you wants me to be brave. I will do that! I will!

My life in the service has not been filled with sweet memories. It is a life of resignation and self-denial, certainly not comfortable. As a raison d'être for service life, I can see only that it gives me a chance to die for my country. If this seems bitter it is because I have experienced the sweetness of life before joining the service.

The other day I received Lieutenant Otsubo's philosophy on life and death which you so kindly sent. It seems to me that while he appears to have hit on some truth, he was concerned mostly with superficial thoughts on the service. It is of no avail to express it now, but in my 23 years of life I have worked out my own philosophy.

It leaves a bad taste in my mouth when I think of the deceits being played on innocent citizens by some of our wily politicians. But I am willing to take orders from the high command, and even from the politicians, because I believe in the polity of Japan.

The Japanese way of life is indeed beautiful, and I am proud of it, as I am of Japanese history and mythology which reflect the purity of our ancestors and their belief in the past—whether or not those beliefs are true. That way of life is the product of all the best things which our ancestors have handed down to us. And the living embodiment of all wonderful things out of our past is the Imperial Family which, too, is the crystallization of the splendor and beauty of Japan and its people. It is an honor to be able to give my life in defense of these beautiful and lofty things.

Okinawa is as much a part of Japan as Goto Island.

An inner voice keeps saying that I must smite the foe who violates our homeland. My grave will be the sea around Okinawa, and I will see my mother and grandmother again. I have neither regret nor fear about death. I only pray for the happiness of you and all my fellow countrymen.

My greatest regret in this life is the failure to call you chichiue *[revered father]. I regret not having given any demonstration of the true respect which I have always had for you. During my final plunge, though you will not hear it, you may be sure that I will be saying* chichiue *to you and thinking of all you have done for me.*

I have not asked you to come to see me at the base because I know that you are comfortable at Amakusa. It is a good place to live. The mountains north of the base remind me of Sugiyama and Magarisaka on Goto Island, and I have often thought of the days when you took Akira and me on picnics to Matsuyama near the powder magazine. I also recall riding with you to the crematorium at Magarisaka as a youngster, without clearly understanding then that mother had died.

I leave everything to you. Please take good care of my sisters.

One setback in its history does not mean the destruction of a nation. I pray that you will live long. I am confident that a new Japan will emerge. Our people must not be rash in their desire for death.

Fondest regards.

Just before departure,
TERUO

Without regard for life or name, a samurai will defend his homeland.[5]

5 Ibid., *pp. 177-78.*

A Great Lesson

It is beyond question that the outlook of the kamikaze volunteers was largely conditioned by Japan's traditions and spiritual heritage. In both soldiers and civilians, the notions of absolute patriotic devotion and mystical reverence for the homeland were so deep-seated as to be almost second nature. This did not, however, exclude reactions quite similar to ours, and the gap between the Japanese mentality and our own is not really so great if one looks back a few centuries in European history. Should we therefore regard Japanese behavior during the war as a survival of the past? Yes, without a doubt.

Japan was closed to Western influences until the second half of the nineteenth century. When she was finally opened to them, her successive rulers tried to assimilate what seemed advantageous and reject what they considered undesirable. To achieve their short-range goals and further their long-range ambitions, they exploited Western science and technology while keeping the population isolated from the great currents of modern thought and maintaining ancient beliefs and attitudes by means of propaganda, education and the Shinto religion. Exposure to such aspects of Occidental philosophy as materialism and nihilism might have impaired the docile obedience of a people conditioned to religious respect for authority and tradition.

When Japan began suffering setbacks in the Pacific war, it was not even necessary to remind her fighting men of their military traditions to make them redouble their aggressiveness and fanaticism. As soon as the Philippines were threatened, the Japanese propensity for self-sacrifice reappeared spontaneously. It was like a powerful torrent that had only to be channeled. Although Admiral Onishi originally intended to use suicide tactics only temporarily, their continuation seemed logical to the Japanese when they became convinced that there was no other way to reverse the tragic turn the war had taken.

An Occidental may not be able to accept the principle of suicide as a military weapon, much less the collective, organized suicide warfare employed by the Japanese, but can anyone be insensitive to the virtues of the kamikaze volunteers? Their courage, selflessness and resolution were admirable, whatever one may think of their ideology.

Perhaps it is because Japan lost the war that we are inclined to judge Japanese fanaticism severely. The winner is always right, the loser always wrong. If Japan had been victorious, would not the kamikaze principle have been praised all over the world?

After the war, some Japanese sternly criticized suicide tactics and the leaders who had ordered them, but it is always easy to pass rigorous judgment after the fact, when conditions are no longer the same. We are not trying to defend the kamikaze principle; fundamentally we condemn it, but it is important to realize its pragmatic aspect, and this book will have achieved its goal if it sheds light on what was also an extraordinary spiritual phenomenon, perhaps unprecedented in history.

Our intention has been to show that Japanese suicide attacks did not spring from a frenzied collective insanity, but that they were the prolongation, the logical outcome of a whole national psychology reacting to a specific situation. It was as if the fruit of a two-thousand-year-old tree had been abruptly ripened by the electric atmosphere of a storm. The kamikaze pilots' sacrifice was useless as are all wars, but those Japanese heroes gave the world a great lesson in purity. From the depths of their ancient past they brought a forgotten message of human grandeur.

Bibliography

Japanese Sources:

Rikihei Inoguchi, Tadashi Nakajima, Roger Pineau, *The Divine Wind*

Masatake Okumiya, Jiro Horikoshi, Martin Caidin, *Zero*

Saburo, Sakai, Martin Caidin, Fred Saito, *Samurai*

Mochitsura Hashimoto, *Sunk*

Tameichi Hara, Fred Saito, Roger Pineau, *Japanese Destroyer Captain*

Kitaro Matumoto, *Battleships Ymato and Musashi*

Aireviews' [sic], *The Fifty Years of Japanese Aviation*

Airefiew's [sic], *General View of Japanese Military Aircraft in the Pacific War*

American Sources:

Walter Lord, *Day of Infamy*

James A. Field, *The Battle of Leyte Gulf* [?]

James J. Fahey, *Pacific War Diary 1942-1945*

Samuel Eliot Morison, *History of U.S. Naval Operations in World War II*

Robert Leckie, *Challenge for the Pacific*

Robert Leckie, *Strong Men Armed*

Chester W. Nimitz, E.B. Potter, *The Great Sea War*

Fletcher Pratt, *The Marine's War*

James F. Sunderman, *World War II in the Air. The Pacific.*

Theodore Roscoe, *Submarines*

Trevor N. Dupuy, *The Air Force in the Pacific. Air Power Leads the Way*

Trevor N. Dupuy, *The Naval War in the Pacific. Rising Sun of Nippon*

Trevor N. Dupuy, *Asiatic Land Battles. Japanese Ambitions in the Pacific*

Robert D. Heinl, *Soldiers of the Sea*

Navy Department, *Abridged U.S. Naval Chronology of World War II*

British Sources:

Courtney Browne, *The Last Banzai*

F.G. Swansborough, Peter M. Bowers, *United States Military Aircraft Since 1909*

F.G. Swansborough, Peter M. Bowers, *United States Navy Aircraft Since 1911*

Paul H. Silverstone, *U.S. Warships of World War II*

Anthony J. Watts, *Japanese Warships of World War II*

French Sources:

Andrieu D'Albas, *Marine impériale*

Georges Blond, *Le survivant du Pacifique*

Serge Ouvaroff, *Torpilles humaines*

Index